THE BARON, THE LOGGER, THE MINER, AND ME

The Baron, The Logger, The Miner, and Me

John H. Toole

MOUNTAIN PRESS PUBLISHING CO.
Missoula 1984

Library of Congress Cataloging in Publication Data

Toole, John H.
  The baron, the logger, the miner, and me.

  Includes index.
  1. O'Keefe family. 2. Ross family. 3. Toole
family. 4. Montana—Biography. I. Title.
CT274.O44T66 1984   929'.2'0973   84-25426
ISBN 0-87842-174-2
ISBN 0-87842-185-8 (pbk.)

Dedicated to
K. Ross Toole

Foreword

When I drive the highways of Montana, I see things that other people don't see. What I see are places and traces of my grandparents and great-grandparents, who came to Montana beginning as early as 1859.

About 80 miles west of Missoula, near Interstate 90, lies the spot where my great-grandfather Cornelius C. ("Baron") O'Keefe spent the miserable winter of 1859-60, while traveling with the Mullan expedition. When the expedition reached Missoula, the Baron was charmed with what he saw, and squatted on 1,500 acres of land 10 miles west of Hellgate Canyon. When I drive by the Schall Ranch on Highway 93 north, I pass the place where in 1874 O'Keefe's eight-year-old daughter Maggie temporarily joined the Flathead tribe in order to escape the violence of her father's ranch.

South into the Bitterroot Valley I am reminded again of O'Keefe, and how, as a citizen volunteer, he whipped up his wagon team to catch the retreating Chief Joseph and his Nez Perce tribe in 1877. In the Big Hole I spot the ridge from which O'Keefe viewed the headlong flight of the Nez Perce warriors and their huge herd of horses.

Over the Divide in Anaconda I can visit the house at 401 Hickory where grandfather John R. Toole lived and jousted with the mighty in the Wars of the Copper Kings. At Monida my thoughts go back to Alan Hardenbrook, John R.'s father-in-law, at the head of a wagon train in 1864, guiding his oxen up the Centennial Valley to Virginia City after a long, grim journey from Council Bluffs, Iowa.

And it is Virginia City where not one but two of my great-grandmothers, and one grandmother, ended wagon trips across the Plains from Council Bluffs. Two were Alan Hardenbrook's wife and baby daughter; the other was a schoolteacher who became Baron O'Keefe's wife.

The Judith River Country is to me the vast open land where my wife Barbara's grandfather, Mathew Dunn, encountered trapper Jake Hoover, a friend of artist Charlie Russell. Hoover guided Dunn to the fabled Yogo Gulch sapphire mines in the 1880s. Over on the Sun River is the country where Matt Dunn became a cowboy in 1874. There, too, he helped lay to rest his beautiful sister, Kate Dunn Furnell, dead in childbirth in 1879.

Westward, across the mountains in the Blackfoot Valley, the scenes come thick and fast, and they are mostly of my grandfather Kenneth Ross—Kenneth Ross floating huge logs down the river, fighting the snowdrifts and wind in 1887, fording the Clark Fork River in a lumber wagon in 1890 with his wife and baby Marjorie. My grandmother had to hold her baby higher and higher as the river poured over the wagon, until in a last desperate lunge they reached the opposite shore. The baby grew up to become my mother.

These people were my grandparents and great-grandparents, or Barbara's, and I have always been intensely curious about them. Why do we have so many forebears who came to Montana at such astonishingly early dates?

When I was young my parents and grandparents told me wondrous tales of adventure about these people, and I decided to re-create their adventures. I hit for the hills in 1933, and for five marvelous summers I worked on the most remote ranches, lumber camps and mines I could find. In some of these places I worked with men whose time went back to the days of the frontier. The events of these summers became documented in my letters home.

I have always wanted to record these happenings, and as the land changes and my fellow workers die, this task seems more and more important.

So this book is mostly concerned with the first two generations of my forebears—Cornelius O'Keefe the Baron, Kenneth Ross the logger, John R. Toole the miner (plus the women they married and the children they fathered)—and one member of the fourth generation, me. To this cast the book, of course, adds the names of hundreds of friends, associates, distant relatives, historical personages, and tangential characters. Among the latter I have given some people pseudonyms to spare them or their memories any possible injury.

Contents

1 *1933: Splendor and Hope*

George F. Weisel I and Thula Toole Weisel

1 *1933: Splendor and Hope*

The Circle W Ranch was a magnificent place, particularly for a boy like me, fifteen years old in 1933. It was situated in a big bend of the Blackfoot River. The Garnet Range unfolded back of it to the south, and to the north, a stately row of huge ponderosa pines marched along the river course. In the distance across the valley rose the peaks of the Swan Range. To the east the Blackfoot River debouched from a box canyon with vertical walls, and every hole in the river there teemed with rainbow trout.

It was not much of a cattle ranch. It produced only 150 tons of hay a year, in green meadows spread out before the ranch buildings and watered by Chamberlain Creek, a tiny, lively brook that gurgled out of the mountains and through the building grounds.

But when my aunt and uncle bought this ranch, it was not destined for cattle or sheep. Instead, they proposed to found a dude ranch. And for this purpose it seemed magnificently suited, except that the operation commenced just as the national economy started to slide into the Great Depression in 1932.

The Circle W Ranch was operated by one of the loveliest women I have ever known. Thula Toole Weisel was the sister of my father, Howard, and the daughter of two of my most notable forebears. Her father was John R. Toole, of famous association with the Anaconda Copper Mining Company, and her mother was Anna Hardenbrook

The Lodge at the Circle W

Toole, who had crossed the Great Plains to Montana in 1865. Aunt Thula had waving red hair and finely chiseled features. She went about in a riding habit and highly polished boots. Her laugh was merry, her outlook optimistic, and she completely charmed everyone who came near her.

Her husband, George F. Weisel, was a big, broad-shouldered man with aquiline features and a mustache. He was gruff and demanding. He maintained strong standards for himself and expected these same standards on the part of others. He was usually called "colonel" because he maintained a colonelcy in the U.S. Army Reserves. He had doubts about the practicability of the Circle W Dude Ranch, but he was so deeply in love with Aunt Thula that what she would do, he would do also.

One of the first things that had to be done was the construction of log buildings. This he could do and do well. Along with his sons, nephews, and various others, he set to work cutting beautiful, straight-grained larch logs, skidding them down to the ranch site, hand-peeling and notching them, and erecting graceful, low cabins.

One of the cabins was a lodge. Its living room was a 36-foot room, perfectly proportioned, with hardwood floors, a huge stone fireplace, and a grand piano. The lodge had a large dining room,

4

kitchen, and bedrooms upstairs and down. Aunt Thula gave this building its tastefulness and beauty.

The buildings, under George Weisel, rose at remarkable speed. During the winter of 1932-1933, the family decided to stay on the ranch. This meant being snowbound, so that sons George and John Weisel would have to be tutored by their older sister Virginia. While the winter wind blew and piled snow to the eaves, Virginia instructed her brothers in the basics: history, English, and math. When they reentered Missoula County High School the next fall, they were ahead of their fellow students.

In the summer of 1933 Aunt Thula asked me if I would like to come to the ranch to work for my board and room. I was crazy to go. My mother, Marjorie, was dubious and feared for my safety. My father, Howard, thought it a fine idea. So I went. Marjorie was right and Howard was wrong. It seemed to me that I was forever in danger of being kicked by a horse, or falling into the teeth of a mower, or being killed by a falling tree.

Aunt Thula was accomplished with water colors. She had an easel and she sat long hours in front of the lodge. Her renderings were variations on a theme: the old barn, a relic of the ranch's previous owner, the bunkhouse, the great trees bordering the river, and the Swan Range, thrusting its peaks to the north. I played a crude jazz piano, whereas Aunt Thula had studied the violin in a Boston conservatory. There was only one piece we could play together: "Roses in Picardy." I can still see her bending over

The big room at the Circle W Lodge

her violin, her delicate hands, her classic features, and her flaming red hair.

Sometimes in the evening I would walk by her bedroom window in the lodge on my way to the bunkhouse. On several occasions I heard a voice and stopped to listen. It was Aunt Thula sobbing softly in her bedroom.

Why was this woman, so beautiful and vivacious by day, quietly weeping at night? I could not comprehend the catastrophes that had rained down on her—the tragic death of her youngest daughter Anna Afton while she was giving birth two years before, the sudden shock of Thula's descent from security and wealth into virtual penury during the years 1929 to 1932.

*Thula Weisel and one of
George Weisel's dude cabins*

During the winters of the late 1930s, when the times were toughest for her, Thula lived in a tiny apartment on East Front Street in Missoula and hungered for something to do to make a little money. She realized that she didn't care for the rouge that most women wore in those days and set about to manufacture a more attractive rouge in her kitchen. After she had finally created a rouge that pleased her, she would leave her apartment on cold winter days, her product in a paper sack, and sell it to friends and drug stores. She had no car, so often she had to trudge through the snow. She laughed merrily about her rouge business, but sometimes her rounds took her past the great colonnaded house and grounds that her father had built many years before on Gerald Avenue. Her life in this house had been carefree and gay, and if she ever thought about the future, I am sure it was not with foreboding.

6

*The Blackfoot River
at the Circle W Ranch*

The house had been sold in 1932 for $15,000 and her share of the money went to pay debts.

I came home on leave from the Army in 1942 and went to see her. She was in the hospital, very ill. Her face was drawn and gray, but her red hair still glistened. She greeted me effusively and plied me with questions about my life in the Army.

Thula died two weeks later at the age of 55.

During the summer of 1933, my grandmother, Anna Hardenbrook Toole, visited us. She was very quiet and sat knitting— knitting, I was told, her own clothes. When she came to Montana in 1865, her father's wagon had had to stop for days while her mother fought the cholera, even though the Arapaho Indians were lurking near. But the Hardenbrooks made it, and Anna had married John R. Toole, who achieved fame and wealth and built the house on Gerald. Now all this had been swept away and Grandmother Toole sat quietly at the Circle W Ranch, knitting her own clothes.

Wherever there's a Weisel, there's a horse. By whatever process the Lord distributes the genes as they descend through the generations, He arranged for plenty of horse genes to land on members of the Weisel family. They had all varieties of horseflesh, from cayuses to thoroughbreds, and whenever a pause came in the daily labors, they would head for the corral to curry and comb their horses and discuss them endlessly.

Virginia Weisel was a most attractive girl, with the straightforward, direct manner of her father. One day she mounted a mean and fractious brute called Frog Eyes. It seemed to me that the Weisels were always trying to conquer this beast, but they never succeeded. On this day, Frog Eyes headed for the timber and Virginia couldn't hold him. The two went charging off into the

7

George Weisel I

brush. Virginia caught a low-lying branch that swept her from the horse and broke her nose. She gamely walked back to the lodge, her face streaming blood.

Colonel Weisel saw to it that my summer was not a pleasant idyll. Everybody worked, and worked all the time. There was wood to be split, hay to be irrigated, logs to be peeled, and septic tanks to be dug. I didn't expect anything else. I had been strongly endowed with the work ethic by my grandfather, Kenneth Ross.

Nevertheless, it was with some relief that I witnessed the departure of George Weisel for Fort Douglas, Utah, where he would attend an army camp for a month. He strode from the lodge and entered the Buick sedan. There was a great racing of the engine followed by a horrendous clashing of gears. The car took off with a jerk and raised great clouds of dust as it bounced over the rough road and disappeared from sight. George Weisel's piloting of an automobile was legendary in the Blackfoot Valley.

During this summer I came to know one of the most memorable characters I've ever met. His name was Charlie Dunham. He was a strange-looking, gnome-like little man. He had a hunched back and a bushy mustache, and he spoke with a twang. No one knew his background, except that he spoke often of the great cattle ranches of eastern Montana—the DHS, the XIT, and the Circle C. He had

Dude cabins at the Circle W

been a cowboy and his days went back to the time of Charles Russell.

Charlie did not accept the coming of the automobile. He never learned to drive one and disliked riding in a car. When he wanted to go someplace, he simply threw a saddle on his horse and was gone. If there were more than one in his party, he'd hitch a team to a buggy, give the horses a click, and be on his way. He wouldn't visit town; the Montana out-of-doors was his home.

Charlie had an innate sense of gentlemanliness. He called Aunt Thula "Missus" and would invariably tip his hat to her. He loved to dance, and every Saturday night he would mount his horse and make for Ovando. He was well-known and well-liked and never lacked for a dancing partner, always holding his chosen lady at a courtly distance. He could look quite rakish in his black suit, white shirt, and black string tie. He was always well-behaved and never touched alcohol. At midnight he mounted his horse and returned to the Circle W, about an hour's ride.

He was a good worker and worked along with the young men at the ranch at a steady pace.

Charlie Dunham

Midsummer in the high mountain valleys of Montana is the time for "putting up the hay." The days must be hot and the heads of the timothy golden; moisture will cause the hay to mildew unless it is quickly stacked or baled. In the thirties, ranches hired extra men and mobilized horse-drawn equipment. The hay was mowed by a

9

vicious-looking machine with gnashing teeth that would chew a man to death if he fell among them. A machine called a dump rake piled the hay into longitudinal rows called windrows. Then along came a strange contraption called a bull-rake, which gathered up the hay and transported it to a swinging stacker. This outfit seemed to violate all the laws of physics. It was operated by a single horse, and lifted the hay to the top of the stack in a kind of tilted, elliptical arch.

In 1933 the Weisels had a team of one-ton draft horses named Bob and Butch. Butch was detailed to operate the stacker, and I was detailed to drive him. This looked like a good, easy, and safe job, but it wasn't.

The stacker had, at its base, a semi-circular steel flange. In the flange was a series of holes into which the operator dropped a steel pin. Choosing a particular hole made the hay drop on a particular part of the stack. From the human standpoint, it was most impor-

George Weisel I and
Thula Weisel

tant that the load of hay be properly placed, so as not to drop on the man on top, the stacker. This fellow toiled in the broiling sun all day, using a pitchfork to distribute the hay. If a half a ton of hay fell on him, the stacker would emerge clawing hay from his person and cursing violently.

The stacker at the Circle W Ranch was a most unpleasant chap named Bill Hand. He had little use for teenagers and promptly dubbed me Goo Goo Eyes, because I wore glasses.

After a rudimentary lesson in the operation of the stacker, I was assigned the job. All I needed to do was slap Butch on the rump with the reins. He would then thrust his powerful shoulders into his collar, the load of hay would rise majestically in its elliptical arc, the dumping mechanism would hit the pin, and the load would

10

drop—I profoundly hoped—in its proper place. Then I would back Butch up and repeat the process.

I have never been good at this sort of thing. I kept repeatedly dropping the load on Bill Hand. He would claw his way out in a frenzy of fury and hurl curses down at me. The angrier he got, the more rattled I became and the more loads came down on Bill Hand's head. At length, he slid down off the stack and started after me with his pitchfork, at which point the boss took me off this job and put me on the dump rake.

I climbed up to a high seat on this machine, clicked at the team, and we started. I immediately perceived great danger. If I were to fall from the seat, I would be caught up in a windrow of hay and the sharp tines would roll me over and over, piercing my body with hundreds of wounds. The machine had two long steel handles, which were maneuvered to dump the load of hay into a windrow. I tremulously guided this contraption around the field, leaving ragged masses of partly piled hay. The bull rake operator glared at me with anger, but at least I didn't have some maniac yelling at me from the top of a haystack.

After the hay was put up, the summer drew to a close. The big event then was the rodeo at Helmville on Labor Day. It was strictly a local affair with local talent. It was run by Harry Kelley, the largest rancher in the valley. Kelley rode a big bay gelding and carried a megaphone to shout his orders. He was most distinguished looking, with a large gray sombrero, a striped shirt, and highly polished boots. The talent consisted of the local cowboys. The Weisel delegation perched on the fence to watch George Weisel II compete.

One of the competitors was a hard-drinking man named Ernie Morgan. His moment of glory came when they strapped a washtub to the saddle of a horse. Ernie climbed into the tub and let out a yell, whereupon the chute opened, and Ernie came jolting out inside the tub on a fiercely bucking horse. When he passed under me at my station on the fence, I could distinctly hear his spine striking the edge of the tub. After a few turns about the arena, he sprang from the tub, took a belt of whiskey, and waved to the crowd.

Another cowboy, Hap Morris, got bucked off and dislocated his shoulder. He writhed on the ground with pain. Harry Kelley called for a doctor through his megaphone. At length, Horace Koessler, a physician, but not a practicing one, stepped down from the stands and ambled over to the injured man. Dr. Koessler was a very large man, and therefore called "Shorty." He said, "I am a physician. What seems to be the trouble here?"

The "trouble" was readily apparent. Shorty placed one large foot

11

in Hap's crotch. He grabbed an arm with both hands and gave a mighty heave. Hap yelled, and then sat up, saying happily:

"By God. He did it!"

Shorty waved a great paw and ambled back to his seat in the stands.

The rodeo concluded with a roaring dance, but we didn't stay. We had to ride back to the Circle W. That night we spread our sleeping bags on the banks of the North Fork of the Blackfoot. As I lay there, looking at a thousand stars and listening to the steady swish of water, I was overwhelmed by the beauty and the glory of my life.

In the waning days of that summer we rode to Ovando several times to the dances. The land over which we rode had been dubbed Prairie of the Knobs by Meriwether Lewis of the Lewis and Clark Expedition in 1806. It was a sea of small hummocks with waving green grass, and in the low spots were a thousand small ponds from which sprang flocks of ducks upon our approach. On one of the higher hills was a lonely-looking stone cairn about six feet high. George Weisel II told me that it was the grave of a sheepherder who had been killed by Indians. No one dared dislodge a single stone. If you did, the ghost of the dead sheepherder would come flapping out at you. The memory of the stone cairn and the flapping ghost have stayed with me for fifty years. But George Weisel had his tongue in his cheek when he told me that story.

I had to get back to Salmon Lake to see Gramp, my mother's father, Kenneth Ross. He was dying. I rode one of the Weisel horses, and was greeted at Salmon Lake by Kenneth Ross II.

I bounded up the stairs to see Gramp. Even outside the house I heard his loud snoring. He was sleeping his way into oblivion.

In the fall of 1933, after school had resumed, a friend of mine named John Coleman and I decided to go elk-hunting in the mountains back of the Circle W. In those days the Anaconda company ran a logging train to Woodworth at night. It pulled empty cars up the Blackfoot and returned the same night with a load of logs. If you were a good friend of Camp Robinson, the conductor, you could sneak onto this train for the ride.

One cold November night John Coleman and I climbed into the caboose, and the train crew let us ride in the cupola. The caboose was right behind the locomotive. The great steam engine chugged up the canyon, its headlight bathing the track ahead with a yellow glow. Snow had been plowed from the track, and wild game of all kinds ran along it ahead of us—elk, deer, coyotes and even, at times, a moose. Shooting game from the caboose was, of course, prohibited.

The caboose was warmed with a cheery wood stove. An amber-colored kerosene lamp cast a pale glow through the interior. When we approached occasional road intersections, the whole train seemed to shudder at the deep-throated roar of the whistle.

The train stopped at Cottonwood to let us off. It chugged on up the valley toward Woodworth, and John Coleman and I stood alone on the tracks as it disappeared. A strong, cold wind blew from the northeast, mare's-tail clouds scudded before a dim moon, and the land seemed great and lonely. We shouldered our packs and rifles and set out across the hills for the Circle W.

We could see no lights glowing from the windows at the ranch, but a short distance below the barn, we spotted a horseman. It was Charlie Dunham, and he was all dressed up, headed for the dance at Ovando.

"What're you young fellas doin' up here?"

"We came up to go huntin,' Charlie." I replied.

"You did, huh? Well, I'm goin' with ya."

"No, no, Charlie!" I protested. "You're goin' to the dance! We can go by ourselves."

"No you can't. You're just kids. You might get hurt or lost or somethin'!"

I protested in vain. He got off his horse, showed us a couple of bunks, built a fire in the kitchen, then regaled us with ancient ballads in a high quavering voice.

We were up at dawn. Charlie fixed us a large breakfast, got us saddle horses, and we were off. The trees were dusted with snow. The cold was oppressive, but there was a strong sense of adventure in the air.

Charlie announced, "We're goin' up on Blacktail Mountain."

We rode for a long time and reached a clearing in the woods. Charlie had us tie our horses and said, "We'll hoof it from here. Now I don't want you fellas stepping on twigs or hittin' limbs. Walk real quiet."

The slope was steep and we crept upward and my heart raced. Every time we made a sound, Charlie glared at us. All of a sudden, John Coleman croaked, "It's an elk! An elk! An elk!"

I croaked back, "Where? Where? Where?"

Charlie skittered around, peering at the ridge. I strained my eyes. John Coleman was thrashing like a wild man trying to get into firing position. All of a sudden we saw the elk. He was trotting along the top of the ridge, head and horns held high, sniffing the air.

"That's not an elk," said Charlie. "It's a beautiful whitetail buck. He can smell us, but he ain't seen us yet. Come over here, Johnny. Rest your rifle on this limb. That buck'll come back. When he crosses your sights, let him have it!"

Sure enough, the buck came trotting back. When he crossed my sights, I pulled the trigger of my Krag 30:40. There was a deafen-

13

ing explosion, the butt of the Krag crashed into my shoulder, and the buck dropped like a stone.

Charlie looked at me with a look of utter amazement on his face and exclaimed, "By God, Johnny, you got him!"

John Coleman and I went roaring up the mountain. Back of us I could hear Charlie laughing. I looked around. He had his hat off and was slapping his thigh in uproarious humor.

John Coleman and I reached the buck in a state of shock. I had to sit down. The animal had a clean bullet hole through his neck. John Coleman grumpily announced, "Nothing but a freak shot." Charlie climbed up and took a different attitude, "Johnny, that was some shot. That buck was movin' fast!"

But John Coleman was right. It was a freak shot. I've never been able to hit the broad side of a barn with a rifle. It was the first big game animal I'd ever killed.

Charlie then gave us a lesson in how to dress out a deer. We soon had a sloppy mass of entrails on the ground. Charlie showed us how to use the knife so that the stomach contents would not spill out and taint the meat. It seemed eery to warm our hands in the buck's steaming guts.

Charlie had brought a rope. We skidded the deer down to the horses on the snow. Charlie rigged a pole so that the carcass would hang high.

"There," he said. "But just for good measure I'll tie this bandanna around his foot. That's got man scent on it, keeps the coyotes away."

We headed back for the ranch. I was still guilty about keeping Charlie from going to the dance and mentioned it again.

He laughed, "Don't worry about that, Johnny. You two kids give me ten times as much fun as I'da had at the dance!"

We turned into bed early. Charlie sat by the stove and sang a ballad called "The Lakes of Pontchartrain."

The next morning would be Monday, and we were due in school. We saddled up, left a hind quarter and a front quarter of the deer with Charlie, and headed for the railroad. The loaded downstream train was due about 9 p.m., and we stood shivering on the track for a long time. Soon we heard a rumble and the engine, now pulling about thirty cars of logs, came in sight from the northeast. The train came to a screeching halt and we climbed into the caboose. Stopping a loaded freight train to pick up two teenagers in a lonesome valley was something that no railroad would do today.

Camp Robinson inspected our venison with approval and sent us up to the cupola. The locomotive swayed down the Blackfoot Valley, the rails and the snow snaked ahead of us, and a delicious drowsiness came over me.

14

2 The Outrageous Baron

*Cornelius C. O'Keefe
in his younger years*

2   The Outrageous Baron

Since who knows when
Indians were in the valley
fishing, hunting, fighting, living in it
free as the winds,
in harmony with nature,
not upsetting its balance,
using its lands, its grassland,
its abundance of good things,
imagining beautiful myths, as if
the Great Spirit were a companion.

The valley was a
good place to be.

A great bowl with space
for a man to gaze into
and delight in.
Ringed by mountains,

with two swift running rivers
lined with cottonwood trees.
Vast blue sky, white clouds, air
fresh and invigorating.
Birds cheeping and singing in it,
animals—wild ducks and geese,
antelope, elk, deer,
with fish flashing in the rivers.
Meadows lovely with long grasses
running in the breezes,
with many flowers.

Paradise.

The Golden Valley, by H.G. Merriam

This is what my great-grandfather Cornelius C. ("Baron") O'Keefe saw when he rode into the Missoula valley with Captain Mullan in the spring of 1860. He had a saddle horse and a rifle. He bought an axe from the Captain and turned his horse north to a little meadow at the mouth of a narrow canyon, the Coriackan Defile. He decided he would settle here, even though there were practically no other white men in the valley in May of 1860.

The story of the life of this shanty Irishman who chose to call himself a baron inspires amusement, disbelief, outrage, and some-times admiration. The essentials of O'Keefe's life story have been told best by my daughter, Edith Toole Oberley, a professional writer. So at this point I turn the book over to her for a while. In an article originally written for the *Montana, the Magazine of Western History*, she starts by telling us about a tattered letter, dated simply "Sept. 2" from "Belmonte" (in Ireland) that bears this closing: "Long life and many a happy Xmas to Mr. and Mrs. O'Keefe. May the 'Baron' *live temperately, make money and Save his Soul* whatever may betide him. *May God Bless you all*.
      Yrs very sincerely,
      Mary Burns,"
and goes on as follows:

This missive traced a tortuous route across the Atlantic, over American plains and mountains, and finally reached its destina-tion a year later in a crude cabin settled in among the hills a dozen miles west of present day Missoula, Montana. Its arrival was no doubt a big event, certainly in the life of Anna O'Keefe, the wife of the self-appointed Baron. A person of sensitive and poetic temper-ament, she saved carefully every reminder of a more civilized existence. This letter was one of several found within the pages of a worn scrapbook, filled with pressed flowers, bits of lace, cards, and original verse, which attests to her awareness of another world. Life with the Baron could not have been easy, although surely it was as exciting, unpredictable and full as ever a life could be.

Who was this Baron, so exhorted to live temperately, make money, and Save his Soul? Mary Burns must have known him well, either personally or through correspondence with his wife, because her admonitions were directed toward certain key aspects of his character. In some ways, he was the prototype of the Irish character; indeed, he cultivated the image. Short and strongly built, red-haired, fiery-faced, and green-eyed, he was feisty, capricious, ingenious, crude, voluble, and possessed of an iron will. His temper, always simmering, frequently flared out in spectacular explosions, as we shall see. He also had the power, when he wished to exercise it, of being exceedingly cosmopolitan and charming, a quality instrumental in winning his lovely English wife, Anna Lester. He could astound his listeners with rich Irish oratory or arouse them to instant fury by firing off original insults that always pierced vulnerable spots. He was a rugged individualist who, by sheer force of personality, will, and determination, carved out a prosperous living for himself and his family and wielded some influence in the politics of Montana.

Whence came this inimitable Irishman and why to the wilds of Montana, in 1860 a territory scarcely settled and full of all the dangers a frontier life held? The story has its beginnings in County Cork, Ireland, a land of mists, stone walls, green fields, and the abject poverty of the peasants in the midst of the potato famine of 1845-46. Cornelius C. O'Keefe was a young political activist, a member of the revolutionary "Young Irelanders." He and his group agitated against the oppressive English government, which, they said, through callous neglect and abuse was exacerbating the potato famine. O'Keefe was caught by the authorities and sentenced to exile in Van Dieman's Land, now Tasmania, a convenient nineteenth century dumping ground for political prisoners. By his daughter's account, he escaped from the prison ship in New York in 1853. Finding passage on a ship that took him around Cape Horn, the Baron settled for a brief period in California.

Moving on to what is now Washington state, he spent a few unsatisfactory years farming, and in 1859 joined the crew of John Mullan, who headed a party commissioned by the U.S. Army to build a wagon road between the headwaters of the Missouri and Columbia rivers. After a miserable winter spent in camp near present-day St. Regis, on Montana's western border, the Mullan crew made its way into Hellgate, now Missoula.

Here is where the story of Cornelius C. O'Keefe as his descendants know it really begins. As the Mullan party passed through the area northwest of Hellgate, O'Keefe's attention was attracted by a green, fertile-looking plain, spreading gently into foothills that in turn swelled into mountains. To the south of this valley marched the Bitterroot Mountains, tumbling together in craggy masses of blue, green, and purple that diminished in the hazy distance. Directly to the northeast loomed Mount Stuart, flanked by the hills and ridges of the Rattlesnake Mountains. Bubbling into this springtime valley from the mountains of the north was a small, pure, rushing stream pouring itself through a narrow defile. This precipitous canyon was known as the Coriakan Defile, named after a trapper who, in the 1840s, was ambushed and killed by Blackfeet Indians.

Montana in the spring is beautiful. The wildflowers, the sweet-smelling air, the rippling streams, the inviting expanse of open, untouched land. . . . O'Keefe's decision to homestead in this area influenced the lives of the many people he came to know, as well as his descendants, who feel a bond with the land unusual in these days of a more rootless society. A vivid description of the spot he chose to settle is provided by his daughter, Mary (Mollie) O'Keefe Ross. She said in her reminiscences, written many years later:

> It never takes a very great stretch of the imagination for me to see Montana, and our locality particularly, as it must have appeared fifty years ago. . . . When I drive along the roads or ride over the hills in our beautiful Indian summer days, I can see it all as it used to look. No white man's habitation in sight, the tall waving bunch grass with buffalo, not cattle, grazing on a thousand hills, the beautiful colored foliage, then as now, and deer and antelope and all wild animals in plenty . . . the country was full of living things. I can see the Indian lodges clustered along some stream, the Rattlesnake or Grant creek. How big and broad and grand it must have been, but how terribly lonesome. . . .

Mollie went on to describe the privations her father endured in those early years: the lack of proper shelter or food, and above all, the deep, abiding loneliness. One winter he had nothing to eat but beans and flour. He warmed the beans with tallow candles he had bought at a dollar a pound. At one point, to assuage loneliness, he traded two blankets for a tiny kitten. One day, when he was leaving for a short trip, the kitten tried to follow him. In attempting to send it back to the yard, he threw a stone that hit the kitten and killed it. Overcome, he sat down and wept. Mollie related that "he always cried at that story."

In spite of these hardships, O'Keefe built a log cabin with a sod roof and settled to the business of raising grain, potatoes, and fruit. His brother, Dave, joined him in 1861, and the brothers became successful at their ventures. Soon they were sending supplies as far

Anna Lester O'Keefe

as Fort Benton on the Missouri River, Corinne, Utah, and the Montana gold towns of Bannack and Virginia City. The O'Keefes are said to have brought in the first modern implements of farming to Western Montana: threshing machine, reaper, and mower.

So far, this tale of C. C. O'Keefe in Montana is no different from the ordinary pioneer story describing determined men wresting a living from the soil. It is not long after his settling at the O'Keefe Ranch, however, that the tales of the Baron's unusual exploits begin.

To clarify one point: why would an Irish peasant who lived in a sod hut be known to contemporaries and posterity as "the Baron"? It is typical of O'Keefe's sense of humor and of personal grandeur that he would let it be known that he was a land baron, a member of the Irish nobility.

It was in this guise that he rode to Virginia City with a load of potatoes to sell one September day in 1865. There he was struck with the charms of Anna Lester, an English girl who had also lived in Ireland and was teaching school in Virginia City. Legend has it that O'Keefe, dashing and gallant with his handlebar mustache ablaze and his green eyes ardent, pressed his suit with great vigor, leaning heavily on his well-known sobriquet of Baron.

He promised Anna, who had just recently arrived across the plains in a covered wagon, a life of ease and plenty in the baronial palace back at the Coriakan Defile. His efforts in this whirlwind courtship met with success. They were married within three days. Imagine Anna's dismay when she saw the real baronial palace!

Anna Lester's own trip westward makes an interesting story. Mollie describes how old tales were told by her parents around the fire at the O'Keefe Ranch:

> One of my pleasantest recollections is of an immense fireplace built in the corner of our big kitchen. It was made of adobe; they had no bricks then. We children would sit or lie on a buffalo robe spread before it and listen, winter evenings, to reminiscences. Many old-timers sat beside that fire—traders from the Hudson Bay Company, miners, packers, and later cowboys. Their stories if in print would entertain as well as some of Jack London's. They did not seem at all out of the ordinary to us children there; we were still in the wilderness.

Virginia City in 1868

Mollie related how her mother came from Council Bluffs to Virginia City, Montana Territory, in 1865 after a three-month trip by ox train: "It was a long, monotonous journey, and not without a good deal of fear." Although the travelers did not encounter hostile Indians, stories they heard caused them to take the precaution of

22

forming the covered wagons into a protective circle every night. Mollie wrote:

At last in September, they arrived in Virginia City. What a haven it was! They treated themselves to dinner at a restaurant that day. The building had a roof of ox hides. It was raining, and as they ate the maggots would drop from the ceiling out of the skins, which had not been well tanned. Everything was a fabulous price, calico a dollar a yard, etc., but they were very glad to be there. Before long my mother married my father and went to live in a little log cabin on a big lonely ranch far away from anyone, never a woman near.

Anna Lester O'Keefe's scrapbook suggests much about her character and temperament. Carefully assembled, it is inscribed "Mary Aileen O'Keefe from Her Mother, Nov. 26, 1882." It was clearly important to her that her daughters grow up with some grace and awareness of a more cultured world, raised though they were in a log cabin with buffalo robes for carpeting. There are several pictures of such contemporary figures as Queen Victoria and the Czar of Russia, people who ruled nations and lived in a genteel society foreign to two little pioneer girls. There are many clippings of poems and articles written in the slightly sentimental Victorian mode, valentines, faded photographs: a loving collection of the rare and tiny treasures with which Anna Lester could instill in her daughters the ideal of "gentle womanhood."

Nevertheless, she greatly appreciated the splendor of her wilderness surroundings, as her own poetry, three stanzas of which follow, shows:

Amidst the dark blue Mountains
    Of my Montana home
I love its sunny fountains
    As through its woods I roam

When wandering o'er its dark green hills
    I sometimes wend my way
I love to hear the murmuring rills
    Make music day by day

And oftentimes entranced I gaze
    Upon the setting sun
Upon its gorgeous tinted rays
    When its day's work is done

The scrapbook as a whole shows a conflict between Anna's love for the purity of the wilderness in which she lived and her longing for a more civilized, ordered beauty. The challenges she faced as a pioneer wife were difficult but often exhilarating. Her character

23

was a good complement to the Baron's. She made him a fine wife, and she was an excellent mother to their two daughters, Mary (Mollie) and Margaret.

The Baron's courting experiences were not limited to his pursuit of Anna Lester, however. One funny story was made public after his death, in a reminiscence by W. H. Babcock that appeared in the March 25, 1893 issue of the *Bozeman Avant Courier*. It seems that the Baron was, at an earlier time, quite interested in a captivating young half-Indian girl whose father, a white man, cast a jaundiced eye upon her multitude of suitors. He was so hostile, in fact, that he "was accused of having poisoned some of these men, not so they died but so that they were very sick. As a consequence, most persons admired the girl at a distance."

The Baron, intrigued by the "dusky damsel's" beauty and her inaccessibililty, sought out a lawyer to intercede on his behalf with the father. The lawyer, named Meredith, returned with glowing tales of the father's pleasure at the suit, claiming that both father and daughter were "eager for the match. In fact he overdid matters by picturing how glad they would be and how easy it was [for O'Keefe] to win her."

A little nonplussed at such instant availability, the Baron "sat in a brown study for perhaps twenty minutes. When he spoke it was substantially as follows: 'Now Meredith, I don't know whether I want that blamed half-breed or not. Me father was a baron before me an what would me family think to hear I was married to a half-breed. A man of me means and dignity. I have $10,000 in cash." And so on.

Although C. C. O'Keefe did not marry an Indian, many Indians became his friends. Except for a couple of rather humorous altercations, he managed to coexist quite peacefully with the native Americans throughout his lifetime. According to Mollie O'Keefe, "the Indians were very kind to Father . . . when he first came into the Missoula Valley. One helped build the little cabin with its dirt roof and also helped split the rails to fence around it. But the Indians would often all go on their hunting trips and he would be all alone. . . . I remember the whole flat at the mouth of the canyon being covered with their lodges and once seeing a grand bear hunt. They drove the bear out of the mountains and killed it on the sidehill just in front of our house. There were fully a hundred Indians chasing him with their dogs."

Close to the O'Keefe house was an old battleground on which the Blackfeet and Flatheads used to fight in earlier times. Mollie remembered one dark, rainy night when what seemed like a hundred Flathead Indians arrived at the door and asked for protection inside the house, fearing attack by hostile Blackfeet. They all crowded inside and stayed until dawn. Mollie recalled being "awfully frightened, but Mother seemed quite calm." Although the girls were frequently alarmed by drunken Indians singing and yelling in the road at night ("a hair-raising, blood-curdling sensation"), the family was never harmed.

The Baron alone, however, had a couple of skirmishes that bear retelling. One day a drunken Indian appeared at the back door of the O'Keefe ranch, looking for food. When no one seemed to be around, he pushed through the door and wandered into the main room, where the Baron (now an older man) was napping peacefully on the sofa. Startled into sudden wakefulness by the boozy smell of an alien presence, the Baron angrily demanded "wat in hell" the Indian was doing there. Sharp words ensued, and the Indian's belligerence became too much for O'Keefe's patience. So he whacked the intruder over the head with his rifle butt, and as the Indian slunk away, he prepared to return to the bliss of his nap. A wisp of smoke wafting through the window jarred his senses again. He leaped up to discover that the Indian, in retaliation, had set fire to all his haystacks!

Another tale that is told and retold with delight is the story of the Baron and his cravat. His granddaughter, the late Marjorie Ross Toole, wrote that this event occurred in 1862, when the O'Keefe brothers were taking a load of potatoes to Bannack by way of Trail Creek through the Bitterroot Mountains. Dave was drunk when they started out, and spent the day weaving all over the trail and mumbling to himself. They were accompanied by a Mexican cook who irritated the Baron intensely by wearing constantly an insolent, lazy grin and refusing to do any extra work. Two days passed with no harm done except to the combined dispositions of the party. But on the second night the three found themselves surrounded by a war party of Bannock Indians who had been attracted by the fire carelessly built up by the cook.

The Indians surveyed the scene with pleased grins, then proceeded to unload the thirteen horses and cook the potatoes in the fire. After the feast, they relieved the O'Keefe party of the rest of their burden by transferring all but one of the thirteen horses to the hands of their own braves. Then they seriously undermined the personal dignity of the brothers by snipping off buttons and removing gaiters. Naturally, the Baron was incensed at all this folly, but he managed to suppress his temper until one of the braves cast a covetous eye upon his cravat, an article of clothing he felt honor-bound to keep. When asked to give it up, he refused and snorted, crimson-faced, "An wat's more, ya big ham, you an' your schoolboys had better trot along, or it's lickin' ye all I'll be."

His Irish fervor so intimidated the Indian that he backed down, unwilling to lose face but reluctant to tangle with such tangible fury. Finally, however, to bribe the Indians into leaving, the Baron surrendered the cravat and the three escaped unscathed. Although they were shorn of horses, goods, and clothing, the indomitable O'Keefes found their way back to the ranch and set out again with a new load of potatoes for Bannack.

Another episode that shows the Baron's feisty spirit is the story of the O'Keefes' hospitality to the road agent. According to Marjorie Ross Toole, in January of 1864, Bob Zachary, a member of the Henry Plummer gang, came to the O'Keefe ranch and asked for food and shelter. The O'Keefes, happy to see a new person whether his reasons for traveling were fair or foul, showed the stranger much hospitality. The morning after Zachary's arrival, the Baron was aroused by an imperious knocking on his front door. There were the Vigilantes, armed and only too anxious to escort this notorious road agent to his final resting place. Without a glance at the owners of the house, they strode dramatically into the room and said, "Come, boy," to Zachary who was lying huddled on the floor in his blankets. The villain of the scene prepared to depart docilely enough, but the Baron was irritated at having his hospitality so rudely interrupted and his guest so summarily dragged forth. His ire was really aroused, however, when he glanced out of the front window and saw the Vigilantes preparing to hang the man on his front gatepost.

Slamming open the window, he bellowed, "Here! Wat's goin' on! There'll be nobody hangin' from me gatepost, and furthermore, ye can't hang a man on an empty stomach! Ye'll be bringin' him back in here this minnit if I have anything to say, an' thin afther breakfast ye'll take him into town an' do the thing proper!"

There was much arguing back and forth before the Vigilantes complied, but Bob Zachary had a hearty meal before he was taken into town and "hung proper."

Lest this portrait of the Baron O'Keefe paint him only in colors of fierceness and pugnacity, another Virginia City incident should show other facets of his character: his sense of honor and personal pride. The *Reminiscenses of Matilda Sevieur* recall how, in 1864, during one of the Baron's trips to Virginia City, he incurred a wound in his leg. A lady who noticed him limping gave him linen, castile soap, and salve to cleanse and bind the wound. They talked for a long time about County Cork. On his next trip, he rumbled into town with his wagon and waved away the miners who had converged and were grabbing at the green vegetables so rarely seen in those parts. "Hold on, boys," said the Baron. "Let me select some of these vegetables that I want to send to a lady up the gulch who saved me leg."

O'Keefe shared this sense of personal honor with his close friend,

Thomas Francis Meagher

Thomas Francis Meagher, who was a famous Civil War general and twice Acting Governor of Montana. His acquaintance with Meagher went back a long way; both were sent away from their homeland on the same ship because of their activities with the "Young Irelanders." We gain a glimpse into Meagher's private feelings and concerns in a letter he wrote to the Baron on September 26, 1866, in which he requested a loan of $1,000 to pay back some "miserable little bills:"

> Having, as I said to you, secured the "public" triumph, I want to complete it by the "private." . . . I want to return to Virginia City a proud and independent Irish gentleman—having no one to insult, or even to give me the cold shoulder, because I owe him a miserable little bill of "50" or "100" dollars—
>
> I want my countrymen to place me up and beyond the sneers of these "blackguards"—who are, ever, so ready to run down an Irishman, whenever, and wherever they have a chance—
>
> It is my ambition—it is indeed, and in truth my heart's desire—to be the representative and champion of the Irish Race in the wild great mountains. . . .

This florid, expansive prose reflects both men's desire for public stature as well as personal honor. Surely the Baron, too, was conscious of the shanty Irish image so prevalent in those times, and sought to change it. He assured the lady in Virginia City that his

27

family back in Cork were "very respectable folks, ma'am." Such feelings (as well as his constant need to be in the limelight) may have prompted him to become politically active in the late 1860s and early 1870s.

One other letter to O'Keefe from Meagher is faded, torn, and difficult to decipher, but it is evident that Meagher, on December 10, 1866, acted on a request by the Baron to secure the job of Missoula County Commissioner for him. "Immediately on receipt of your letter of the 6th November, I called upon the Governor and handed the communication to him. The result was he made out your commission as County Commissioner, and sent the same, right off, to the Council for Confirmation."

Thus, through the offices of a good friend, the Baron O'Keefe's short but colorful political career was launched.

Although there is not much known about the Baron's work as Missoula County Commissioner, there is no doubt that he made waves. An article on Missoula government in 1866 by A. L. Stone which appeared in the *Great Falls Tribune* in September, 1944, describes how O'Keefe refused to show up for two months at County Commissioners' meetings, irritated because the county government had been transferred from Hellgate to Missoula Mills, thus necessitating a longer trip to get to meetings. Then, when the other men present seemed to take very little interest in some minor issues he raised, he "bolted the session" just after becoming reconciled to the new meeting place.

The Baron seems to have met with greater satisfaction in his role as legislator. The January, 1952 issue of the *Montana, the Magazine of Western History* described how the Baron referred to the legislature as "parliament." "Until a few years ago there were those who could recall seeing the Irishman astride his horse, in formal dress, on his way to the legislature. He was wont to shout to passers-by 'Out of me way! I'm on me way to parliament!' "

O'Keefe's sojourn in the legislative halls lasted only two years. He was elected to the Territorial Legislature for an extraordinary session in 1873, and returned in 1874. He was defeated when he ran in 1876. The specific reasons for his political downfall remain obscure, since the citizenry evidently appreciated greatly his introduction and support of certain popular bills.

What scanty correspondence the Baron left to posterity is something of a study in invective. For example "Shanahan," he wrote to Martin Maginnis in 1874, "is a sneaking, low, contemptible rogue. No word of honor, no pluck, or no fight in him. He is a miserable, lying creature. He says he is a cousin of Cavanaugh's. He lies. He'd have more man in him if he had any Cavanaugh blood in him." Having thus blasted Shanahan, the Baron remarked: "Ivrybody wants me to go to parliament again, but I won't as it is a loosing game." Perhaps to one of the Baron's intransigence it was, indeed, a "loosing" game.

Research into the House Journals of 1873 and 1874, though, is enlightening: the Baron's name is mentioned with some frequency, but it appears that our illustrious statesman is recorded most often as having moved for adjournment or recess of the various daily sessions.

Bills that would directly benefit the Baron and his constituents received his strong support; in 1873 he moved to repeal the dog tax law, and through some deft maneuvering managed to have Missoula County exempt from an act restricting "the killing of game and catching of fish." In 1874 he advocated a bill to "regulate the fees of doctors and lawyers."

His efforts were well received after the 1874 session. A quote from the *Helena Daily Herald* of March 12, 1874, describes how the Baron, returning to Missoula, received "a salute of ten guns . . . fired by the citizens of Missoula, who assembled in immense numbers, and a grand demonstration took place, which is said to have been the most enthusiastic within the recollection of the oldest inhabitant . . . as the Baron . . . stood proud and erect before the crowd, a happy, contented smile radiated his features. . . ." Apparently Missoulians were pleased by the Baron's support of "the Toll Road and Bridge Law, the new Apportionment Law, and others." It is not known exactly what role the Baron played in the passage of these laws, but legend has it that the absence of state toll roads and bridges in Montana is attributable directly to C. C. O'Keefe, since he opposed such inconveniences so vehemently. There is a story of how the Baron, who made frequent trips to Fort Owen, once refused out of principle to pay toll at a bridge across the Clark Fork, and instead swam the river.

The culmination of his political career, the "grand demonstration" in Missoula, took place in 1874, when the Baron was an established figure, a "solid citizen." Montana was a developing territory, fitted out with all the proprieties of a legislature and judiciary system.

But the most famous story about the Baron comes from a dozen years earlier, when Montana was raw and unsettled, the Vigilantes and road agents were rife, and legislatures and judicial systems were niceties thus far unheard of in those parts. This story has been documented by several sources, including the Baron's daughter, his brother, and his granddaughter, and it is of genuine historical significance. It describes the first trial in what is now the State of Montana.

The defendant was, naturally, the Baron O'Keefe, and the plaintiff was one Tin Cup Joe, a half-breed French Canadian trapper

Henry P.
Brooks

Frank H.
Woody

who had come down into the valley from his trapping lines in the
Bitterroot with his Indian wife and a half-starved horse. This was
in January or February, 1861 or 1862. They came to the O'Keefe
cabin and asked permission to stay all night. The Baron granted it
on condition that Tin Cup Joe take care of the place while he and
his brother went up the Blackfoot to see Captain Mullan. He
cautioned his guest not to let the horse get into the seed oats, which
he was carefully saving to plant a crop in the spring.

All appeared in order upon the Baron's return, until he glanced
in the direction of the barn and saw the horse contentedly munch-
ing on the oats he had stored. His Irish temper raging, he drove the
horse from the barn, whereupon the frightened creature fell into a
partially excavated root cellar and died before it could be gotten
out.

Tin Cup Joe, highly incensed at having one source of his livelihood so suddenly gone, went immediately to Hellgate to talk to his
friend, Henry Brooks, who was Justice of the Peace. Brooks advised Joe to sue for the killing of his horse. So a trial was arranged,
which was scheduled to take place in Bolte's Saloon. According to
Marjorie Ross Toole, "Bolte's was a little log building not far from
the Higgins-Worden store—the first store to be built in the state.
The windows were very small; there was just one door. And in the
dark interior was the scene of the first formal administration of
justice in Montana."

This trial was formal in name only. The court session opened
with Brooks acting as judge and Frank Woody as self-appointed
prosecuting attorney. (According to Dave O'Keefe, Woody acted as
the judge. In Mrs. Toole's version, Woody was prosecutor while
Brooks acted as judge. In both accounts, however, Woody was the
person to whom the Baron presented his "credentials.") The Baron
was there, prepared to conduct his own defense. As Granville
Stuart observed in his *Journals* under the date of March 20, 1862,
"Anyone knowing the Baron would feel confident that he was well
able to look out for himself."

The proceedings began, with Tin Cup Joe's lawyer contending
that the Baron had attacked the horse with a pitchfork. (The Baron

has since been exonerated of this charge; its falsity rests primarily on the fact that there was no such implement in that part of the country at the time). O'Keefe was becoming prickly with anger at hearing himself accused of such indignities. He sat there, growing more crimson every second, then suddenly stood up so fast his chair fell over with a crash. Stalking over to Woody, his eyes blazing and his red hair sticking up in tufts, he demanded to know who gave him the right to defend a case and where were his credentials? Woody reached coolly into his pocket and produced a pack of cards.

Fanning them out with a flourish, he smiled confidently at the Baron and responded, "Here are my credentials. And by what right, may I ask, do you find yourself duly constituted to act in your own defense? May I see your credentials?"

"You really want to see my credentials?"

When Woody replied in the affirmative, the Baron's fist shot forward, striking that distinguished attorney between the eyes. "Here are my credentials!" roared the infuriated defendant. Then the melee began. Another Frenchman struck the Baron over the head with a stool, and although the redoubtable O'Keefe was ready to fight every man in the place, he might have been in sad shape if a man named Skinner (according to Dave O'Keefe, a road agent), hadn't happened along. He took the part of the underdog and the fight raged for some time. Finally the Baron, disgusted, left.

After his departure, some semblance of order was restored. Amid shattered glass and splintered chairs, it was decided that the Baron should pay $40 in damages to Tin Cup Joe. It is universally assumed that the settlement was never made, and that Tin Cup Joe still has the $40 coming!

Typically, Baron O'Keefe maintained his humor, courage, and strength up until the last minutes of his life. An article from the *Helena Daily Herald*, dated June 10, 1871 and signed JHM, characterized him at one point in his career: "The Baron is brave as steel, will fight in a minute, and I believe always gets 'licked,' but his courage is never the weaker for that."

A. L. Stone, in a series of articles on Montana history in the *Great Falls Tribune*, described the Baron on the day of his death in 1893 in a story which deserves to be quoted here:

As the Baron passed into the last moments of his life he asked for the presence of his brother and knew that death was imminent. But Dave had gone to Frenchtown and couldn't get back that day. When the Baron heard this he went into a rage against his brother. Mr. Eliakim M. Ross, who knew that the Baron had Bright's disease and was paying him a neighborly call on that day, tells the story:
"Upon the answer to his question as to the whereabouts of Dave,

the Baron exploded, 'Gone to Frenchtown! What the hell does he have to go to Frenchtown for on the day I'm going to die?'

"The comment that followed upon the lack of fraternal feeling on the part of Dave is better not repeated here. It was fierce and vindictive and lasted a long time. When the sick man's breath gave out Ross ventured the natural assurance that it was nonsense to talk about death, there was no immediate prospect of it.

" 'Of course I'm going to die today,' was the comeback. 'Look at my hands, they're turning purple right now.' Ross looked. The Baron was right. His fingers were blue. In a few hours he was dead."

Marjorie Ross Toole

Claude Elder relates that Dave O'Keefe, upon returning from Frenchtown, built a coffin for the Baron. They loaded the coffin into a wagon for transportation into Missoula, while Dave, presumably out of sentiment, got roaring drunk. He rode the coffin into Missoula, flourishing a pint of whiskey and singing Irish ballads all the way. It was certainly a more appropriate send-off for the Baron than a lugubrious funeral march. The Baron was buried at St. Mary's Roman Catholic Cemetery in Missoula.

Cornelius C. O'Keefe was a man molded by the rigors of his age, yet he helped shape his world and make it what it was. I often wonder what he would be like had he lived today. Could his character have made such a strong imprint on our memories if he had lived within the last few decades? Would he have been as free to exercise his ingenuity, his courage, his eccentricity? As that redoubtable Montana lady, the late Jeannette Rankin, observed once during a television interview, "People have to conform so much more today. In the old days we did what we pleased." The Baron certainly did what he pleased, and in doing so he made some significant contributions to the pioneer west, and created some legends that are remembered today with laughter and delight.

A mournful conclusion bemoaning a lost spirit and glorifying the pioneer days would be as inappropriate, however, as a sedate funeral train would have been after the Baron's death. True, the O'Keefe Ranch stands in danger of being engulfed by pastel housing developments, but O'Keefe Creek still gushes out of the Coriakan Defile and the contours of the hills around Hellgate remain constant. We can still hike up to the Top O'Deep where the Baron's descendants struggled to find gold during the Depression, and find peace in the beargrass and the sunlight. This bond of the land's beauty is something that links Baron O'Keefe with his most remote descendants, and we are grateful for the legacy.

That is the end of my daughter's account of the life of her great-great-grandfather. Since she wrote it, a little more has come to light about the fabulous Baron, most notably a story about the time he went to war.

One day, in August, 1877, the Baron came charging into the ranch house. "Anna! Anna! The Indians are comin.' I'm takin' you and the little girls into town so you'll be safe. We've got to go right away!"

Anna was bewildered.

"What Indians?"

"Anna, it's the Nez Perce. They're invadin' the Bitterroot Valley. I'm a Citizen Volunteer and I've got to head up the Bitterroot."

Anna said calmly, "Baron, you know the Nez Perce would never harm us."

"That I know, Anna, but I'm a Citizen Volunteer. I've got to go!"

"Why did you volunteer to fight the Nez Perces? They're our friends."

"Anna," said the Baron in exasperation, "how did I know what tribe was comin'? For all I knew it might have been the Blackfeet!"

Anna resignedly piled the two girls into the Baron's wagon and the Baron whipped the team into a gallop. They picked up Uncle Dave on the fly. The Baron was in his element.

In less than an hour, he unloaded Anna and the girls at the Eddy Hammond Co. store (now The Bon) in Missoula. A large crowd of women and children were in the basement, many crying with fear.

The Baron and Dave turned south and the team clattered across the Higgins Avenue bridge. They headed south and the Baron whipped the team to such a speed that Dave was moved to say, "Hell Baron, ye'll have the team wore out before we get to the battle!" The Baron laughed and replied, "Aw, we'll put 'em up in Stevensville and give 'em some oats. Then you and I'll have a shot of Irish whiskey, eh?"

They reached Stevensville and put the horses into a livery stable. The Nez Perce tribe with all their women, children and baggage had gone through the day before, but they had been fairly peaceable. The warriors had made a few forays, and they had stolen some cattle and horses, but the Nez Perces had no quarrel with the valley residents. The O'Keefe brothers headed for the nearest saloon, which was full of excited men, talking and gesticulating.

In the morning, the Baron was anxious to be on his way but Uncle Dave decided he would go no further. "I've got nothin' against the Nez Perce," he said. "Let the Army catch 'em. That's the Army's job."

The Army indeed. The first column of regulars, the U.S. Seventh Infantry, began marching into town from the north. The Baron hung around for a while. Finally he could stand it no longer. He hitched up the team, and headed south where the soldiers had disappeared.

He made it to Sula but at that point he had to tie up the team

Chief Joseph of the Nez Perce.

because of windfalls. The little valley was full of settlers riding around in all directions, talking excitedly and pointing south to the great mountains of the Continental Divide where Chief Joseph and his Nez Perces had disappeared ahead of the Army troops.

The Baron didn't know what to do. He had foolishly signed up as a Citizen Volunteer to fight a tribe of Indians that he could not fight because he was a Nez Perce blood brother. But he tied up his team and headed up the mountain to the south all alone.

Darkness caught him and he spent a shivering night curled up in a hole in the rocks.

He could hear the sound of rifle fire before dawn. He roused himself and went on. Then he heard the loud boom of artillery and he said to himself, "Faith, and it's cannon they got!"

As he drew near the battlefield, he veered out to the south and crept cautiously down the nose of a ridge that overlooked the Big Hole Valley. He saw a thrilling and amazing sight.

There before him, streaming out to the south, were a thousand Nez Perce horses. They were galloping at a hard run, their manes flying and their tails flaring out behind them. On either side of the herd, rode the Nez Perce warriors at full speed, their war cries echoing as they whipped their horses into a frenzy. Behind came the squaws; the hastily loaded travois bounced across the rough ground; the baggage piled high, and on top the little Indian children hung on for dear life. Some squaws rode, others ran; their skirts flew up and their pudgy legs carried them over the ground at astounding speed.

The Baron was struck with awe and he said to himself, "Begorra, the Nez Perces gave the Army the slip!"

Thus did Chief Joseph and the Nez Perces escape destruction in another battle in their famous retreat to find refuge in Canada. The battles would end in the cold fall months at the Battle of the Bearpaws within sight of the Canadian line, and Joseph would say at the conclusion of his famous speech:

"From where the sun now stands, I shall fight no more forever."

34

The Baron turned and made his way up the ridge. He picked up Dave in Stevensville, and in Missoula he retrieved his little family who were still hiding in the basement of the Eddy, Hammond Co. store.

O'Keefe's daughter Mary (Mollie) married a tough and enterprising young logger and builder named Kenneth Ross, whose fascinating life story is the subject of Chapter 4. Their daughter Marjorie was my mother. The O'Keefe's other daughter Margaret (Maggie) married a man named Fitzell, and they had a daughter named Mollie who grew up to marry J. Harold Matteson, an educator.

Mollie Matteson now lives in Florida, but her memory of the things Maggie told her about her life with Anna Lester and the Baron are vivid. In a long letter to me a few years ago, Mollie Matteson related with great poignancy the struggles of the young mother and the two little girls as they coped with the violent Baron and the continuous parade of Indians and frontiersmen who haunted their lonely ranch home.

Mollie was born many years after the Baron died in 1893, but her mother, Maggie, was with her off and on until Maggie died in 1956. Maggie was reticent about discussing the Baron, as were all the members of this family who knew him. Kenneth Ross never mentioned him. Mary (Mollie) O'Keefe Ross never mentioned him. But over the long years, Maggie began to talk and her memories came out, particularly of her mother, Anna Lester O'Keefe. The two daughters loved and respected Anna, and were proud of the heritage she gave them.

Anna was definitely English and Scottish—she came from a prosperous English family near Glasgow. She was educated; her letters and poetry leave no doubt about that. In the little writing desk that she carried across the Plains, there is a postcard showing a promenade at Brighton-by-the-Sea. It comes from one of her suitors and the writer asks: "Do you remember, dear Anna, when we strolled in bliss along this walk by the sea?"

On her mother's side, Anna was a descendant of Mary Stuart, Queen of Scots. This would make her a Catholic, the right religion for the Baron, but she is not buried with him in St. Mary's Cemetery. Maybe she had joined the Scottish Presbyterian Church. Her two daughters were Protestant.

Anna's mother died on the sailing ship bound for North America, after she had been forced to take some "horrible black medicine" for cholera. Anna landed with her father, Richard, in Ontario. She came to Virginia City by covered wagon to be "with friends"; the *Official Register of the Montana Pioneers* pinpoints the date as 1864. Alan Hardenbrook was on the same trail at the same time.

In Virginia City, she became a seamstress for a time, and once the prostitutes there offered her some hand-me-down dresses of magnificent velvet, brightly colored and trimmed with fur. She found them repulsive and haughtily turned them down.

In 1864 Anna was twenty-two, time to be married in those days, and when the green-eyed Irishman who ostensibly bore a title of nobility wanted to take her to his castle, she succumbed and he carried her off to a one-room cabin with a dirt floor.

Maggie told her daughter that the one thing which enraged the Baron most was to be thought of as a shanty Irishman. Maggie felt the same way, and she claimed that the O'Keefes of County Cork indeed did have money.

As Maggie described it, life was hell for her mother Anna in O'Keefe's one-room cabin.

In his early years, the Baron was gregarious. Every Indian, drunk or sober, every bandit, road agent, mountain man and trapper stopped to hoist one with the Baron. His ranch bordered the main trail to the Flathead country and the procession was endless.

The Nez Perce were his favorite Indians. Chief Joseph dandled little Maggie on his knee. One day Anna and the two little girls witnessed the ceremony in which the Baron became a blood brother of the Nez Perce. The Baron faced a Nez Perce chief and thrust out his arm. The chief thrust out his own arm. Each took a knife and slashed the forearm of the other with a deep gash. They joined forearms, and each man squeezed as much blood as he could stand into the wound of his brother. Thus, did the Irish and the Nez Perce become blood brothers in a savage ritual signifying that each thought the other a brave and indomitable warrior.

Maggie said that when the Baron was sober, he was kind and generous, but when he was drinking, he was cruel and frightful. When he went on a rampage, Anna always hid the two little girls. In the 1870s the girls were attending Sacred Heart Academy in Missoula. One day Anna rode in from the ranch in a highly nervous state, with a kerchief tightly bound around her head. She told the girls that it was the only way she could calm her nerves. This was probably the result of either Indian trouble or Baron trouble.

In her childhood, Maggie said, there was a warning system arranged by the people of Missoula to signal the arrival of Joseph and his Nez Perces in the Missoula Valley. When the Nez Perces were spotted riding down Lolo Creek, two huge white flags were flown from the ridge north of Lolo Peak. The women and children were taken to safety, and the men prepared to do battle. Once some boys hoisted the two white flags as a prank, and all the Missoula people went into hiding again.

I met Maggie once myself. I went to Seattle in 1941 and called on her in the apartment where she was staying with her daughter Mollie. I found her to be a friendly, loquacious, elderly lady. I also noticed that she had a pronounced limp. It turned out that in the 1870s Maggie was bucked off a horse and broke her leg. Anna took her to a doctor in Missoula, who announced that the leg had to be amputated. Anna wouldn't hear of this. She knew of a good surgeon in Helena, so she loaded poor suffering little Maggie into the wagon to go there. On the way, they were accosted by some drunken miners who demanded a ride. Anna could do nothing but accede to their demands. One miner sat on the driver's seat, pulling on a quart of whiskey. When he finished the quart, he carelessly tossed the bottle into the back of the wagon where little Maggie was reclining in great pain. The bottle landed right on the fracture in Maggie's leg.

It took Anna three days to reach Helena. The surgeon saved the leg, but Maggie limped around for the rest of her life.

But Anna seems to have been up to any emergency. When the Northern Pacific Railroad was completed in 1883, the main line ran only a few hundred yards from the O'Keefe Ranch. One day, Maggie and Anna were up near the tracks picking flowers. Anna noticed that a rail was broken and a tie removed. She rushed up the tracks and flagged down an approaching train, averting a bad accident. The Northern Pacific officialdom offered her a lifetime pass on the railroad, but Anna declined, saying that any good citizen would have done the same.

My mother, Marjorie Ross Toole, was born on the Baron's ranch in 1890 and lived there for the first six years of her life. One rainy night, she and Anna heard a pathetic crying, a wailing human, someone in distress. It went on and on and on. My mother became frightened and distressed. She was only four years old, and she kept asking Anna what the haunting cry was.

The Baron was asleep on the couch. Finally Anna went over and shook him to life. He was irritated, but he rose and Anna said firmly: "Baron, go out on the road and see who's making that noise. Little Marjorie's terribly frightened." The Baron arose grumpily, donned his coat, and stumped out into the rain. The county road was only a few hundred yards from the house. Within a few minutes, he returned and Anna asked: "Well, Baron. What is it?"

"Aw," he replied, "it's just a drunk Indian beatin' his wife." He plopped down on the couch.

After the Baron died in 1893, Anna moved to Missoula and stayed with her son-in-law Kenneth Ross. In her last years, she was blind. She died in 1900 and was buried in the Missoula cemetery, about one mile from St. Mary's cemetery where lies the body of the Baron.

In his first years at the Coriackan Defile the Baron did well. He and Dave worked hard at their vegetable garden and made continuous trips to the burgeoning mining camps. Granville Stuart's journal records several of the Baron's passages through Gold Creek. Fortunately he never caught the mining fever.

Major Washington J. McCormick would become one of Montana's leading citizens as his life progressed, but in the early 1860's he was the Indian Agent for the Flathead Tribe and his headquarters were at Arlee, about 15 miles north of the Baron's place. His monthly stipend originated in Washington, D.C. and had to come to Montana by the perilous route across the Plains or by the savagely dangerous and slow voyage up the Missouri by steamer, thence by freighter or express rider to Arlee. The Republicans were rampantly in power and Major McCormick was known as a "red-hot Democrat," so there was no particular hurry in sending out his monthly checks. The Major became embarrassed financially to the point of insolvency. Knowing that the Baron was a Democrat and prospering, the Major went down to see him. He informed the Baron of his plight and asked the Irishman for a loan of $1,500 to tide him over. Ever suspicious, the Baron raised his eyebrows and asked, "And what can ye be givin' me for security, now?"

"Well Baron, I can give you a mortgage on the Flathead Reservation. That should be sufficient, wouldn't you say?"

Sufficient indeed. The Flathead Reservation is an incomparably rich, well-watered valley of excellent soil, threaded by a large river, containing the largest fresh-water lake in the west, and bounded by the Mission Range on the east, a chain of alpine peaks that rival any scenery in the world. It covers one million acres.

But the Baron wasn't particularly impressed. No one lived on the Flathead Reservation except the Flathead Tribe, which came and went. The only white men were a few priests at the St. Ignatius Mission. This magnificent land was worthless without white men to extract its wealth.

Major McCormick whipped out a mortgage and showed the Baron his appointment papers, which gave him broad authority to hypothecate the Indian land for any purpose. The Baron went to the table and weighed out $1,500 in gold dust, the only universally accepted medium of exchange in Montana in 1865.

Major McCormick immediately took off for Washington, D.C. It is not known whether he caught a boat going down the Missouri or made his way across the Plains. It is known, however, that the distance is 3,000 miles and that it took almost two months to reach Washington from Montana.

After five months, the Baron became irritated and concerned about his money. His letters to McCormick went unanswered, so he addressed a letter to the Montana Territorial Delegate, James Cavanaugh, a fellow Irishman, and soon received a letter from McCormick:

Dear Baron, as distance lends enchantment to the view, so does time lessen the weight of financial obligations. Upon my arrival in Washington, I found that Congress had adjourned without appropriating funds for my salary. However, I anticipate that they will convene again next fall and I have secured a promise that maximum efforts will be made to re-open the Indian appropriation bill so as to pay me one year's back salary. I am also sending you another mortgage which covers all the personal property on the Flathead Reservation. This includes all the items at the Agency such as feed grains, tool, horses, cattle, pack saddles, and a wagon. This security for your loan is of much more value than the previous mortgage which covers only the land. [Ahem!]

Please do not bring foreclosure proceedings until my return which I hope will be about Christmas time. Oh, what a sad day it was for this nation when the perfidious Republicans usurped the power!

McCormick was as good as his word. He showed up at the Coriackan Defile in the cold, closing days of 1865 and peeled off a roll of U.S. Treasury greenbacks that paid off the principal of the Baron's mortgage and interest at 3 percent per month.

The value of the Flathead Reservation today can be said to be in excess of $1 billion. Had the Baron perfected his mortgage and foreclosed (and this could well have happened in 1865) and, if one goes back to 1865 and takes the extracted value of crops, timber, minerals, tourism and energy production, plus the appreciation in land value, the net worth of the descendants of Baron O'Keefe would be about $20 billion. Thus they would be the richest family in the world.

As we have seen, living with the Baron at Castle O'Keefe, as he sometimes called it, was trying and at times fearful. There was much fighting and shouting and even shooting and Maggie O'Keefe hated it. So in 1875, at the age of eight, she made a perfectly rational decision. She had come to like the life of the Indians better than her own, and decided to go live with them.

Early one spring morning she set out northward toward the Coriackan Defile. She knew that the Indians always disappeared into this dark canyon when they left the ranch, and she was sure she would find them up there someplace.

When she entered the canyon, she found O'Keefe Creek pouring its way down over rocks and boulders. The trail was steep but well marked. She reached the top of Evaro Hill and crossed the little meadow at the top where the Indian women had their annual foot races. On the other side of the pass she found Finlay Creek and followed it down to its mouth where it joins the Jocko River. Ahead of her there was nothing but a great, wild country, with the Mission Range thrusting its white peaks at the sky. She saw no Indians but she resolutely pushed along down the west bank of the Jocko. She was getting a little tired when she reached the spot where the Schall Ranch is today, but looking across the stream she saw a fairly large Indian village. Smoke was coming out of the teepees, and several squaws were digging for bitterroots in the fields near the village.

The Jocko is not an inconsiderable stream, but she plunged in, and though she was swept from her feet a couple of times, she emerged dripping wet on the other side.

She walked over to the nearest squaw, who was on hands and knees digging roots. The squaw stood up, put her hands on her hips and stared at little Maggie. Maggie said:

"I've come to live with you."

The squaw couldn't understand English, so she grasped Maggie by the hand and led her to the village and up to the lodge of Chief Arlee, who could. Arlee took one look at Maggie and laughed.

"You've got the Baron O'Keefe's little girl, Maggie."

Then he said to Maggie, "What are you doing up here, Maggie? You better go home."

Maggie shook her head, saying, "I've come to live with you."

Arlee remonstrated, "Maggie, you've got a nice house and family. You better go home."

Maggie would not change her mind.

Arlee laughed again and said, "Well, all right, you can live over there in McDonald's lodge. But Maggie, you've got to work just like the little Flathead kids work."

Maggie was overjoyed. Mrs. McDonald could speak some English, and she told Maggie that her man was away hunting buffalo across the mountains. She put a deerskin dress on Maggie to replace the gingham one that had been soaked in the Jocko, and she showed Maggie where she was to sleep.

On the day that Maggie left, Anna O'Keefe and her daughter, Mollie, Maggie's older sister, were alone on the ranch. The Baron was away hauling vegetables to Fort Benton, but he was expected back any day. Anna started looking for Maggie. As the day wore on and she came to realize that Maggie was nowhere near, a cold fear came over her. She ran down the road to Dave O'Keefe's cabin. Dave immediately saddled a horse and galloped off for Missoula, thinking that somehow Maggie might have been inveigled into visiting that metropolis. He reported the disappearance to the sheriff, who promised to raise a posse.

Anna was now frantic with worry. She put little Mollie on a

horse behind her and set out for Frenchtown. She called on every French settler, then headed for the barren hills north of the town and entered the timber, calling constantly for Maggie. It was long after dark when she returned and put little Mollie to bed, but she slept not a wink herself. Anna was desperate.

In the morning, she once again put Mollie behind her on the horse and rode into the hills where the Missoula Snowbowl is now located. All day she rode, helplessly calling Maggie's name. Uncle Dave rode up the Bitterroot, where he killed a bear and examined the contents of its stomach.

On the evening of the next day, the Baron clattered into the ranch on his wagon, which bore bales of buffalo robes. Anna met him in front of the house and said desperately,

"Baron, little Maggie is gone!"

"What d'ye mean, she's gone?"

Anna breathlessly poured out the story.

The Baron quickly rode to the barn, saddled his horse and headed for the Coriackan Defile. He pounded his horse up the narrow canyon, across the meadow containing the squaws' race-track, and made a beeline for the Flathead Indian Agency and Major Peter Ronan.

The major said that Chief Arlee had brought his band through several days before, but that no little white girl was with them. Concluding that Maggie could not possibly be further north, the Baron turned toward home, but upon arriving he did not stop. He took the Mullan Road for Cedar Creek, where an immense gold strike had been made. Cedar Creek was a full 50 miles from Castle O'Keefe.

The next day, Mollie was sick and Anna was forced to stay home and take care of her. She was all alone on the ranch and spent most of the day in prayer.

Maggie was getting along just fine with the Flatheads. She learned how to tan deer hides and how to dig for bitterroots. She wandered far in search of firewood. She watched the little Indian boys trying out their small bows and arrows on gophers and squirrels.

She learned how to reach into a pot for a buffalo rib and how to tear the meat from the bone with her teeth. And there was some white man's food, too—coffee, bread, and pork. Mrs. McDonald was kind to her, but firm.

Maggie dreaded only one thing. When the warriors returned from the hunt, there would be whiskey and fighting, and men and women would act strangely. Maggie had learned to detest whiskey.

In a few days, the Baron returned from Cedar Creek, but he could not stop looking, so he turned east and went up the Cokahalahishkit, the River of the Road to the Buffalo (now the

Blackfoot). Uncle Dave searched the banks of the Clark Fork River.

Anna had a strong feeling that if she could just get to the top of the highest mountain around and view the whole country, she might get a clue to Maggie's whereabouts. So she put Mollie behind her on the horse and headed for the top of Stark Mountain, the huge timbered ridge that hoists itself into the sky just north of Castle O'Keefe. After climbing endlessly through brush and fallen trees, she emerged at the top by afternoon and found a small clearing in the trees.

She looked in all directions, studying the floors of the great valleys. At length she spotted Chief Arlee's camp and its teepees, with smoke coming out their tops. She and Mollie guided the horse down the north face of the great ridge. When they hit the floor of the valley, they forded the Jocko, and emerged just a short distance from Arlee's camp.

Arlee was in the midst of breaking camp to head north for the Flathead Mission at St. Ignatius. Maggie was tussling with a long pole in order to carry it to the horses to be used as a travois. Teepees were coming down and confusion was everywhere.

Anna did not spot Maggie in her deerskin dress right away, but then she saw a pair of blue eyes. She rushed to Maggie and clasped her in her arms.

"Oh, my baby, my little girl! I've found you. Oh, thank God! Thank God! You're safe at last!" She held Maggie to her breast and sobbed.

Chief Arlee came over and Maggie looked at him questioningly. Arlee explained to Mrs. McDonald in the Indian tongue, "That's the O'Keefe woman. She's come for her little girl."

Anna looked up at Chief Arlee through her tears and said, "Thank you, thank you, Chief, for taking care of my darling little girl."

"That's all right, Mrs. O'Keefe. Maggie's a good worker. She'll make somebody a good squaw someday." Then he laughed.

Maggie didn't really want to leave Chief Arlee's camp, but parental authority prevailed and soon Anna's horse was headed south with two little girls riding in the rear instead of one. They made their way to the Flathead Indian Agency, arriving about dusk. Major Ronan put them up for the night and in the morning Anna headed for Castle O'Keefe.

The Baron was standing in front of the house when they arrived. He reached out and grasped little Maggie to his breast. He buried his face in her neck, then held her out in front of him as the tears streamed down his face.

Maggie looked back at him and smiled—an uncertain smile, yet a smile.

Always in the background at the Baron's ranch was his brother Dave. They got along well and worked together in the ranch's customary tasks of raising vegetables and transporting them to markets in Fort Benton and Virginia City. Usually the two went together on these trips, but sometimes Dave went alone.

In the year 1875, Uncle Dave made such a trip to Fort Benton alone. He took the Mullan Road. The shorter route up the Blackfoot Canyon was impassable for a wagon because of the narrow gorges on the lower Blackfoot River. After Dave crossed the mountains, he turned his wagon north and drove down Canyon Creek, thence northward across the prairies to the Dearborn and Sun rivers, both of which he forded, thence on to Fort Benton.

Dave O'Keefe had never owned a suit of clothes and he wanted one. He sold his produce, then went to the T. C. Power Co. store to visit the clothing department. There he found a fine-looking black suit, brought to Fort Benton by a Missouri River steamer that had come 2,000 miles from St. Louis. He sought out T. C. Power and asked if he could buy the suit on credit. Power replied:

"No, O'Keefe, I won't sell you that suit on credit. But I'll tell you what I'll do. I'll give you that suit if you'll go home and bring me a load of potatoes and vegetables, like I saw you bringing in to I. G. Baker's store yesterday. How about it?"

"I'll do it," responded Uncle Dave.

So he got into his wagon and headed home across the plains, carrying a load of buffalo robes and wolf hides the 250 miles to the Coriackan Defile, full of danger. Blackfeet warriors roamed everywhere, and they were angry. The Army was waging war against Blackfeet men, women and children. Only recently the famed American Fur Co. trader, Malcolm Clarke, had been killed by Indians near Wolf Creek. But Uncle Dave made the trip safely both ways. When he reached Fort Benton again, a chill wind was beginning to blow across the plains. Fall was coming.

He carefully wrapped his new suit of clothes, tucked it under a buffalo hide and set out for home. By the time he got there he had driven 500 miles in forty days. He celebrated by putting on his painfully acquired suit and attending a dance in Frenchtown.

After the Baron died in 1893, Dave O'Keefe stayed on at the ranch alone in his house across the road from the Baron's buildings, where the O'Keefe Creek road turns east. He farmed there until about 1912. Then he started to go blind and, like Anna O'Keefe earlier, moved in with Kenneth and Mollie Ross in Missoula.

Uncle Dave had always occupied a special place in the heart of Mollie O'Keefe Ross. He was kind and helpful when problems came up for the young mother, Anna, and her two little girls. As a small boy living in the same house, I too came to know and love Uncle

Dave. He would bounce me on his knee and sing strange songs, some in Gaelic. One went: "Rumpstye, pumstye, piddle eye, winkum. Sing, song Polly won't you Chimeo."

But Uncle Dave could be a trial at times. He was a frontiersman and always kept a loaded 30:06 rifle handy. The big house was heated by slabs from the logs at Bonner. A college boy was hired to heave the slabs into the basement. He made quite a noise, and on several occasions it occurred to Uncle Dave that the boy was a burglar. Although Uncle Dave was completely blind, he took his rifle down, stumbled into the basement, and fired in the direction of the noise. His aim, naturally, was rather poor, and he was always wide of the mark. Nevertheless, the college boy became quite nervous. He finally went to Kenneth Ross and said, "Mr. Ross, I think I've got to quit my job. Every time I go into the basement, that old man shoots at me."

Ross replied, "Now, Tom, I think things will be all right. Just hold on a few more days."

In a day or two, Uncle Dave said to Gramp, "Kenneth, what with all those burglars in the basement, I'm running out of ammunition. Get me another carton, will you?"

Kenneth Ross bought some more ammunition and then told Tom, "You don't need to worry, Tom. I just bought Uncle Dave some more ammunition, and they're all blank cartridges."

Despite the fact that 905 Gerald was a huge house with eight bedrooms, there was no bathroom on the ground floor. But there was a long pantry just off the kitchen and at the end of the pantry a small sink. Poor old Uncle Dave, once he got downstairs, found it difficult to climb the stairs to the second floor bathroom so he took to surreptitiously urinating in the sink.

My mother was not a fierce woman, but this practice outraged and horrified her. The business became such a problem that when she caught Uncle Dave in the act, she would fly in and whip his legs with a dish towel. Later, the maid took it upon herself to do the same thing, and poor old Uncle Dave would totter out of the pantry onto the porch.

What to do about it? All Uncle Dave could do was simply to wet his pants. Ross and I were warned not to use the sink under any circumstances. It was quite a problem.

One night in 1923 my brother Ross and I were awakened by a sort of plop. It sounded like someone had fallen down. Then there were more plops and it sounded like someone had fallen down the back stairs. But whatever it was, the plops were soft and whatever it was, the plops were slow. Something was plopping slowly down the back stairs from one step to another.

We peeked out the door and saw my father, Howard, leaving his

44

bedroom, tightening the belt on his bathrobe and striding down the hall. Then Gramp came out of his bedroom, and both went down the back stairs.

We ran to the head of the stairs and peeked down and saw Uncle Dave's dead body lying crumpled at the foot of the stairs.

Howard was talking on the telephone. When he finished, he came into the kitchen, sat down and lit a cigarette. Gramp lit a cigar and the two men sat there and smoked and gazed at Uncle Dave's body. Finally, Gramp said, "You know Howard, Uncle Dave was a fine old man. He was always a bright ray of sunshine to Mrs. O'Keefe and the two girls out on that lonesome ranch."

Howard didn't reply right away but finally said, "I've often wondered why he never married."

There was a knock at the door. Two undertakers came in with a wicker basket. They picked up Uncle Dave's wasted little body, dumped it into the basket, and left.

Howard saw Ross and me at the head of the stairs. He was startled and said, "What are you two boys doing out of bed?"

"Dad! Dad!" we said, almost in unison. "What happened to Uncle Dave?"

Howard replied, "Boys, Uncle Dave died and went with his soul to heaven. He's probably already there. Now you boys get back to bed."

Ross and I talked for a long time about how wonderful it was that Uncle Dave went to heaven, and we knew it was because he was so good and kind to everybody.

And so departed Uncle Dave O'Keefe, frontiersman, rancher, and freighter. At eighty-eight he had outlived his brother the Baron by thirty years. In his old age his greatest joy in life was to have dinner at the Florence Hotel. He couldn't believe that anything so sumptuous had actually come to his valley.

Uncle Dave was the last of the first generation of my family in Montana.

In one of her letters, Mollie Matteson enclosed an amazing, faded photograph taken in 1895. It is a picture of O'Keefe's last house and the lane leading to it. A row of cottonwood saplings had just been planted. My mother, helped plant these saplings when she was a girl five years old. By 1980, they had become so big and scruffy that the present owner had them cut down.

The photograph shows, on the north side of the Baron's road, a dike that impounds a large lake. The dike extends half way across the valley. It is a monumental engineering effort when one considers the construction tools available in the later nineteenth century. The lake no doubt stored water for irrigating the lower pastures.

The last home of the Baron O'Keefe. In the thirty-three years that the Baron lived at Coriackan Defile he had three homes. The first was a one-room cabin with a sod roof. The second was a little more pretentious and had several rooms. It was the second in which Maggie and Mollie were born. The house above was built in the 1880s. Marjorie Ross Toole helped plant the row of cottonwood trees in 1895.

Also shown in the photograph is a huge barn, so massive and so well built that I always assumed that a subsequent owner constructed it. But the photograph proves it was there in 1895. The Baron built it.

After this photograph arrived I drove out to the subdivision known as "The Meadows of Baron O'Keefe." Ranch-type homes typical of the 1980s, painted in various hues, were beginning to spread across the O'Keefe meadows. I turned in his gate and drove down to the barn. It is now filled with box stalls used by horse fanciers. The barn is 100 paces long. The ridge pole is 15 feet off the ground. The barn sits on a massive stone foundation of the kind built in the 1890s. There is not an inch of sag in the roof.

I looked for the dike and the meadow where reposed the Baron's lake. The dike had been obliterated and there is no remaining sign of the lake.

It was a cold and blustery day and no one was around. I sat on a stump of one of the giant cottonwoods and thought of this man who rode his horse into this valley 132 years ago, when the valley contained virtually no white men.

I realized that I had perhaps done this man a disservice when I mentioned his heavy drinking. No drunk could have constructed his fine house, his huge barn, his dike, and his lake. Obviously, he was a hard worker who tried to do his best for his family. Sitting there, I hoped I might hear his voice, but the voices of the pioneers are always ephemeral. What I did hear was a review of his incedible career:

An Irish revolutionary. Arrival at New York on a British prison ship. Escape. The dangerous voyage around Cape Horn. His unknown activities in California and Washington. His signing on with Captain Mullan. His squatting on 1,500 acres of land at the Coriackan Defile. His serving as first County Commissioner of Missoula County. His two terms in the Territorial Legislature. His self-defense in the first trial in Montana. His narrow escapes from the Bannock Indians. His becoming a blood brother of the Nez Perces. His friendship with Chief Joseph.

Any way you look at it, the Baron was quite a guy.

The Baron in his later years

47

3   1934: Faith and Desperation

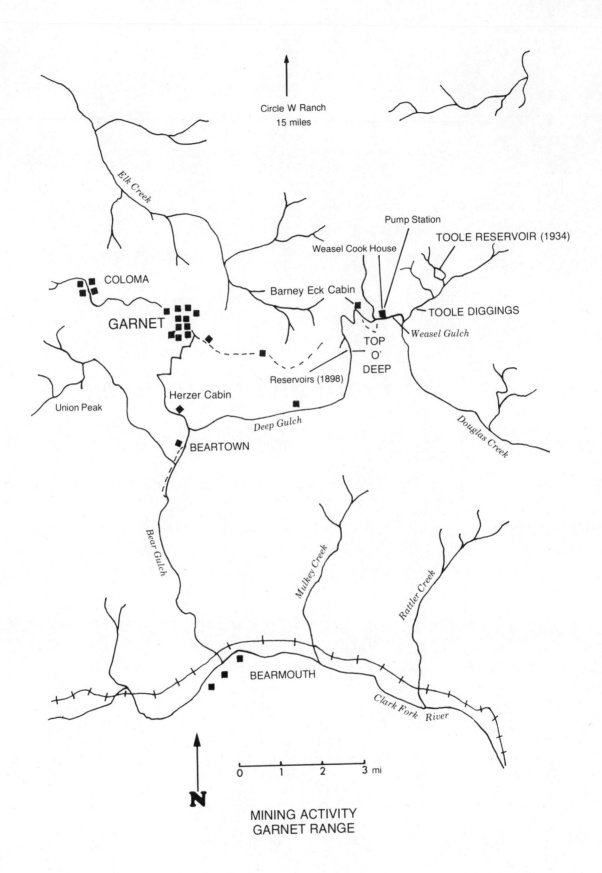

Circle W Ranch
15 miles

Elk Creek

COLOMA

GARNET

Union Peak

Herzer Cabin

BEARTOWN

Bear Gulch

Deep Gulch

Barney Eck Cabin

Weasel Cook House

Pump Station

TOOLE RESERVOIR (1934)

TOOLE DIGGINGS

Weasel Gulch

TOP O' DEEP

Reservoirs (1898)

Douglas Creek

Mulkey Creek

Rattler Creek

BEARMOUTH

Clark Fork River

N

0   1   2   3 mi

MINING ACTIVITY
GARNET RANGE

50

Cabin at Cave Gulch, Spring 1934. Left to right: Mining engineer (name unknown), Mrs. Herzer, Dick Herzer, Frank Wolfe, Herzer son-in-law, Marian Wolfe, John Brown. Seated: Geologist (name unknown).

3   *1934: Faith and Desperation*

It was late March, 1934.

Dick Herzer was standing on the steps of his cabin at Cave Gulch, a few miles below Garnet, the historic gold-mining town high up in the range of the same name. He was watching a beautiful English setter that my uncle Brice Toole had left with him to board for the winter.

The dog was running madly, with its nose under the snow, searching for small rodents or birds. The snow streamed out behind him the way it does behind a highway plow. Dick put his hands on his hips, turned to me, and said, "That dog hits a stump and he's gonna come back a bulldog!"

Dick Herzer was a prospector par excellence. All his life, he had roamed the western states, including twenty years in Alaska, always searching for the big gold strike. He had made some strikes, but had never stayed around to work them. He always sold his interest and went on prospecting. Only a few days before, he had dug behind a big rock on Cave Gulch and extracted a four-ounce nugget.

He was a short, roly-poly man, with arms and legs like tree trunks. His unvarying garb was black rubber gum boots, wool pants, suspenders, checked shirt, and billed cap.

Douglas Creek

That spring he was conducting a mining operation on First Chance Gulch just below Garnet. My dad, Howard Toole, had arranged for me to spend two weeks with him. Every day we would rise early and ride up to the First Chance diggin's in a Model A Ford pickup owned by John Brown, one of Herzer's men. Herzer's was a hydraulic mine. His crew, manhandling a fire hose equipped with a nozzle, directed a powerful stream of water at a vertical bank. Great hunks of the bank fell off, broken by the water's force, and dirt and water roared into sluice boxes, where the gold would stick and the light material would rush out the end. It was kind of thrilling: the clear blue sky, the steep canyon with its timbered slopes, the roar of water, the men shouting at one another, and in the sluice boxes, a treasure—maybe.

One night, Dick Herzer said to me, "Tomorrow we gotta take a load of grub over to Douglas on a sled. You wanna go along and help?"

I jumped at the chance. I would see the fabled Douglas mine! I remembered that my grandfather, Kenneth Ross, had hauled his own grub on a sled across the Bitterroot Range to the Coeur d'Alenes in the silver strike of 1883. I couldn't foresee that this would be one of the most grueling expeditions of my life.

The Douglas mine was virgin ground, ground that had never been worked before. Dick Herzer had discovered it. It lies just northeast of the crest of the Garnet Range, down a dizzying trail to Weasel Gulch, thence down to Douglas. The distance from Cave Gulch to Douglas is ten miles, the vertical rise almost 3,000 feet, the descent, 1,000 feet. You reach it by traversing the entire Deep Creek Canyon to a meadow on the crest of the range known as the Top O'Deep. In summer, you could drive to the top, if you had enough power and clearance in your car and were willing to ruin it on the unspeakable road.

Word had gotten around that Douglas was the famed Lost Silverthorne mine, discovered in the 1850s, the location of which died when Silverthorne himself cashed in. Indeed, in the summer of 1934, we unearthed a cast-iron teakettle, which analysts at the University of Montana declared was manufactured in the 1850s. An aura of mystery enveloped the Douglas properties.

52

Our sled was a homemade affair with sawed-off skis for runners. Dick's load of provisions seemed to weigh about 200 pounds. John Brown and I hooked our torsos to the sled with ropes. We started at dawn. Dick walked ahead to break trail. We passed Plez Oxford's cabin; he came to the door and waved us on. Oxford was noteworthy because of his handlebar mustache. It was so wide you could see its protruding tips when he turned his back.

I was soon floundering. The heavy load, the narrow trail, and my first attempt at showshoes made my breath come in short gasps; John Brown, a short, wiry outdoorsman with immense shoulders, was in his element. On we labored, through Springtown, now a ghost town with few buildings left, and at last we reached Billy Miller's cabin. This old prospector greeted us warmly; Dick broke out a loaf of bread from the sled and Billy poured hot coffee. I flopped on Billy's bed, but Dick put us back on the road immediately.

"Come on boys, four miles to Douglas!"

Now the trail steepened. It was just one lunge after another. Backbreaking! We heaved past Chris Lennon's and John Stuart's cabin, past the Pearl mine; the trail sloped up forbiddingly and finally we emerged on a snow-covered meadow. It was the Top O'Deep. Dick stopped for a blow, announcing, "Boys, you're in the Blackfoot Valley."

The Blackfoot Valley! My whole world in those days consisted of the five valleys that radiated out of Missoula. The upper Blackfoot was my favorite place on earth, and it seemed strange and wondrous to enter at one of its headwaters. I could look down and see the rolling prairies around Helmville, the great cattle ranches, and above and beyond, the peaks of the Swan Range. I turned, and Montana's great mountain ranges ringed the horizon in all directions: the Continental Divide, the Pintlars, the Granites, the Sapphires, the Swans, the Bitterroots, and the Missions. The mountains were pure white; the sky a bright blue. It was dazzling.

Dick wasted no time. "You in a trance or something, Johnny? Let's get goin'! It's all downhill from here!"

The trail plunged down the Blackfoot slope at a nauseating angle. The sled pitched forward between John Brown and me, dumping me into a snowbank.

"Easy does it, boys. Now hold 'er!"

Dick planted his solid body in the snow, downhill from the sled. We slithered and fell down the trail, the sled simply dragging us along, snowshoes askew, gasping for breath. "Jeez!" I thought to myself, "What an ordeal!"

We leveled out on Weasel Gulch, the snow deeper but the grade easier. At about 4:30, we broke into a level spot where stood the abandoned, timbered, multi-storied pumphouse of the Weasel

Placers, idle since 1898, and beyond it, the long, log bunkhouse, still in good shape after thirty-five years. Emerging from the door came its smiling occupant, Chuck Cook. He shook hands all around, glad to see us. He hadn't seen a human being in four months. I slumped down on the porch, completely done in. Dick came up, kicked my foot, and laughed, "Now you know what a day's work is, eh, Johnny?"

Chuck unloaded the sled.

Dick had hired Chuck to guard Douglas against claim jumpers, men who come in, squat on a claim, file the necessary papers, and acquire mining rights. Claim jumpers were run off with a rifle. Today, I think Dick's fears were unfounded; he was kind of paranoid about it.

Chuck started whipping up supper. I was shown my bunk and fell into it. Chuck had a primitive phonograph, powered with a chain drive. He played two scratchy records over and over again: "I'm Looking Over a Four-leaf Clover" and "Ivan Skavinski Skvar." We wolfed down supper, then sat around for a jaw.

Chuck wanted to install another stove. He got into a discussion with John Brown about where the stovepipe should go through the roof. Soon they began to argue, and the argument became strident.

All of a sudden, Dick pulled out his pistol and fired a bullet into the ceiling. As he shoved his pistol back into its holster, he said, "Put the goddamn thing right there!"

I was thunderstruck. Chuck and John stared at Dick, their mouths wide open. Chuck broke the silence, "Jeez, Dick. Now I gotta patch the roof."

Dick got up and wound the phonograph, changed the record from "Ivan" to "Clover," and muttered something about foolish arguments. John Brown and I figured it was time for bed and Chuck went out to patch the roof. I had always romanticized about the frontier; now I was actually living in it. What a day!

The next day, we snowshoed down to Douglas, a few hundred yards away. I was a little disappointed. There was so much talk and mystery about the place that I expected something else, temples and grottoes maybe. Actually, it was just another mountain gulch.

Chuck showed us his diggin's. He had sunk an untimbered shaft down about twelve feet. Water from melting snow was cascading down the sides. Across the top of the shaft was a windlass and a rope. The rope was tied to a bucket. Chuck would lower the bucket to the bottom; then he would climb down a ladder to the bottom of the shaft, fill the bucket full of dirt, climb back up the ladder, windlass the loaded bucket to the surface, and dump the load into a wheelbarrow. He repeated this process six times. After six bucketsful, he had a wheelbarrow loaded with dirt; he would then trundle the wheelbarrow down to the sluice boxes and dump his load. At this rate, he could wash only about two-thirds of a cubic yard per day.

I saw nothing outmoded, inefficient, or backbreaking about this procedure. Quite the contrary. I envisioned a treasure in each wheelbarrow load. Nor did I realize that Chuck was in terrific danger. A falling rock could hit him, or the shaft wall could collapse and trap him, bringing death from exposure within forty-eight hours.

At age fifteen, I couldn't foresee the day when men would never willingly do what Chuck Cook did alone in that hole in 1934.

What did he earn out of it? No one will ever know. He and Dick stepped to one side, had a low conversation with much arm-waving and finger-pointing. There was a furtive exchange of bottles. Then Chuck came out smiling. Chuck had an "arrangement" with Dick. Dick couldn't pay him wages, so Chuck agreed to spend the winter at Douglas in exchange for a percentage of the gold he mined. Prospectors are wary and close-mouthed with outsiders, but among themselves, honesty is essential. I suspect each received his share as agreed.

Chuck was working rich ground. I knew that Dick had taken $1,200 out of an adjacent shaft in the winter of 1932-33, when the price of gold was $20 per ounce. He had washed less than 100 yards of dirt. Try the arithmetic at $35 per ounce; then, for the hell of it, try it at $600 per ounce, the 1980 price.

In the afternoon we trudged back to the bunkhouse. Chuck started a fire. "Can you fellows stay a few days?" he asked. "We could wash a lot of dirt with four of us."

"No, Chuck," replied Dick. "They're cleaning up at First Chance today, and I gotta get back and see that them highbinders don't steal us blind."

Before bed, I stepped out on the porch. A gigantic mountain covered with alpine fir rose right in front of me. There were a million stars in a blue-black sky, and utter silence. My love affair with Douglas was just starting. It continues today.

Dick roused us early. Chuck whipped up a ham-and-eggs breakfast. We fastened our snowshoes, waved good-bye to a smiling Chuck Cook, and set off up the mountain at a vigorous pace. We left the sled with Chuck. Dick was worried about the clean-up at First Chance, and his short legs chopped the snow with rapid rhythm. Laboring up the steep pitch, hanging onto branches, and finally emerging from the forest onto the meadow at the Top O'Deep, I stopped for a last look at the stupendous panorama. Dick and John Brown went on; Dick stopped and hollered at me, "Quit your daydreamin,' Johnny. Come on!"

We pulled into the Cave Gulch cabin about 3 p.m. Slim, the foreman at First Chance, was waiting. "Well, how'd we do?" Dick asked.

"Not good, Dick. About fifty bucks." He put a small bottle of gold on the table.

"Fifty bucks? Only fifty bucks?"

Then Dick's words came tumbling out: "Them highbinders stole it, didn't they? They been up there at night, ain't they?"

"No, Dick. Nothin' like that went on."

"Hell, that ain't even enough to pay the crew. Go on up and let 'em go. Let 'em all go!"

Slim left.

Dick walked to the window and looked out. It was beginning to snow. He drove a fist violently into the palm of a hand, then quietly said, "That's the way it's been all my life, Johnny. These are hard times, hard times. Them men at First Chance can't get no jobs. They ain't even got a car. All they can do is hoof it to Bearmouth, hook a freight, and head for Deer Lodge or Missoula, and go on relief." He paused a moment, then said, "You know, your Uncle Brice Toole was a partner in First Chance. It'll go hard on him, huh?"

Then he turned around, broke into a smile, and patted his pocket where he had placed Chuck Cook's gold. "Well, we got enough to keep us in groceries for a while. And now Douglas. We got to concentrate on Douglas, the only piece of virgin ground in the West! There's a mine for you!"

His depression was gone. He went to the cupboard, took down rags, oil, and a short ramrod, put his pistol on the bed, and proceeded to clean it, all the while whistling "The Girl I Left Behind Me."

Two months later I was back in the Garnet Mountains.

I had a Model T Ford touring car. The minute school was out in early June, I loaded it up and headed east on U.S. 10 for the Douglas Creek mine. I had the promise of a job there that would pay me $50 per month and board and room. I had just turned sixteen.

In a Model T, the driver and the car become one. I could tool along the new highway at 35 miles per hour, but the curves were not banked and the high center of gravity on the jalopy caused it to tilt dangerously. My right arm was wrapped around the steering wheel, the fingers of the left guided the sensitive hand throttle. Ears were carefully cocked to listen for the fatal sound of a loose crankshaft bearing or the ominous grinding of a faulty differential. Every trip was an event, an expedition.

I was tense. I was determined to drive my Ford clear to the Top

O'Deep, although everyone had said it couldn't be done. At Bearmouth I turned north up Bear Creek. My tension wasn't relieved when a four-foot rattlesnake slithered across the road in front of the Ford. But then I remembered—no rattlers at Douglas, too high and too much snow.

Bear Gulch was humming with human activity—log cabins, tents, men slaving feverishly in the creek bed with their little sluices and cradle washers, frantic to take advantage of the pitiful flow of water, which would disappear in July. Bear Gulch had been discovered way back in 1866. A mad rush of miners took $5 million in gold. Beartown, its capital, was a wild mining camp of four thousand souls, situated at the mouth of Deep Creek canyon.

I turned up Deep Creek, roared by Plez Oxford's cabin; he poked his mustache out the window and waved. Now the road was covered with vicious, sharp talus rock. I flinched at the likelihood of a blowout.

The first really steep pitch loomed ahead. I stopped the Ford to inspect the road. It rose on a 20 percent grade, rutted and slanting; then it leveled out. I put the Ford at full throttle, then pushed hard on the "low" pedal of the planetary transmission, and rocked vigorously back and forth with that silly body motion drivers used to use to urge a car forward. Halfway up, the engine quit and we stopped cold. Ah-hah! I knew the trouble. She had no fuel pump. At a certain angle, gravity would not carry gas into the engine. The answer? Back up the hill; then the gas would have to pour into the engine.

I started backing rapidly up the hill with a perilous careening and tilting. Halfway up, the rear wheels began spinning. There was no way to go on; the Ford was too light.

I disconsolately pulled off the road, got out a chain, and padlocked both front wheels to a tree. The mountains were full of roaming, unemployed, would-be gold miners. But I wasn't really worried about the Ford. The distressed victims of the Great Depression were strangely law-abiding. And the wanton vandalism common in the twentieth century's latter half wasn't even thought of.

I shouldered my 75-pound pack, which had an accordion, a guitar, and my dad's 30:40 Krag rifle strapped to it. I trudged up the road, and when I approached Billy Miller's cabin, he stepped out of the door, stared bellicosely, and asked, "What are you, a gypsy or somethin'?"

I had to mollify him because I wanted a cup of coffee and a sandwich. When I left, I looked back, and he was standing in the road shaking his head.

Johnny Stuart and Chris Lennon were sitting on the porch of their cabin, smoking and basking in the sun. I stopped to visit these

57

two old veterans of the 1890's boom.

The road sloped upward sharply. To the left I saw dirt flying out of a vertical shaft. It was Dave and Tom Eliot sinking a prospect hole for hard-rock gold ore. All the great rich gulches radiated out from the Top O'Deep, and every miner figured that a fabulous "mother lode" lay close to the surface. If it exists, it's still there. The Eliots were great, powerful, brooding men. An inner fire burned in them and it frequently burst out in fits of violence. They glared at me malevolently. What with the guitar and other paraphernalia strapped on my back, I guess I looked like a 1934 hippy. I would witness the Eliots' violence before summer's end.

Upward and onward I trudged, breaking out finally on the little meadow at Top O'Deep. The sweeping snow field of March had yielded to waves of tall, green grass studded with a myriad of wild flowers. A gentle wind kept all in motion and murmured through the gnarled branches of the ancient Douglas firs. Still white were the great mountain ranges piercing the horizon in all directions. The place looked like heaven.

To my discomfiture, I saw John Brown's Model A pickup parked over in the trees. John and Art Periman were transferring supplies from the Ford to Art's wagon—40 gallons of gasoline, lumber, tools, nails, and canned goods. Art's big, powerful horses stood quietly, switching their tails. Art Periman was a cowpuncher from Drummond—a quiet young guy, not much older than I. He rode broncs in the Helmville rodeo—a Charlie Russell type.

"Hop in the wagon," Art said to me. "I'll haul you down to the diggin's." I threw my pack in the wagon.

John Brown laughed and waved goodbye, saying, "Careful, Art. You got a one-man band on board!"

I perched myself on the high seat beside Art. I was a little apprehensive. How in hell could he maneuver the ponderous wagon and these big horses down that treacherous road? At the first steep pitch I found out. He hopped down and "rough-locked" the wagon wheels—that is, he tied the front wheels to the axle with a chain. The wheels couldn't turn; they dragged. He hopped back in and slapped the team with the reins. I held on for dear life. The wagon scraped down, tilting and careening. Sparks sprayed from the steel-tired wheels rasping over the rocks. The horses lowered their big rumps over their extended hind legs, front legs stiff, necks bowed, foaming mouths open. Art, his jaw clenched, a Bull Durham cigarette clamped in his teeth, his Stetson hat cocked to one side, held back firmly on the reins. We leveled out at the Barney Eck cabin on Weasel. It was a magnificent little experience—the elegant horses, the silent, competent cowpuncher—a distillation of the West.

Art spoke to me only once on the whole trip. Looking straight ahead, he said, "They got two women down here now."

"Two women! What are they doin'?"

"Cookin.' "

And that was that.

We unloaded the grub at the Weasel cookhouse and took the rest of the wagon load down to Douglas. I was introduced to the crew and shown my bunk, which was in an army squad tent down by the creek. Dick Herzer, the discoverer of Douglas, was not there. An ebullient Chuck Cook had stayed on after the snows disappeared. I asked him about Dick.

"I don't know what happened, Johnny," he replied. "I guess he had a falling out with the Toole brothers."

It would have been difficult to have had a "falling out" with my father and uncle. Both Howard and Brice were generous to a fault. Both were anxious to please, made an inordinate effort to get along with associates, and possessed an infectious enthusiasm about Douglas. The same syndrome—"If father could do it, we can too"—dwelt in both of them. The only thing about it was that their father, John R. Toole, had gotten in on the world's richest mine in Butte, Montana. He had made a fortune, but in the shuddering economic collapse of 1929, that fortune had been swept away. Howard clung to his small law practice in Missoula, but Brice, also an attorney, had chosen to throw up his hands and go to gold mining. These buffetings seemed to have had no effect whatsoever on their bubbling faith in the future.

They had no money, but they had attended eastern colleges and had "contacts" with eastern capitalists. Under the influence of Dick Herzer's unwavering optimism, they contacted the contacts and got some financial commitments. First, they had to buy out the interest of Dick Herzer.

Pumphouse and privy,
Douglas Creek, 1934

Dick Herzer

59

A perusal of old letters reveals what happened. Dick walked away with $2,500, a munificent sum in 1934. And, indeed, there had been no "falling out." Dick wrote to Howard: "I guess I'm a fool to turn loose—but you know I got this claim over on Harvey Creek. . . . Thanks for your many, many favors."

Dick had been the only smart one; a prospector at heart, he knew that Douglas had a few fabulously rich pockets, but the mine as a whole could never justify the kind of investment planned by the Toole brothers.

And so it came about that Brice Toole was in charge at Douglas in 1934. Brice was a genial chain smoker, of medium size, and had a small, carefully trimmed mustache. His background as an attorney scarcely equipped him to operate a mine, but he attacked the job with good cheer and an effervescent sense of humor. In World War I, he had joined the French army before the United States' entry in 1917. He had a bad heart, and the grueling climb up to the Top O'Deep exhausted him. Most important to me, Brice Toole did not snore. I shared a tent with him.

Marvin McDonald

Marvin McDonald half crouched on the seat of the mighty gasoline hoisting engine that powered the gin-pole dragline. Marvin was a tense, handsome, strong man. He radiated energy. He was always on the run, skipping from rock to log. Short-fused, he could veer rapidly into violence.

Marvin had skidded the huge engine all the way from Beartown. He would drag the three-quarter-inch cable out ahead of the engine, which was on timber skids, hook it to the base of a big tree, run back to the engine, start the reverse drum, and pull the engine ahead by its own power. He then repeated the process until he had covered the full eight miles. The scars on the trees are visible to this day.

Slim Madden was a great slab of a man, hawk-nosed, silver-haired, with immense shoulders and long, sinewy arms. Slim slept outside in a bunk contrived by stringing planks between two big fir trees with boards for a mattress. When it rained, he pulled a tarpaulin over himself. Slim was a man of the outdoors, who said he hadn't slept inside for forty years—"except winter, o' course." He liked to tell dirty jokes and went on for hours about his exploits in whorehouses. One day he challenged me to a "wrassling" match. He picked me up and threw me in the creek. The old bastard!

Ed Fisher was the only man at Douglas who knew what he was doing. He had two burros. He was given some ground to work in exchange for the use of the burros in freighting. He had a little sluicebox and had sunk a deep shaft. I'd visit him every night, and every night he had another bottle of gold. He was getting old, yet he remained a movie version of the typical prospector. Montana was wide open in those days. When he quit in the fall, he just got on a burro and headed for Marysville or Clancy or maybe Blackfoot City. No dragline, washing plants, or hoists for him.

Diminutive Chuck Cook was the general roustabout, adviser, and clean-up expert. He slept in a sheepherder's cabin that had a floor paved with sheep manure.

Elsie McDonald was Marvin McDonald's wife. She came up to be with her husband and to help with the cooking. A small, trim, wispy blonde, I think she found the rough life and isolation grim, but she had Pearl Hanson for company. Pearl was a short, curvaceous brunette with a saucy manner. Pearl was a good camp cook, but she griped because she had no ice, no electricity, no vegetables, no milk, and no running water. Besides, the outdoor john was plumb filled up.

I went to work the day after I arrived. My duties were to keep the Weasel cookhouse supplied with water, split wood for the cookstove, haul supplies down from the Top O'Deep with Ed Fisher's burros, and in my spare time help Slim Madden shovel big boulders out of the sluiceboxes.

The operation at Douglas in 1934 was a desperate, agonizing race—a race to beat the October snow, a race against the daily diminishing volume of water in the creek, and a race to produce a good showing of gold soon, so that the money spigot from the East would not be shut off. It was a race terribly complicated by problems of communication and supply. And it was a race being directed by a heroically hardworking, but inexperienced, man.

John Brown and Art Periman had hauling jobs for other mines. Frequently, John Brown and Art would not make connections at the Top O'Deep. John would then dump his load under a tree. If Art happened along soon after, fine. If not, the grub was attacked by bears and coyotes, and the camp, 1,000 feet down and 2½ miles away, would run short of gas, spare parts, and food. Then I would be detailed to head for the Top with Ed Fisher's burros, in the faint hope that the supplies had been delivered and were still in good shape.

There was no telephone or radio. Often Brice labored to the Top and down Deep Gulch to a crank-type telephone owned by the Blackfoot Forest Protective Association. The line ran first to a lookout on Union Peak, thence to Bonner. The operator at Bonner would relay the message to Howard in Missoula. Then Howard would somehow procure what was needed and somehow get it delivered to the Top. If the gas wasn't delivered, the dragline stopped and the financial hemorrhage became a torrent.

One Saturday night Brice and I were in Garnet to play for a dance. Jim Malone, a miner whose cabin was hidden in dense woods at the Top O'Deep, came over and said, "Brice, I was lookin'

The bottomless bucket

Brice Toole on the penstock pipe

your outfit over yesterday. You ain't gettin' much gold, are ya?"

Brice shrugged.

"Brice, your drag bucket ain't got no bottom. You know what happens when gold hits water that's agitated. It goes down, Brice. It goes down!"

Brice gave him a vacant stare.

"I'm tellin' you, Brice, when you pull that bucket through the water the gold goes right out the bottom. Brice, can you hear me? You gotta get another bucket, one with a bottom in it!"

Brice muttered something and then said to me, "Come on, John. We better get to the dance. They're waiting for us."

As we walked away, Brice said, "You know, John, that conversation made me shiver."

My heart went out to him and also to Howard who, late at night, was penciling his long, enthusiastic letters to the eastern money interests.

An emergency—Marvin jumped off the dragline, ran up the creek. The dragline bucket was stuck on a reef of solid rock.

"Hey, Brice," he hollered. "We're hung up. We gotta blast that rock out!"

Brice went to the tent and packed out three cases of dynamite. He set one on the rock reef, then ran back down the creek, and said, "John, get your rifle, hide behind this rock, and fire a coupla rounds at that box of powder." (Miners, loggers, and construction men always call dynamite "powder.")

I said to myself, "This is great!" I ran to the tent, got Howard's Krag, took careful aim from behind the rock, and pulled the trigger. I hit the dynamite box, fair and square. Nothing happened. Sticks of dynamite flew every which way, but did not explode. I tried several more shots, the same results. Finally, Marvin called to Brice, "Christ, Brice, you can't detonate dynamite that way! You got to have blasting caps!"

The other men turned their faces to hide their amusement.

Brice shouted in reply, "We don't have any caps!"

Then he turned to me and pulled a $5 bill out of his pocket, saying, "John, take this over to Tom Eliot and buy some caps."

I took off on the run for the Top, then down to Eliots' mine. Their shaft was now deep. They were working out of sight in a drift, a lateral tunnel extending from the bottom of the shaft. I hollered down, then heard Tom Eliot's voice.

"Who's up there?"

"It's me. John Toole. I need blasting caps."

Tom came into sight wearing a carbide light on his hat.

"Ya got any money?"

"Yeah."

"Come on down."

I climbed down a rickety ladder and showed him the $5 bill.

He said, "Well, money's scarcer'n caps," took the bill, and then put some caps in a red bandanna handkerchief, saying, "Be careful with them, kid. They're dangerous."

I put the caps in my pocket and headed for Douglas. I knew the need for caps was urgent, so I ran, the caps jangling in my pocket. When I reached Douglas, I pulled out the handkerchief. Some of the caps fell on the ground. Marvin jumped back about ten feet like a scared jack rabbit.

"Jesus, Johnny, you can't handle caps like that! You'll kill us all!"

I'd pushed my luck to the limit, largely out of ignorance.

The next day was spent drilling holes for dynamite in the rock reef. Marvin and Slim stripped to the waist. It was to be a double-jack operation. Each man grabbed a heavy steel sledge hammer. Chuck Cook held the drill steel and placed the cutting edge perpendicular to the rock so that the drill would go straight down. Marvin swung first with a full circle, bringing his sledge crashing down on the drill. Then, on Marvin's back swing, Slim brought his own sledge down. And thus it went all day—clank-clank, clank-clank, clank-clank. Chuck turned the drill slightly with each blow and occasionally poured a little water down the hole.

I watched, transfixed—the perfect rhythm, the synchronization, the rippling muscles of the two powerful, sweating men, men welded to steel. It was more inspirational than any ballet, than any moving work of art conceivable. They never missed. Chuck's hands were safe.

And that evening, we attached the caps, loaded the holes with powder, lit the fuse, and the rock reef disappeared in a mighty explosion.

We all looked forward to Saturday afternoon. That was "cleanup day." The water was slowed to a trickle. The riffles (parallel poles) were gently lifted out of the sluice boxes. Brice and Chuck Cook steadied a large wash tub at the end of the boxes. By controlling the

Garnet 1897

volume of water, the heavy concentrates were slowly forced down the boxes into the tub. As the heavy material went down, it would leave behind its receding edge, the heaviest of all—gold nuggets!

The men gathered round, and when a nugget appeared, they would all pounce on it, shouting, "There's one!" Brice kept a sharp lookout to be sure that no one slipped a nugget into his pocket.

When the tub was full, a marathon of gold panning ensued. It was slow work because every pan was full of dense, heavy material. At last each pan was reduced to a ring of black sand surrounded by a ring of brilliant yellow gold.

The pans were taken to the Weasel cookhouse; a vial of mercury was poured into each pan, and the pan was jiggled around. By some strange chemistry, the mercury picked up the gold until each pan contained a big hunk of amalgamated mercury and gold. The black sand was removed. A fire was lighted in the cookstove, the amalgams placed in a frying pan, the windows and doors opened, and Brice said to me, "Out you go, John. Quicksilver fumes will kill you!"

After some time, we tentatively entered the cookhouse. In each frying pan was a tidy pile of gold, the elusive metal for which men have fought, drowned, frozen, and starved for eons. The mercury had vaporized.

The gold was carefully poured into bottles. It looked like a great quantity to me, but it was only five to six ounces per week, not enough to pay expenses. Brice hid the gold, and he must have

64

hidden it well, because every Saturday night we evacuated the camp and headed for a dance in Garnet.

This little town was hauntingly beautiful. At almost 7,000 feet, its weathered buildings were scattered here and there along a winding street. Garnet had lain among the green pines for forty years, almost unknown to the outside world. The road to reach it, called the China Grade, was devilish. Winter snows completely buried the town.

Garnet had everything: a two-story hotel, a large dance hall, a post office, and a saloon. All thumped to life in 1934. In place of skinners cracking their whips over the rumps of their horse and ox teams, there was now the roar of Model A Ford pickups.

The Nancy Hanks mine (situated right in town) had fifty or sixty men, the Dandy mine about the same, and droves of prospectors, part of the great army of the unemployed, roamed the mountains. They all converged on Garnet on Saturday night.

Some Saturdays, John Brown picked us up at the Top to haul us to Garnet. Often, we hoofed it.

Brice and I were an integral part of the band for the dance. Brice

Garnet 1959

was a marvelous banjo player. He had played his way around the world on a luxury liner. I can still hear the loud, melodious, metallic slap-slap of his music. An old guy with a fiddle joined us, and I played the accordion or guitar.

The dancers were there when we arrived. We were ushered in, carrying our instruments, with extravagant yells and backslapping. We unlimbered, broke into ragtime; feet started stomping, the old hall swaying, the men yelling, "Ho! Ho! Ho!" and we were off.

We played ragtime, jazz, waltzes, polkas, and schottisches. Men outnumbered women two to one and some men danced together. The placer miners were bronzed by the sun; the deep-mine men were pale. All were vigorous, lusty, muscular, and enthusiastic.

Many were veterans of World War I. It became a ritual that, at midnight, we would play "My Buddy," the poignant song of death in the trenches sixteen years before. Everyone would rise, heads bowed, and silently gaze at the floor. The song would end; a miner would boom out, "Parlez vous!" and we would launch into the rollicking "Mademoiselle from Armentieres." The miners would sail across the floor, yelling "Hi-yee! Hi-yee! Hi-yee!" and the old hall would begin to shake and sway again. Was there an economic collapse in America? At this moment of the blending of rhythm, music, and pure mountain air, these superbly strong people were happily unaware of it.

The orchestra was paid by taking up a collection. A gent wearing a derby took it off and held the hat in front of him, soliciting money. As he danced—danced all by himself, waltzing, sashaying, jigging—the hat began to fill with coins, quarters, half dollars, silver dollars. The bar was just down the street; the miners kept going back and forth, and whiskey brought forth generosity.

One night the gent danced by the orchestra, tipping his hat for us to see. It looked enticing. He went on dancing, dancing. He danced to the front door and danced right out. Brice rose to his feet, pointed to the door, and yelled, "Stop that man!"

The crowd surged to the door, but the thief had disappeared into the woods. Oh, well.

At 2 a.m., the music stopped. Brice and the fiddler went to bed down with Billy Liberty, an old miner. The miners grabbed me, saying, "Come on down to Lars's place, kid. You can't quit now!"

I could play the accordion all night, so I went. Lars Ness's little saloon resounded with the thump, thump, thump of the dancers. Lars was a nervous Scandinavian. The rush of business got him all shook up. His cash drawer had no stop on it. When he frantically pulled it out to deposit coins, the drawer fell out and coins spilled all over the floor. Miners scampered for them and used them to buy more drinks. Lars was a flustered human wreck by morning.

Just at dawn, it happened. Marvin McDonald and Dave Eliot were arguing at the bar. Suddenly, Dave swung at Marvin. Marvin ducked and Dave missed, the force of his swing carrying him across the narrow room. Dave glowered and came charging back at Marvin, but the miners closed in and thrust both men out the door, yelling, "Fight! Fight! Fight!" We all poured out. The sun was rising. It was to be the most primitive, savage encounter I had yet seen.

The creek ran right in front of the saloon. Both men stood ankle-deep in the water. Dave swung first, caught Marvin with a glancing blow to the head, and Marvin went down. Dave lunged at him, but Marvin cocked his knees and caught Dave fair and square in the crotch. Dave staggered back and flopped on his back in the creek. Marvin was on him like a cat, trying to turn the big man over and press his nose into the water. But Dave hauled himself loose, struggled up, and wrestled Marvin down, pushing his face into the stream. Marvin wriggled out, pulled away, his face covered with water and mud.

Dave had the weight and strength; Marvin had the speed and agility. Both men sought the coup de grace—a kick to the testicles. George McDonald, Marvin's father, raced back and forth with the fighters, shouting encouragement to his son. The miners cheered the gladiators on. The crowd surged back and forth along the creek. I was appalled. I'd seen this in the movies, but never for real.

The fight raged up and down until both men stood glaring at each other, their faces streaked with blood and mud, their breath coming in short gasps. Big, brooding Tom Eliot stepped in beside his brother, and "Pinky" McDonald, Marvin's brother, a tall, straight, broad-shouldered miner with red hair, took his place beside Marvin. It looked as though the brawl might erupt again when the sheriff stepped timidly between the contestants.

Yes, Garnet had a sheriff. He was a pot-bellied character who wore a huge badge and a pistol.

"Well, boys, you had enough? Heh! Heh! I reckon the fight was a draw, eh, fellas?"

The miners agreed that it was and slowly dispersed to their diggin's to sleep the day through. I was a little worried about Marvin and his wife, Elsie, who had disappeared. My worry was baseless; both appeared for work Monday morning.

But I had one hell of a time with Slim Madden. He was falling-down drunk, and there was no vehicle to take us home. I had my accordion strapped to my back, my guitar over my right shoulder and Slim hanging onto my left arm. In this way, we staggered the six miles back to Douglas. Slim kept wanting to lie down and sleep, but I always kicked him awake. A couple of times I thought I might challenge him to a "wrassling" match to get even with him for throwing me in the creek, but I thought better of it.

I didn't drink in those days, so I felt O.K. But it was noon before I rolled old Slim into his outdoor bunk.

One afternoon, a band of about two thousand sheep came traipsing through the camp. The miners snorted in disgust at the sheep, the infernal bleating of lambs and ewes, the smelly droppings covering every inch of bare ground. Our beautiful mountain stream turned into a muddy, chocolate torrent, but there was nothing we could do. The sheep rancher had government grazing rights on this place.

Behind the band of sheep came the dogs, their cream-colored tails flashing in the sun, driving the band up the canyon with uncanny teamwork, shifting responsibility back and forth like hockey players. And at the rear, there were two sheepherders sporting black mustaches, dressed in black clothes and hobnail boots, with 30:30 rifles crooked in their arms.

They set up camp on the creek above us, and that night came down to our cook shack for dinner. They fascinated me. I'd never seen men like these before.

There was little conversation at the dinner table, but that was not unusual. Taciturnity at meals was expected of men of the out-of-doors in those days so many years ago.

After dinner, one of the herders handed me a harmonica and asked, "Can you play that, kid?"

Playing the harmonica was one thing I could do, and do well. I nodded enthusiastically.

"Well, come on down to that old stone boat, and I'll put on a dance for ya."

A stone boat was a sled built of big timbers. It was used to haul heavy rock behind a team of horses. Its bottom was a single sheet of quarter-inch steel, like a toboggan. This one was lying inverted down the trail a way below camp.

When we reached the stone boat, the sheepherder rested his rifle against a log, took off his hat, and stepped lightly to the steel surface. He took a few tentative hops, then commanded, "Play fast."

I launched into "Yankee Doodle," "Turkey in the Straw," and other tunes. He picked up the beat immediately and became a transformed man. He whirled, stamped, and gyrated. He put his hands behind his head and kicked his legs to the front, then swung round and kicked the other way. Next, he leaped upward, clicking his heels in the air. His timing was perfect. His hobnails clattered on the steel deck, now lightly, now with a roar. I was fearful that the steel on steel would make him slip, but he was never off balance for a second. He stopped once or twice, mopped his brow, then tossed his head at me to start again.

The sun was behind the mountain when he finished. He put on his hat, reached for his rifle, put out his hand for the harmonica, and said, "You play that pretty good, kid."

He didn't say another word as we hiked back to camp. Finally, I asked, "Why don't you dance for a living instead of herding sheep?"

"Nothin' to do in this country now but herd sheep."

He went on up the canyon to his sheep camp, and I went into our shack and asked Slim who he was.

"Oh, that's Dancin' Jack," came the reply. "He's crazy to dance. I wouldn't walk across the street to watch him."

The next evening, I hung around camp in hopes that he would return. He did. He tossed me the harmonica, and down we went to the stone boat again. It was another wild and dramatic performance: the clattering hobnails, the tossing black hair, and my own feeling that the man was possessed by some sort of strange and turbulent spirit.

I never saw him again. The sheep moved on up the canyon to the divide. The creek cleared up. The infernal bleating was gone. In a few days, a string of pack horses came up the canyon behind a cowboy carrying a rifle in a saddle scabbard. He was the camp tender for Jack's band of sheep. He stopped to visit for a minute. He said the band was now over in the Chamberlain country. As he left, I called to him: "When you see Dancin' Jack, say 'hello' for me, will you? I played the mouth harp for him."

The cowboy laughed, "He put on a dance for you, huh?" Then he put the spurs to his horse and was gone.

As I look back now, almost fifty years later, this experience is dreamlike. But it was no dream. Some years later I spoke to Helmville rancher Paul Peterson, who had owned Jack's band of sheep. He remembered Jack well.

"Oh, yeah, Dancin' Jack! He was crazy to dance. He disappeared a few years ago. Never knew where he went. He was a good herder, but he never talked much."

In 1934, I knew nothing about Basque sheepherders, but it seems to me that Jack must have been a Basque. That black hair and mustache! Yet I'm still not certain. The Basques I knew in later years could speak scarcely any English. Jack, though taciturn, could speak very well.

The rapidity with which modern man can destroy places of beauty and wonder is incredible. In the late 1930s one man on a bulldozer punched a road into the Douglas Creek mines in a matter of days. Burros, pack horses, and wagon teams disappeared overnight. Where men had labored ten hours per day in the depths of the Great Depression, buoyed by President Franklin D. Roosevelt's increase in the price of gold from $20 to $35 per ounce, no one at all

69

now labors for gold priced at $600 per ounce. The great bands of sheep no longer invade the canyons, the dogs no longer flash their cream tails against the backdrop of green trees, and the mysterious armed men in black have disappeared forever.

The rotting timbers of the old stone boat are still there, but the steel bottom was the victim of a World War II metal scavenger. I stand there and try somehow to recreate the wonder of the intense, lithe, dark sheepherder; his almost frenzied, whirling dance; and the chubby sixteen-year-old kid puffing vigorously on a harmonica.

But all I can contrive is a kind of jewel-like memory now wreathed in wonder and mystery.

In early August, another of those lethal emergencies started bearing down on us. The water level in Douglas Creek dropped alarmingly. The bucket (still bottomless, because Brice had no way of getting another) dragged miserably through mud. The water that was sprayed into the bucket on the top of the grizzly (ore screen) with a fire hose, lost its pressure. Something had to be done. Brice decided to build a dam up the creek a mile, store the water at night, and let the stored water out during the day in time to reach the diggin's. We moved bag and baggage up the creek. Art Periman rented himself and his team to us for a week. Brice went to Missoula to consult with Howard in a desperate effort to raise money. Marvin, with no dragline to operate and with the dark clouds of failure lowering, decided to seek his fortune elsewhere. As he and Elsie hiked away from the cookhouse, I waved at him sadly. He was everything I wanted to be—handsome, athletic, and courageous.

The dam would be built by Art's team pulling a "slip." This was a horse-drawn scraper that could load one-third of a cubic yard of dirt. The operator grabbed two handles protruding from the back of the open-topped slip. The handles were about one foot off the ground, so the operator stooped and stumbled behind the team.

Chuck hollered, "O.K., Johnny, get on that slip!"

I threw the knotted reins around my neck, yelled, "Giddap," grabbed the handles, and pulled up. The lip of the tiny scraper bit into the dirt. When the team felt the load, they hit their collars with a jolt, tore the handles out of my hands, and the slip turned over. They pulled the inverted, empty scraper up to the top of the dam. The reins came near to cutting my head off as I floundered in the rear. Art Periman hollered, "Hey, you ain't supposed to do it that way! Here, I'll show ya."

The slip required a "feel," just the required upward and downward pressure on the handles to make it dig, but not enough upward lift to make it flip over. It required a strong back and strong arms. The workingmen of those days never had back trouble.

While we were building the dam, a kid from Garnet came running up and said, "Johnny Toole's old man wants him to come to Missoula right away. His Grandma just died!"

I grabbed a sandwich and took off for the Top O'Deep. I rushed down past the Eliot boys' shaft, past Johnny Stuart's cabin, down, down, down to Billy Miller's, and down to my Ford. It wouldn't start.

It was now dark, so I crawled into the back seat and went to sleep. Before dawn, I started descending the long, long road down Deep Creek. The mountains enveloped me, and everything was silent. The big cottonwoods at Beartown were motionless and drooping.

"I should get a ride here," I thought, and I turned down Bear Gulch. But no car came. Bear Creek was dry; the little tents and cabins seemed deserted. The silent canyon, the awareness that Douglas Creek was failing, the totally unexpected death of my grandmother, all filled me with an inexpressible sadness. It seemed that everything was being swept away before I even got a start.

I had to reach Missoula by 2 p.m., the hour of the funeral. How? Hitchhike? As I topped the little hill north of Bearmouth, I saw, to my amazement, a Milwaukee freight train slowly pulling through the village and heading west. I raced across the highway, across the little red bridge, sprinted to the train, and hopped on a flat car. I sat on the edge of the car and dangled my feet over the side as the train picked up speed. It was late morning.

We clattered down the Clark Fork Canyon. The river curled beside the track, deep and blue. The great, timbered mountains pressed in on both sides.

I jumped off the train just before 2. The Milwaukee Railroad was only two blocks from the Presbyterian Church. Large groups of solid citizens dressed in black were entering the church. I was in work clothes, dirty and unshaven. I hid in the alley. When the organ music started, I slipped into the church and sat in a back pew, forgetting to remove my hat.

In the casket under the lectern lay the body of Anna Hardenbrook Toole. Howard had told me of her life, and I recollected what he said.

It was only a month after Robert E. Lee surrendered to Ulysses S. Grant at Appomattox Court House in Virginia. It was the same month in which Mollie O'Keefe was born on the Baron's ranch, nine miles west of far-off Missoula, Montana.

Alan Hardenbrook lifted his little daughter, Annie, into a covered wagon at Council Bluffs, Iowa. His small wagon train headed west, but was soon stopped by the U.S. Army. The Army officers said that the Indian danger was so great that all emigrant trains must organize into companies of forty to sixty wagons for protec-

71

tion. The Hardenbrooks joined with other trains and Alan Hardenbrook was named captain of a train of forty-five wagons. At every stop, they would circle the wagons into a "corral" for protection against Indians.

Little Annie soon acquired a babysitter. She was a young woman named Sarah Raymond and she kept a diary. It is only through the pages of Sarah Raymond's diary that we know what little Annie saw and must have felt.

Monday, June 12, 1865

We stood by the graves of eleven men that were killed last August by the Indians . . . [a] frightful tragedy. We are in the worst place for Indians. The captain [Hardenbrook] says, "Stay within sight of camp." And I must obey.

Tuesday, June 13

A narrow escape. . . . Neelie [Sarah's best friend] found some beautiful wild flowers, and she insisted upon gathering them. Of course, we waited for her. When the captain saw that the train would soon be out of our sight, he went to Mr. Morrison and said, "Ride quietly back and warn those girls of the danger, there are Indians around. They [will] not be safe one minute!" Mr. Morrison started, but not quietly; he snatched off his hat, whipping his horse with it [and] went on to Neelie, who was looking all about to see the Indians. He gave her pony a cut with his whip, and we went flying over the ground, Neelie's merry laughter pealing forth.

Many of the emigrants weren't even sure where they were going. Some favored California, some Oregon, but many were lured by the "rich gold mines" of Montana. A prolonged discussion took place on Saturday, June 17.

I said, "Why not go there?" [to Montana], but Hillhouse [Sarah's brother] said, "I do not like for you and Mother to go there for it will be rough living.

[Sarah's mother spoke up.] "Well . . . we are going. How many women are on their way there in these trains? I reckon it will not be any worse for us than it will be for them.

It was settled there and then that Montana will be our destination.

On July 1, the wagons approached the crossing of the South Platte, and the great Rocky Mountains loomed ahead.

When the sun shines on the snow-capped mountains the effect is thrilling; they are great altars of earth raised up to Heaven for the morning sacrifice.

Sunday, July 2

I was sitting on the bank of the river watching with anxiety the wagons as they ploughed through the deep waters [but] there has been no serious accident nor any lives lost although thousands of cattle, hundreds of horses, and more than a thousand human beings have crossed the river since yesterday morning. . . . There is to be a praise and thanksgiving for our safe conduct through the deep waters and our protection from the Indians.

Monday, July 3

We suffer agony when our boys are away from camp guarding stock or hunting. There were Indians seen this morning by men looking for feed for the stock. It is almost dark and the boys have not come. [Captain Hardenbrook] is getting anxious. . . . We passed the graves of two men this morning who had been killed by Indians. . . . The Captain's orders are, "Do not leave camp this evening."

Thursday, July 13

Mrs. Hardenbrook had a sick headache this afternoon. I took little Annie that she might not disturb her mother. She is a dear, sweet child and seems fond of me.

Sunday, July 16

We saw—just before we came to Rock Creek—a station that had been burned and all the inmates killed; . . . there were none to tell the story. Soldiers [are] stationed there now.

Just after we crossed [Rock Creek], where there is a sudden turn in the road, we saw where two men had been killed and two wagons burned last week. There they were—dead and scalped—the horses gone, and wagons on fire.

Yet Sarah was captivated by the beauty of the country.

Tuesday, July 18

Why try to describe or picture anything so entirely impossible? The masses of fleecy white clouds, with the brightness of the morning sun shining upon them as they floated around and over the top of the mountain, made an ever-changing, beauteous panorama that I cannot describe.

The Hardenbrook train was not attacked by Indians. There were just too many wagons. But travelers on the Bozeman Trail, the short route to Montana, were savagely attacked by Sioux and Northern Cheyenne Indians, and two years later it was closed by the U.S. Army.

The train therefore continued west on the Oregon Trail to the crossing of the North Platte River. During the crossing, little Annie rolled up the canvas to peek out and see a wagon on its side in the middle of the river. Sarah drove the Raymond wagon and unhesitatingly plunged it into the stream.

Friday, July 21

[While my brothers Hillhouse and Winthrop drove the ox-team into the river], I drove the horse-team right in behind them. The current is very swift; they had all. they could do to keep the oxen from going with the current, and did not know I had followed them until they came out on an island in the middle of the river. Hillhouse smiled a sickly little smile, and said, "You should not have tried that. Wait on the island and I will come back and drive you over."

But of course I could not do that. I drove in with fear and trembling for there lay a big freight wagon in the middle of the stream. It was more difficult than the first since the banks were higher and steeper, and the water deeper. We got over without mishap. I wandered off alone and climbed to the top of a near-by mountain.

The train crossed the Continental Divide at South Pass (elevation 7,550 feet) in Wyoming, and headed for the Green River.

Monday, July 24

We passed the summit of the Rockies today. The ascent has been so gradual.

Tuesday, July 25

I know from the doctor's tone and manner that he thinks Neelie dangerously ill.

Wednesday, July 26

Sim Buford is quite sick; very much like Neelie. . . . Oh, the dust, the dust; it is terrible.

Friday, July 28

Mr. Kerfoot [Neelie's father] said, "Miss Sally, why don't you and your folks come [with us] to California?"

"Why, Uncle Ezra, you know the reason. We think Montana the better place to get a start."

"Tut, tut; Montana is an awful place. Why the only law they have is mob law."

Neelie was better on Saturday, July 29. The doctor told Mr. Kerfoot that if they did not move until Monday, he felt sure she would be out of danger. But Mr. Kerfoot was "very much afraid of the Indians," and in a few days, they would be out of the Indian country. Mr. Kerfoot decided on a half-day's drive. "He cannot believe that a calamity such as Neelie's death can befall them while he is trusting in a merciful Father."

Monday, July 31

Mrs. Hardenbrook has been quite sick to-day. I have been taking care of little Annie.

Tuesday, August 1

Mrs. Hardenbrook is no better; her symptoms are the same as Sim's and Neelie's, and we fear she is taking the fever.

Wednesday, August 2

Several head of Hardenbrooks' and Walkers' cattle were missing this morning; the men have been hunting them all day.

Thursday, August 3

I rode in the wagon the greater part of the day, so I could take care of little Annie Hardenbrook; her mother is very sick.

Friday, August 4

Mrs. Hardenbrook is very sick; I fear we are going to have another case of serious illness in our camp.

Saturday, August 5

We saw someone coming on horseback. It was Frank. He shook hands without speaking. I asked, "How is Neelie?"

"She is very low. I came after you, doctor."

Doctor Fletcher rode away at a gallop.

We rode a while in silence, then Frank said, "Frazier was shot and killed yesterday evening."

Murders were not uncommon on the Oregon Trail. The danger, the frayed nerves of the men striving to protect their wives and babies, erupted in violence often visited on their companions.

Hofstetter, a freighter, was arguing with Frazier about a shipment of flour he was freighting to Virginia City. Frazier stepped out of his wagon with an axe to fix a wagon wheel. Hofstetter thought Frazier was going to attack him and shot Frazier through the head. A "wagon-train" jury exonerated Hofstetter on the grounds of self-defense, but the U.S. Army sent out a squad of soldiers from Green River to pick Hofstetter up, stating that his trial was not legal.

The Hardenbrook train was now bogged down with illness. Captain Hardenbrook could go no farther because of the precarious condition of his wife. The Raymonds and a few others wanted to go on. They spoke to Captain Hardenbrook. He thought it was a good idea, because the Raymonds' wagons and teams were in good shape and the danger from Indians now minimal.

Sunday, August 6

I climbed into Mrs. Hardenbrook's wagon to tell her good-bye, kissed little Annie as she was sweetly sleeping. Mrs. Hardenbrook seemed so sorry to have us go.

And so we leave the indomitable Captain, his seriously ailing wife, and little Annie, stranded on the Green River.

The resolute Raymonds, now in a tiny train, pushed north, up the Ham's Fork of the Green River and crossed the divide into the Snake River valley. They had more adventures: horses stolen; a meeting with a surly band of Bannack Indians, now cowed by the U.S. Army. They thoughtfully gazed on the many graves and were shocked by Mormon polygamy.

Then, distressingly, they started to meet droves of men returning to the States from Virginia City mines.

Thursday, August 24

George Mays says he worked just one day, got five dollars, and took the back track the next day. "Mining is the only work a man can get and it would kill an ordinary man in less than a week."

[We have heard] a doleful account of hard times in Montana: "There are a few fortunate ones who are making money like dirt, but they are the exception, about one in a hundred."

Sarah had to sell her bay pony, Dick, at Snake River. She had ridden him most of the way. A miner from Virginia City wanted him. Much bargaining and finally the man tossed a leather pouch with $125 in gold dust into her lap. Family finances dictated the sale and Sarah flung herself on the bottom of the wagon and sobbed.

The train wound up Monida Pass, into the Centennial Valley—"scenery is magnificent"—and down the Ruby River. Montana at last!

Monday, September 5

We are camping in the suburbs of the city, in Alder Gulch, where the miners are at work. There is a temporary bridge (very shaky) across the gulch. Standing on this bridge, looking up and down, and even beneath my feet, the scene is a lively one. So many men in each other's way, like bees around a hive. Such active work: not one of that great multitude stopped for one instant shoveling and wheeling dirt, passing and repassing each other without a hitch. It made me tired to look at them. The ground is turned inside out; great deep holes and high heaps of dirt. The mines are said to be very rich.

A woman interviewed me. Her name is Neihart. I presume I did not make a very favorable impression, for after she called across the street to her neighbor—so we could hear what she said: "Some more aristocrats. They didn't come here to work. Going to teach school and play lady," with great contempt in her voice.

Virginia City is the shabbiest town I ever saw, not a really good house in it. We found a log cabin with two rooms for eight dollars per month. It has a dirt roof. There is a floor in it, which is better than some here.

We found quite a budget of letters at the post office. Oh, sad, sad news in Frank [Kerfoot's] letter. Neelie is dead. Oh, the anguish of soul, the desolateness of heart.

[Frank wrote that] Mrs. Hardenbrook was much worse. That hot, dusty drive was terrible for sick people. When Neelie died she was very low, but she rallied and the rest of the train will move on. But Captain Hardenbrook will stay at Green River with his wife until she is entirely restored and they will go to Virginia City on the stage coach.

Tuesday, September 6

And thus ends our first day in Virginia City, and brings the "Crossing the Plains and Mountains in 1865" to an end.

Hardenbrook and grandchildren

Unlike Ezra Kerfoot, who moved his daughter in the covered wagon because of his fear of the Indians, Alan Hardenbrook would not budge until his ailing wife rallied. But by the time Captain and Mrs. Hardenbrook and little Annie arrived in Virginia City in the fall of 1865, Mrs. Hardenbrook had completely recovered.

Sarah Raymond married a man named Herndon in 1868 and settled on a ranch north of Virginia City. She lived a long and productive life. The *Rocky Mountain Husbandman*, a frontier newspaper, serialized her diary in 1880. The following letter from an earlier emigrant appeared when the series was concluded:

I have felt a deep interest in S.R.H.'s, "Crossing the Plains in 1865," all through these long series of letters. Many a familiar spot has been brought back to me that has long been forgotten. And as some of the actors in the play live in Challis, Idaho, I will say to S.R.H. that Mrs. Hardenbrook is still loved by a large circle of friends, and that little Annie is now a blooming young lady, and ever worthy the good-bye kiss; that the Captain has never disgraced the title bestowed in 1865.

I am, Mr. Editor, respectfully yours,

O. E. Penwell

I spent the evening with my family. Howard was distraught and preoccupied with the death of his mother. The next morning I hightailed off for the Milwaukee tracks and caught a freight headed east. The train was loaded with unemployed men wandering the country in search of a job. We rolled through Bearmouth at high speed and went on to Drummond. There I got off and went back to Gambler Gulch for the long hike to Douglas. I reached the diggin's after dark. Sarah Raymond's diary had been published in a little book. I had it with me. She had autographed it for Mollie O'Keefe Ross.

The dam had been finished and the flow of water slightly improved. Brice was back and that evening he called a meeting of the men. He squatted on one heel and toe and the men squatted around him. John Brown and Art Periman were there.

"Boys," Brice began, "we've run out of money. We can't pay you any more, but we can keep on giving you board and room, such as it is. If we hit big, we'll catch up on your back pay, and we'd like to keep going until the first snow flies. How about it?"

The men looked at each other. Chuck Cook spoke first, "You can count on me, Brice."

Then the others: "I'll stick with you, Brice."

"Can't get no job on the outside, Brice. I'll stay, too."

"I'll give you the team and me, Brice."

John Brown spoke last, "I'll keep on hauling for you, Brice. If you could chip in on the gas, it would help."

Brice nodded.

I didn't say anything. I figured I'd get fired, but I guess Brice realized that he had to have someone to haul water and split the wood. And I desperately wanted to stay.

Sadly, Pearl Hanson watched Art Periman's wagon head up to

the Top. She wanted very much to leave, but the poor girl was in a kind of trap. She was a little too chubby to make that climb, and even if she reached the Top, she would still be in a wilderness full of wandering miners. Brice induced her to stay and promised her a ride out in the fall.

I had to haul water twice a day. This onerous task was accomplished by saddling a long yoke that was notched to fit my neck and shoulders. I hung a five-gallon can from each end of the yoke and staggered up Weasel Gulch about one-fourth of a mile. When I donned this contraption, I always felt like Spartacus, the slave.

At the cookhouse, I stopped to split wood each morning.

One of my jobs was to hike about 1½ miles up the gulch, close the floodgates on the dam in the morning, then go back up at night to open them. During the night, the excess water would flow down to the diggin's and arrive in time for the day's mining. When I first started these hikes, a coyote followed me, yapping all the way. I told Chuck Cook about it. He responded, "You better kill that little bugger. They kill deer. Take your rifle next time."

I carried the rifle for several days, but the coyote stayed away. I finally got tired of packing it. The first day I hiked to the dam without the rifle, the coyote reappeared with his nerve-wracking yap. I started packing the rifle again. He didn't show. Fascinated, I kept up the game, but I never got a shot.

I told Chuck about it, and he laughed: "Them coyotes are clever little beasts."

Pearl had a boyfriend named Fred. He must have really loved her because one day he hiked in all the way from Bearmouth to spend the night with her. The next morning, I went to work splitting wood outside Pearl's bedroom. I heard all kinds of weird noises coming from within—giggles, moans, sighs. I knew what was going on, but I was the victim of a strict, Scottish Presbyterian upbringing, and I highly disapproved. I kept on splitting wood.

At length, a disheveled Pearl appeared at the door and rasped, "Get back down to the diggin's, Johnny!"

I glowered back at her and went on splitting wood, grimly and noisily. Soon a ruffled Fred appeared at the door and started hiking up the trail. Pearl, one stocking sagging below her knee, called to him, "Fred, come back. Please come back!"

"I can't, Pearl. I got a job. Pearl, I got a job. Can't you figger that out?"

Pearl glared at me and turned away sadly.

Poor Pearl! She was a brave little gal, stuck in the wilderness with rough miners, none of whom dared make a pass at her. She had saved herself for Fred, the man she loved, and my righteous puritanism had, in part, spoiled her one romantic moment of the summer. I have often regretted my behavior.

The mine was gradually slowing to a halt. The bottomless bucket lay sullenly idle in the muck. The men went out prospecting on their own. Ice appeared around the edge of my wash basin in the morning.

Then Nick Sheridan appeared. He was a tubby mining engineer who came up to "test the ground." He puffed and panted around, digging little holes here and there, and panning the dirt in the creek. He did strange things with a transit and a level. He was told to sleep with me in my bunk in the squad tent.

Sheridan's snoring was monumental. When he inhaled, he sounded like a giant diesel truck. Then there would be an exquisite moment of silence before the exhale, which closely resembled the high-pitched scream of a Boeing 747. At the end of this single breath would come a series of grunts, moans, and a brief gnashing of the teeth, before the swelling roar of the giant diesel truck started as he inhaled again.

I punched him and coughed in his face. But he just went on snoring.

His final report was wildly optimistic. He seemed able to find gold in his little holes when nobody else could. He casually dismissed the problem of the dwindling water supply. His longhand report was rushed to Howard, who promptly had it typed and mailed to potential investors.

Unable to stand his snoring, I decided to build myself a cabin. I borrowed Ed Fisher's burros, cut and skidded about fifty alpine fir logs, notched them, placed rocks for a foundation, cut doors and windows, and topped it off with a roof gleaned from old sluice-box lumber. The cabin had no floor, but I put in a bunk bed and removed myself from the tumult of Sheridan's snores. I was two weeks building it.

My last trip to the Top was a disaster. I was to pick up a load of gas, grub, and supplies. I had the burros. At the Top, I found that John Brown had filled our forty-gallon drum. I had only two five-gallon cans and no funnel, so I had to siphon out the gas with a rubber enema tube.

I started the siphon by sucking on the tube. I swallowed a lot of gas and got sicker than hell. I loaded the gas, grub, and supplies into the panier-type pack saddle that hung from sawbuck pack saddles.

You can't lead burros; you have to drive them from the rear with a long set of reins. I was too sick to hold the reins, so I thought, "Oh, hell, I'll just let them go on their own."

The stupidity of this idea rapidly became apparent. The burros started to run. I crashed into the timber beside the road to head them off. The faster I ran, the faster they ran. I became bogged down in windfalls and heavy brush. When they reached the steep pitches, the jolting caused the loads to start spilling out. My heart sank. I ran on down to the Barney Eck meadow. The beasts were there, peacefully grazing, the packs askew. One panier was full of ketchup. Practically everything else was gone except, thank God, the gas. I went up the trail to view the damage.

Vast quantities of nails were strewn about, pairs of boots, hammers and saws, gloves, socks, and—good God—the grub! Broken jars of peaches, plums, peanut butter, applesauce, strips of bacon, and a river of Log Cabin syrup oozing down the trail. Potatoes rolled about.

I had a mad desire to head for Bearmouth and clear out of the country. But I painstakingly picked up the nails and everything else I could, and headed for the cookhouse carrying a broken jar of peaches in one arm and a broken jar of peanut butter in the other.

Pearl and Chuck were waiting for me. As I approached, the ketchup was streaming out of the packs, blood red. Pearl exclaimed, "Good God, Johnny! What happened?"

Chuck just shook his head. Tomorrow I would head for home and school. I felt dismal.

I was up at dawn. All the men were sleeping. The creek barely murmured. Wisps of mist curled up the gulch and over the great pile of rock we had created. The bottomless bucket was buried, never to move again, its long steel cables looping over the mud.

As I gazed out over the diggin's, a stray recollection came to me from Sarah Raymond's diary:

"Worked just one day, got five dollars. . . . Mining is the only work a man can get and it would kill an ordinary man in less than a week. . . . There are a few fortunate ones who are making money like dirt, but they are the exception, about one in a hundred."

It was only sixty-nine years since Sarah had met the disheartened miners leaving Virginia City, but so much had happened that Howard could tell my brothers and me: "You three boys have more members of the Society of Montana Pioneers than any other family in Montana. Somehow, it seems to me, that this should tell you something."

Well, in 1934, it didn't tell me much. I was a timid kid, and the thought of a Blackfeet warrior hurtling down on me with tomahawk upraised made my blood run cold. I could not have done what Alan Hardenbrook did: leave a secure home in the Middle West and load my family into a covered wagon to endure the miseries and dangers of crossing 1,800 miles of mountains, plains, and rivers.

My mind drifted to Anna Lester, the English girl about whom we

81

know so little, losing her mother from disease on a sailing ship in the North Atlantic. She came to Montana by covered wagon in 1863, almost casually "to be with friends." Who cared for this little girl of twenty years? Of course, the wild, uncouth Baron "cared" for her after he swept her off to his one-room, sod-roofed cabin at the Coriackan Defile, so that she could live the rest of her life with this violent, ill-tempered, hard-drinking man.

I wondered and wondered how these people could get along. They were my forebears, but that was just accidental. It was just accidental that they all ended up in Montana. It didn't tell us something, as Howard had said. It was just there, an indisputable fact, and it would be foolish to say that it didn't bear down heavily on our lives.

It didn't seem to matter to these people that Montana was huge, stark, cold, and forbidding, and that a virtual state of anarchy existed in the mining camps. The thing that mattered was what Sarah Raymond had said when her fellow immigrants were trying to divert the Hardenbrook train to sunnier, safer California: "We think Montana is the best place for our boys to get a start. Montana is our destination."

I thought of Brice and Howard and of half-remembered conversations:

"Hell, Brice, there's no reason that Douglas can't be one of the richest gulches in Montana. The old timers didn't find it because it's so hard to reach. Look, Brice! Think of it. You've got to go all the way up Bear Gulch, then all the way up Deep Gulch, then over the Top O'Deep at 7,000 feet, and down Weasel Gulch to Douglas. It takes an honest to God prospector like Dick Herzer to find a place like that."

"Yeah, I know Howard, and Dick is the kind of guy who'd never fool us. You know, I trust that old guy, Howard!"

"Well, Brice, here's some mail, a letter from Jewett Orth in Maryland, and here's the best part of it, a check for $500!"

"I knew we could count on good old Jewett, Howard. You know, we won't have any trouble getting a dragline in there. Marvin McDonald told me that all he has to do is run the cable out ahead, hook it to a tree, reverse the drum and pull it ahead on skids by its own power. That's all it takes. Ingenuity!"

"You bet, Brice. And Dick says that when the water gets low in August we can just build a dam and use the same water over and over again. We're lucky to have somebody like old Dick with us."

"Howard, I don't see how we can miss on this one. Just look at the gold Dick's hauled out of those little pockets in the dirt!"

Then the spring came. Brice enthusiastically headed the machinery up Bear Gulch. It was agonizingly slow; the dragline crept forward, scraping itself along on skids, breaking down, snapping

Howard Toole, Douglas Creek, 1934

82

Brice Toole

cables and wedging itself between trees. The men's wages went on and he had to hire Art Periman with his team and John Brown with his Model A pick-up. Brice's heart bothered him; he sat down and thought of the water which was beginning to rush down Douglas Creek. They should be there now . . . now! . . . and take advantage of that water! But the dragline just crept slowly along, the noise of its engine swelling and dying.

Howard drove up and they sat and talked. They were discouraged that day, and they didn't talk of moving machinery or dried up streams. They talked about next fall and of stalking the elk and grouse on the high ridges, stopping to rest among the wild flowers in the little meadow at the Top O'Deep, and of harking to the whisper of the wind in the age-old trees.

Brice looked up as John Brown's pick-up went by loaded with gas cans, and said: "Anyway, Howard, it's a great country." Howard nodded and replied, "It sure is."

But the moment of truth was on them. Their Eastern prep school friends had put up some money; there were men to be paid, and there were immense problems of supply. The pleasant fantasies about the great wealth and huge nuggets hidden in the Garnet Range must wait.

The risks now began to weigh on them. Howard got in his car, turned it around and headed for Missoula. Brice strode up the road.

The dragline had now gone as far as Secret Gulch. He was not easily discouraged, and he told himself: "Hell, there's only 15 miles left. Maybe this is not such a crazy scheme after all!"

And he began whistling that buoyant song from World War I, "Over There."

And only 25 miles away at the Circle W Ranch, Aunt Thula was sitting in front of the big lodge with her easel, brushes and water colors. She was reproducing the sweep of the land before her, the meadows, the river and the great mountains; and some of her family were gathered around her. She spoke.

"You know, boys, I just *know* that this ranch will be a success. When the guests come and can sit here and be inspired by this view, they are going to want to stay and stay and stay. This is a real western ranch, you know, but it is the most beautiful ranch in the west. Just look at that sight! I know we're going to have another beautiful sunset tonight.

"When our guests have had a chance to see this sight, they will go back to the east and tell their friends. The Circle W will be known as the most beautiful place in the west, and there will be more people who want to come here than we can accommodate.

"And we don't want to overcharge them. I have a vision that our guests will be rather like our own family. We don't want to commercialize the ranch. We will just have to arrive at a fair rate so that our guests will know they're not being victimized. Oh, I'm just full of enthusiasm about the whole thing!"

Just then, Colonel George F. Weisel strode around the corner and said brusquely: "Thula, will you step in here a moment? I want to talk to you." Aunt Thula followed him into the bedroom. There was a long, hard talk about money, about Lester Perro's wages, about Charlie Dunham's wages, and about a note at the bank.

Aunt Thula came out and sat again before her easel. She brushed a lock of her lustrous red hair away from her forehead. She had a bad heart, but those around her were only vaguely conscious of it. She never spoke of it.

Last winter, she had stayed at the ranch, snowbound. The harsh winter wind piled snow to the eaves, and the Weisel boys had to saw firewood day after day to keep warm. One wonders if she had that terrible feeling of loneliness that comes with being snowbound in a vast and empty land.

Thula, Brice and Howard Toole had lost practically everything in the Depression. Somehow, with them, this overwhelming fact never seemed to sink in. It seemed such a short time since there had been a great colonnaded house with gardeners and housemaids, since they had taken trips around the world and kept blooded horses.

But bright and cheery, the three of them struggled on with their impractical projects, light-hearted about what they considered to be the certainty of their success. When the days ahead seemed impossibly bleak, Brice could say, "Anyway, Howard, it's a great country!" And Aunt Thula would say, "Just think of the hardships that Gramp Hardenbrook and his family endured when they came across the Plains in a covered wagon! We should never be discouraged."

That was it. We should never be discouraged. There were ineffable voices speaking to these people, voices coming across the years from that day in 1865 when Alan Hardenbrook lifted little Annie into his wagon.

They were ingenuous about how other people would treat them. They totally lacked hard-heartedness, and naively assumed that all would turn out well, just as it had for Alan Hardenbrook and John R. Toole. Losing their material wealth was just a momentary set-back.

They loved and were loved, and a legion of friends shook their heads in wonder at their striving. But they went cheerfully on, ever enthusiastic, ever optimistic. Their bodies all carried weak hearts, but no one knew. All too soon, the curtain would descend on their lives as the flagging hearts collapsed.

I turned away and trudged up Weasel Gulch and soon was at the Top O'Deep. I desperately wanted the ranch and the mine to succeed and to help these floundering people. All around me in Montana were the giant smelters, the mines, the railroads, and the sawmills which had produced such great wealth for the parents of these people. But now, all that had been swept away, and I was only vaguely conscious of how hard the world had become by 1934.

John Brown met me at the Ford and together we got it started. I sadly turned down Deep Gulch and tooled down the highway to Missoula.

At our house, Brice Toole was taking his leave. He had gotten a job with the New Deal as an attorney for the Department of Justice in Washington, D.C. He didn't want to leave Montana, but he had come to a dead-end. He took off in a little car with his wife, Eleanor, and his two small sons. Ever cheerful, he waved as the car pulled away. My returning wave was mournful.

And the next day, Howard did something he had promised my mother he would never do. He went down to the bank and borrowed $1,000 to clean up all the delinquent bills at Douglas Creek.

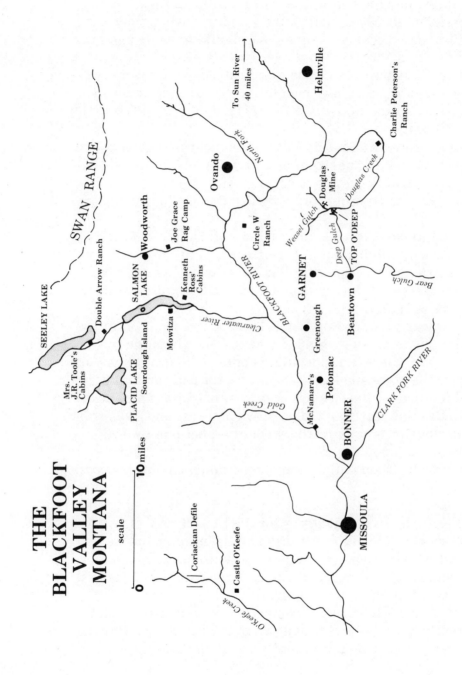

THE BLACKFOOT VALLEY MONTANA

scale

0 [10 miles

SWAN RANGE

SEELEY LAKE

Mrs. J.R. Toole's Cabins

Double Arrow Ranch

Woodworth

Joe Grace Rag Camp

SALMON LAKE

Kenneth Ross' Cabins

Mowitza

Sourdough Island

PLACID LAKE

Clearwater River

BLACKFOOT RIVER

Ovando

Circle W Ranch

North Fork

To Sun River 40 miles

Helmville

Charlie Peterson's Ranch

Douglas Mine

Douglas Creek

Weasel Gulch

Deep Gulch

TOP O'DEEP

Bear Gulch

GARNET

Greenough

Beartown

McNamara's

Potomac

Gold Creek

BONNER

MISSOULA

CLARK FORK RIVER

Castle O'Keefe

Coriackan Defile

O'Keefe Creek

86

4   The Hardheaded Logger

The Brothers Ross

4   The Hardheaded Logger

COVENANT

*WE, THE UNDERSIGNED, the sons and daughters of Alexan-
der D. Ross and Mary McCabe Ross, in memory of our dearest
departed mother, late of Green Hill in the Province of Nova Scotia in
the Commonwealth of Canada, do hereby legally and mutually bind
ourselves to make to our beloved Father, the said Alexander D. Ross,
an amount of money, to be paid annually, equal to ten percent of our
annual incomes.*

*We do this in recognition of the affection and generosity he bes-
towed on us to the detriment of his own prosperity, health, and
station in life, and as a tribute to our dear mother who brought to us
the teachings of Jesus Christ in the Holy Bible and taught us to fear
God in all things.*

*Solemnly sworn to by each and all of us this 26th day of December
in the year of our Lord, Eighteen Hundred Ninety Nine.*

/s/ *George E. Ross*	*Chinook, Montana*
/s/ *Malcolm M. Ross*	*Missoula, Montana*
/s/ *Kenneth F. Ross*	*Bonner, Montana*
/s/ *Alexander D. Ross*	*Missoula, Montana*

My grandfather Kenneth Ross engineered this covenant, which was found in his papers after his death, and he wrought better than he knew. The aging Alexander Ross suddenly was deluged with more money than he'd ever seen. He did something that was, for him, bold and unprecedented. He got on a train and journeyed to Montana to visit his five sons. He had never in his life been out of Green Hill, Nova Scotia, where he had raised the sons and three daughters in desperate poverty on a hard-scrabble farm.

In 1929, my mother, Marjorie Toole, induced her father, Kenneth Ross, to dictate the story of his life. It took much coaxing, but at length, he set to work. I can still see him, his eyes closed, a huge cigar in his hand, resting in his great rocker, summoning the memories of a rags-to-riches life.

The journal is a priceless historical document. It sheds light into the lives of men such as the Fisher brothers in Detroit, the Weyerhausers, John D. Ryan, H. H. Rogers, Marcus Daly, A. B. Hammond, and John R. Toole. The journal has huge gaps. The reader is tantalized by occasional omissions, and wants to know more of Ross's ranching experiences in eastern Montana, his hassles with Marcus Daly, and his war with the Industrial Workers of the World. But he wrote about the things he considered important, and what was important to him may not seem significant to us. He wrote at length about the Molly Maguires and the violence in the Pennsylvania coal mines where he was employed as a miner at the age of sixteen. He expounds on religion and philosophy and puzzles over the strong anti-Catholic bias implanted in him by his strict Presbyterian upbringing, finally concluding that his previous teaching "had been all lies."

Kenneth Ross's writings seem ingenuous, almost childlike. He had an inquiring mind, uncluttered by education. In these gropings, he stumbles on the main thread running through the thinking of leading nineteenth-century philosophers. Kenneth Ross could not even read, let alone understand, Ralph Waldo Emerson, and he certainly did not pronounce with certitude anything close to an Emersonian credo. He was just nibbling around the edges, and as soon as he had gone far enough to reconcile the conflicts within himself, he promptly adopted an optimistic, tolerant, sunny view of life, a view based firmly on his own sense of values. And he would be governed by this view until the day he died.

One used to hear the phrase, "only in America." It applies to Kenneth Ross. There had never been a time or a place in human history in which an illiterate fifteen-year-old boy could leave home and find spread before him a rich continent, occupied sparsely by a free people living under a free economic system. These conditions combined in the North America of the nineteenth century—and the largesse was indeed spread unequally—but for Kenenth Ross,

90

born on March 29, 1863, it was all there. The only limits on him would be the limitations he carried within him. And so, in 1877, he trudged away from the Nova Scotia farm into a time of magnificence. The time was like a bright ray of light, a light that would shine only briefly and would be snuffed out in August 1914, before he was sixty years old.

All our family were reared on the farm that was our birthplace. It was impossible, however to raise enough on the farm to support us and my father was obliged to work away from home part of the time. My father was a very remarkable man and was well educated although he never went to school. He often told us that the only slate on which he had to figure was the stone hearth in front of the fireplace, using for his pencil a soft stone that he had picked out of the creek. He was a very good violinist and taught music besides conducting a number of singing schools and training church choirs for many miles around. My mother, of course, was kept very busy at home where she, with the help of the family, sheared the sheep, washed and carded the wool, and made it into rolls, later spinning it into yarn on an old-fashioned spinning wheel. From this yarn she wove all the cloth to make our clothing, knit our stockings and underwear, doing all the sewing and tailoring herself. She was a kindly mother and a great reader.

None of our family secured much of an education. There was a small country school about two miles distant from our home where school was held only in the winter time, and when the weather got very cold and the snow very deep, only the larger ones in the family could attend. I went to school very little, so little in fact, that when I left home at the age of fifteen, I could read and write very little. When I left home my father addressed a number of envelopes to himself as I could not write plainly enough to direct a letter home.

It goes without saying that we were very poor. My father was always in debt, and it made my heart ache to know that he was always worried about finances. I can remember lying awake nights when a mere boy, planning to go out west and make a lot of money to send Father and Mother in order to relieve them of this worry.

My brother, George Ross, decided that he would go west with me, so on the fourteenth day of January, 1877, we started our journey to Houtsdale, Clearfield County, Pennsylvania, to a coal camp. When Mother realized that I was really going, she started to rig me out with stockings, mittens, and knitted underwear. I bought a little trunk for which I paid a dollar and a half. It was very little larger than a big suitcase, but in it I found ample room for my belongings. The day for our departure came at last, and I remember that the last thing my father did before I left was to give me a Bible, which he wanted me to keep and which I still have. It was rather a sad leave-taking, especially for Mother. She told me as we left the house not to look back as she felt it was a bad omen.

We arrived in Houtsdale on Saturday, and upon getting up on Sunday morning I found, to my great surprise and horror, that everyone was working as though it were a week day. Trains were running and everything was moving along regardless of the fact that it was Sunday. I decided that these people were very wicked to disregard the Sabbath in this fashion, as it was very much different from what I had been accustomed to at home where all kinds of work, including the running of railroad trains, was stopped on Sunday. We were not even permitted to clean the stable on that day, and the womenfolk always baked enough bread on Saturday to last over Sunday. If you did such a thing as play a musical instrument or whistle a dancing tune on the Sabbath, you were surely doomed to go to hell. My mother and father were Presbyterians and believed that there should be nothing but church and prayer on Sunday.

My brother, being an old experienced miner, was put to work at once in the mine. I got a job at a dollar a day burning coke. It goes without saying that I was delighted to get a job at such a good salary, compared with what I had been working for at home. My first payday I received thirty dollars, as I had worked every day, Sundays included. I paid my board and the balance I sent home to Father and Mother, and I will never forget how happy I was when I sent home my first money. After a time there was a vacancy in the mines for a miner, and I was given a job working with an old experienced miner. I had to mine as much coal and load as many cars as he did in order to get the same money. We were paid by the ton, loading the coal into small cars which held about two tons, and it was hauled out of the mine by small mules. Each drift had its number and our cars were tagged and weighed on the tipple where it was dumped into cars, and we were given credit for the amount of coal we mined. The veins of coal lay horizontally, some veins being only four feet thick and others six. They would lay off a drift 35 feet wide and run a small car track right up to the center or breast of the coal, and two men worked in this drift, each mining the coal on his own side of the track. So you can readily see where it was necessary for me to mine just as much coal as the experienced miner in order to keep up my side of the drift, and in order to get the same pay as my partner. The first month I worked at this job paid me eighty or ninety dollars. I thought I was getting rich very fast. This time I was able to send some more money to Father and Mother.

Things went well for about two months, my pay checks amounting to about one hundred dollars each month. We were mining the coal for 50 cents per ton. There was a very strong miners' union headed by the notorious Molly Maguires. I will say that there was more justice in the miners' union of that time than there is today. This was

92

due to the fact that all members of the union who came out on strike had to stand together, win or lose, and were not allowed to enter any other occupation or take any other man's job until all their differences were settled and the strike declared off. Any one deserting a strike was called a "blackleg," and if he was caught, he was beaten up and oftentimes killed. These men were treated much worse than the strikers of the present day treat the "scabs" as they call them.

Thus does time, change of status, and wealth alter one's perspective and attitude toward organized labor. By 1916, Kenneth Ross would command one thousand sawmill workers and lumberjacks. The Molly Maguires were long forgotten. The shoe was now on the other foot. The union he confronted in 1916, using violence against violence, was the revolutionary Industrial Workers of the World. It spoke and acted for the lumberjacks of the Northwest, who were imprisoned in wilderness camps, under conditions not unlike those in the slave labor camps in the Gulag Archipelago. Kenneth Ross "cleaned out" the I.W.W., but as we shall see, he then promptly reversed his labor policy, bringing labor peace that lasted long after his death.

One of the grievances the miners had was that they wanted a union representative to see the coal weighed before it was dumped into the cars. This man was known as the check-weighman. A strike was called for an increase of 10 cents per ton, making 60 cents, and the employment of a check-weighman, whose salary was to be paid by the operators. The day was set for the strike to be called, if the company did not accede to the demands of the men. These demands, of course, were turned down, and the strike was on. The miners began immediately to hold a great many meetings, the agitator always being very much in evidence and having the most to say, predicting that we would be out only a short time as the company would be obliged to grant our demands. In the course of two weeks, they began circulating subscription lists for needy families, and all miners who could do so were supposed to contribute something to help feed these people. With the small amount of money I had, and feeling that I must subscribe to each list that came around, I soon found myself getting pretty low in funds. The boarding houses all called upon single men to pay a month's board in advance, as the company store had shut off all credit and the boarding houses had to pay cash for their groceries. We had been out on strike about a month, and things had begun to look pretty serious to me and to some of the others who were afraid to express themselves where the agitators might hear them, when we were told that Mr. Whitehead, the man who owned the mines in which we were working, would arrive there to make us a proposition. The agitators, of course, were very much elated, saying that the operators had to come to terms and that the strike was practically over. Many of the miners got drunk and had a pretty lively time of it, but to me things still looked pretty serious. Mr. Whitehead finally arrived, and as the union hall was not large enough, he made his talk from the platform at the railroad station. I was very much impressed by his appearance. He was a tall man with long, white hair, which turned up at his coat collar. He had a kindly face and an unusually lovely voice. He explained to us what he was willing to do, but he said that it was impossible to meet all the demands made upon him. He said that one of the demands he would grant was regarding the check-weighman, but went on to explain that coal was being sold to the big railroad companies and big industries at very close figures.

He said the price of coal had gone up some for the contracts made a year before, but other contracts had to be made in the near future, and he did not know whether the price would go up or down. But he made us a proposition that from then on he would pay 55 cents per ton until the new contracts were let and then, if the price of coal advanced above the present market price, which we all had an opportunity to know, he would pay 60 cents per ton, but if the price were lower, we would have to go back to 50 cents. I thought it was a very reasonable proposition and I was delighted, thinking that the strike was over and that we would all go back to work the next morning. He closed his speech by saying that unless we accepted this proposition, the mines would close indefinitely, as they were under a big expense and losing money.

After his departure, as usual the men gathered in groups and discussed the pros and cons, some arguing that we stay out until we got our demands, while others, like myself, thought we should accept the proposition made us and take our chances with the mine owner. A meeting was called that night and we assembled in the miners' union hall, and it seemed there was no one in evidence to talk except the agitator. The president of the union, a man by the name of Hoover, claimed we had them on the run and that it would only be a matter of a few days until they met our demands. A great many other talks were made along these lines by officials of the union and men who were not working. I should judge there were 250 or 300 men in the hall. The matter was put to a vote, and when the ballots were counted, they claimed that it carried by 90 percent to stay out on strike. You can imagine what a sick boy I was. Hoover later took the first strike breakers into the mine, and when coming out the first night was shot at the mouth of the drift.

Just before the strike had been called, my brother George had gotten the western fever and, together with a man by the name of Tom Sunderlin, started for Butte, Montana. I stayed around for a week or ten days. Many families were destitute and a lot of the single men who were drinkers had spent their money and were actually going hungry. My money was all gone but $2.50, and I decided to blackleg. It was 20 miles from Houtsdale to the main line of the Pennsylvania Central, the junction being known as Osceola. I still had part of a month's board coming to me, but I could not ask for that as I was afraid they would find out that I was going to blackleg and I would be beaten up or killed. One dark, rainy night about one o'clock I left, putting the Bible Father had given me in one pocket and a pair of socks Mother had knitted for me in the other. The only food I took with me was two doughnuts I had smuggled from the supper table that evening. I think the distance between Houtsdale and Osceola was the fastest 20 miles I ever made in my life on foot. I think I ran most of the way.

I arrived there shortly after daylight and climbed into a boxcar of a freight train that had just come along. I rode a station or two when two brakemen came along and wanted to know how much money I had. I told them I had $2.50 and that it was all I had in the world. I also told them I was blacklegging and wanted to get away, that I had had no breakfast, and asked them not to put me off the train until I was far enough away so the miners could not catch me. They made me give them a dollar. I rode some distance to a little station called Ben's Creek, which was halfway between Johnstown and Altoona. There was a mine about two miles up the creek, so I got off and walked up to the mine. I got a 15-cent breakfast at a boarding house and then went over to the mine to look for employment. When I arrived there I was fortunate in finding the foreman at the mouth of the drift. I asked him for a job and was told that the mine was full. I told him I must have work, that my money was just about gone and that I was willing to do anything. He asked where I came from. I told him I had just come from Houtsdale and was blacklegging, and that I had walked all night the night before to get away, leaving my belongings, and that he must try to do something for me. He told me to come over and sit down on a bench, which I did. He asked me a lot of questions. I told him everything, where I had come from, how long I had worked, and I also told him about Mr. Whitehead's speech and about the union men advocating the holding out regardless of the fact that many families were starving. He finally told me that there was a man in the mine working alone, and that he would speak to him about me and see if he would take me for a partner if I could get some tools, as it was necessary for the miners to buy their own tools such as hammer, drills, shovels, etc.

I went to a storekeeper and told him that I was broke, but could get a job if I had the tools and a little money for such things as I needed until the first payday. I could not get board at the company boarding house and had to go down to the mouth of the creek, a distance of

*about two miles from the mine, where I got room and board with
John Bradley and his wife. They had an old-maid daughter and a
boy who was old enough to work in the mine. John was an elderly
man and did very little work around the place. Mrs. Bradley and her
daughter cooked for the men, and I noticed that both of them wore
around their necks large Catholic crosses suspended from long
chains. As I have already stated, though it had not been discussed at
home, I left there with the idea that an Irish Catholic was as near
hell as a human being could get, and, quite naturally, I had my
suspicions about the Bradley family.*

*I went to work in the mine and had worked a little less than two
weeks when a fall of coal came down and broke my ankle and
mashed my foot. The tunnel I was working in was a mile and a half
into the mountains. They put me in a small car and took me out to
the mouth of the drift and then took a spring wagon and took me
down to my boarding house. Of course, a coal miner gets just as
black as the coal itself, so the men took me to the bathroom, gave me a
bath, and I was put to bed. They sent for a doctor, and after a long
wait he came and put my ankle in splints and bandaged up my foot.
Mrs. Bradley left the daughter and her husband to take care of the
boarders as best they could, and she came and took care of me. You
can imagine what distress I was in, having no money to pay doctors'
bills, board, or anything else. It goes without saying that I suffered a
great deal of pain, and oftentimes would wake up at night to find
Mrs. Bradley changing the position of my leg in order to give me a
little rest. She started off so very attentive to me both day and night,
that I was wondering how a Catholic could be such a good woman.
John, the husband, would come to the bedside often to inquire about
me, but I had my suspicions about him. I still thought he might be a
devil in sheep's clothing.*

*Things went on in this manner for two or three weeks when one
day Mr. Bradley came to my room and examined my foot. He said he
didn't like the looks of it and wanted to take me to another doctor, so
they got me up on crutches and I got to a little railroad station a short
distance from the boarding house, where I took a train for Altoona.
The doctor to whom they took me in Altoona took one look at my foot
and then got very angry and wanted to know of Mr. Bradley what
doctor I had had. He said there were two bones in my foot that had
been shoved down out of place, and that cartilege was forming in the
joint which made it impossible to put them back in place. He said he
would have a shoe made for me, and he told Mr. Bradley to make me
put it on every morning and lace it very tight up to the knee, and that
I must step on my toes all I could stand in order to put the bones back
in place. Otherwise I would be a cripple for life. You can imagine my
frame of mind at the thought of being a cripple, away from home,
without money and without friends. I had in mind what my Father*

had said to me when I was so anxious to get away, that I might be like a lot of other boys who had sent to their parents for money to get them home, so I made up my mind to stay where I was and not let them know I was hurt. I would hobble out to the bank of the river on my crutches, where I would put in my time stepping on my toes to get the injured bones back in place. Owing to the pain I suffered, my loneliness and the worry of not having any money, I think I must have shed several barrels of tears. However, I made myself very useful around the house. Mrs. Bradley would put my foot up on a pillow and I would dry the dishes for her. I became very much attached to the Bradleys, especially Mrs. Bradley, so it was quite natural that I commenced to think more or less about the Catholics and their religion. I was not very sure about John and the rest of the family, but when I thought of Mrs. Bradley, I was convinced that there was one good Catholic..No mother could ever do more for her own boy than Mrs. Bradley, the Catholic, was doing for me, so it was only natural that I began to wonder. I knew there were other religions besides the Presbyterians, and there must be a lot of good people in the world.

One Sunday about this time I went with the Bradleys to a little church at a place called Sonman, about two miles from the boarding house. We went in, people got down on their knees, and after a while a man, wearing a handsomely decorated robe and followed by two or three boys carrying candles, came out of a room at the front of the church. This was the first priest I had ever seen. He went up in front of the altar and went through a great many contortions, finally turning to the congregation and saying "high cockolorum" and a lot of other things like that, which neither I nor any of the others understood, and the service was over. We went out. A lot of the Bradleys' friends came around and Mrs. Bradley introduced me as "the boy she had told them about." They were very friendly, and it seemed to me that they were just as good-looking and appeared just as kindly as the Scottish Presbyterans from my neighborhood.

This caused me to begin to consider, even more seriously, the subject of religion. I wondered how it was that I wanted to be a good boy, and though I had done a great many things wrong, I did not seem to be able to help them, and all the preaching I had ever heard was to the effect that we were born in sin, and there was nothing for us but hellfire and brimstone. This worried me a great deal. The question arose in my mind that if God was the Creator of all things, why did he create the devil. It had always seemed to me that the devil had a lot more power than God, when he could doom us to go to hell. I could not understand why it was that, if God was good, he should have created the bad in us. In my boyhood days, I had been under the impression that God was a personal God, a big man who sat on a throne and judged us poor devils when we came up for judgment. I studied and worried over these things for some time and finally, one day, a new line of development had taken place in my mind. I began to regard all the previous teachings I had had as lies. I got away from the personal-God idea, and thought of him as a good God and that what he created was right and good. I decided that the reason we condemned a great many things created and brought to pass by God was that we did not have the proper understanding and that we must learn that everything that had been created was good. I saw the error in the teachings I had had that God created me and all other human beings, knowing our imperfections, but that he would punish us for all our mistakes, regardless of the fact that our making such mistakes was due to ignorance and lack of understanding. I made up my mind that I had nothing to fear. Whatever bad came to us, came from our lack of understanding, and we must learn by experience. Thus, it was up to me to acquaint myself with my own bad traits and try to eliminate them, as this was my only show to develop. The thought struck me that if we had been created perfect, then perfection would mean nothing, that it was right that we were created imperfect and that there was no such thing as perfection. I was convinced that we had come on since creation and that we were developing in the right direction. This led me to decide that all religions were all right with me. It made no difference what was worshipped, whether a stone or a horse, so long as one did what was right. I further decided I would never question any misfortune that might come to me. Everything on earth that was governed by the Creator must be right or it would not be. Thus I felt that everyone was as good as he could be, taking into consideration the handicaps put upon him by his ancestors. I figured everyone was putting up a gallant fight to eliminate the bad in themselves, which was due for the most part to characteristics inherited from their ancestors, the uncovering and overcoming of which imperfections constituted their development and the building up of stronger character. It oftentimes appears to us that some people are not making much of an effort to eliminate the evil in themselves, but were we able to judge, we would find they are doing the best they can with the intelligence and strength of character they have.

The foregoing line of thought came to me when I was about seventeen years of age, and since that time I have been very much criticized for suggesting that people were as good as they could be. I used to argue with a great many people that, physically I was a big, powerful man, but was not responsible in any way for physical or mental development, which was also true of a person of weak frame or mind; that this was the way they were created and were left to their own free will as to development, therefore claiming that all people were as good as they could be. I believed that there was a certain amount of goodness in everyone, no odds how bad they were, and that the goodness, no odds how little it was, could never be taken away from them or destroyed in any way, though it might take ages to develop it. Nothing could destroy it, and it was bound to develop. I have oftentimes wished a lot of good people could know the fight I myself have put up all my life to eliminate in my character traits that I believe were passed on to me by my ancestors, and also that they could know how very grateful I was to anyone who would come to my rescue and help me.

No doubt there is much evil in our characters that has not yet been discovered by ourselves, and of which we become aware only by experience. I also began to discover at this early age that a great many of the best things that come to us are things that are forced upon us and against our wills, and that after we had been forced to accept the new condition, we gradually came to see how wrong we were not to accept the condition that had proven itself to be right instead of wrong. An outstanding example of this is the compulsory adoption of the automatic coupler now in use on all railroads. The railroads fought the bill for two years, stating that it would bankrupt them to make the change, notwithstanding the fact that every court in every county through which the railroads ran was trying personal injury suits for loss of life or limbs, much of which the adoption of the new coupler would eliminate. It might also be stated that in this connection statistics showed at that time that funds collected from these damage suits never reached the wives and children of those who had been killed or injured.

Another example along this line is our present compensation law whereby the state pays a part of the compensation, hospital or doctor bills to any man in any industry in the state, during such time as he is disabled owing to injury, and in case of death, pays to the widows and children a substantial sum. This bill was also fought, likewise regardless of the fact that 50 percent of our courts' time was taken up by damage suits against these same industries, which, in many cases, were forced out of business when some such case was decided against them. I am of the opinion that there is no operator paying compensation to the state who would want to go back to the old state of affairs and undertake to either fight or settle damage suit cases.

In the fall of 1883, my brother Malcolm M. Ross and I left Eau Claire, Wisconsin, where we made our headquarters for a few years, coming directly to Missoula. [In Eau Claire, Kenneth had worked as a "river pig," driving logs down the Chippewa River.]

There were but few dwellings on the north side of the river and none at all on the south side. Where the Missoula County High School [now Hellgate] stands was a sheep corral where they used to round up the sheep at night so they could be safe from coyotes. So you can imagine how interesting it has been for me to watch the wonderful development that Missoula and the surrounding country have had in the past forty-six years.

We stayed in Missoula but a few days and went to Thompson Falls. As the stampede into the Coeur d'Alene country had started, there were a thousand or fifteen hundred people in Thompson Falls, all living in tents of course, but it was sure a wide-open town. All the toughest characters that ever went on a gold stampede were congregated there, as one of the main trails into the Coeur d'Alene started from Thompson Falls.

My oldest brother, George Ross, together with a man named Tom Jordan, went in early in the winter of '84 to a point called Raven on Pritchard Creek, where they claimed that gold had been discovered in the fall of '83. All their supplies and belongings they had to haul on toboggans up over a very high range of mountains and down the other side to the camp on Ryan Creek. My brother M. M. and myself outfitted with our toboggans and supplies went in to join my brother George and Tom Jordan.

Raven, of course, was a tent town, and the tents were pitched over ten feet of snow. Some enthusiastic prospectors were digging down through this depth of snow to see if they could find gold in the gravel.

We stayed there but a short time, as there was no work to be had, and we started back to Thompson Falls, leaving my brother and Mr. Jordan behind, as they wanted to stay until the snow went off, so that they could be at the head of the great rush and stampede that was waiting at Thompson Falls and at Rathdrum, Idaho, where another trail brought them into the Wallace district, and from Coeur d'Alene, another point of entry. So you can imagine what kind of a congregation of men was in these towns waiting to get into the new district at the first sign of spring. This was the spring, of course, of '84.

The snow that winter was very deep all over the Coeur d'Alene and Bitterroot mountains. On our way back to Thompson Falls, on the summit of the Bitterroots, the snow was just 30 feet deep. Someone had built a fire in the top of a dry tree which burned to the ground, leaving a well hole of ice about 30 feet in diameter. I happened to have a tape line, and it measured just 30 feet exactly from the ground to the top of the snow. It was really a strange sight in the spring of the year when the snow went off to see the tops of trees lopped off 30 and 40 feet from the ground.

We came out to Thompson Falls and were employed by Hugh Kirkendahl, the old-time railroad contractor who had taken a contract to build a trail into the Coeur d'Alene and transport a lot of machinery, among other things a saw mill, and all kinds of wares such as wagons and some building material. A. B. Cooke, who afterwards became a very large railroad contractor, was timekeeper

100

for him at that time.

We stayed on the job until we got the trail to the summit, where at times we would have to shovel through a great depth of snow, and of course, the people with their supplies pushed on as fast as the trail was completed.

I came to Missoula and went on to Wallace, which is now called Clinton. Henry Hammond, a brother of A. B. Hammond, was running two sawmills for Eddy, Hammond & Company, one at Wallace and another one about four or five miles west. They had been in the lumber business and furnished the bridge timbers for the construction of the Northern Pacific Railroad Company when they built through this section of the country. I went to work for Mr. Hammond, and after working for a short time for him, we discovered that we had worked in Pennsylvania on the same logging job, but did not happen to become acquainted. We became very good friends. I worked for him only a short time when the man who ran the mill, called No. 2, which was two miles west of Wallace, quit and he put me in charge of the whole operation. You can imagine what an undertaking this was for me, a boy about twenty-two years old, without any education whatever. I never tried to figure a piece of lumber in my life. The only thing that came easy to me was the handling of the logging outfit, the teams, the men. You can see what a problem I had on my hands, to fill specified orders for different kinds of lumber, load it on the cars, tally it, and make out invoices, and I did not know how to figure fractions. Many is the time I had to quit my little office and take my problems to the woods with me, where I had nobody to bother me, but I finally mastered it even though I had some very peculiar ways of getting at the fractions. I surely must have made good, as I stayed in this position for some time, increased the capacity of the output of the mill, and seemed to give very good satisfaction.

After the timber was pretty well cut out around the mill I had charge of, I was instructed to move it to Bonner, and set it up for the purpose of cutting out lumber for a dam, bunkhouse buildings, and for timbers for a sawmill that they contemplated constructing. I put up the little mill on the flat near where the company's stables now stand, and the first logs were cut from timber growing around where the Margaret Hotel is now located, which was a very nice stand of timber. There was also another nice stand of timber further up the river.

We cut a lot of trees 75 feet long out of the biggest timber we could find, and floated them down the river for the foundation of the dam. A man by the name of Walter Comes, a dam builder, came and took charge of the construction of the dam. We laid these timbers up and down the river, 12 feet apart, and then put on cross-timbers 12 feet apart, pinning them together, which made cribs 12 feet square. This, of course,

101

was carried up all the way from the bottom of the river and filled with rock.

After the dam was well under way, along about the first of October, I took a layoff, as I had not heard from my brother George, who was in the Coeur d'Alene. There was really no mail communication. He had been sick with pneumonia, and the last I had heard of him was that he was in very poor health. So I went in.

By this time, a great many small towns had sprung up in the Coeur d'Alene, such as Murray, Wallace, Eagle City, and Raven, and several other towns, and there were thousands of men in there, a big percentage of whom were gamblers. Very little rich diggings had been found up until that time, but they had found some very rich quartz, and had commenced to take on the form of a real mining district.

I got my brother George, who was in very poor health, and brought him out with me. Of course, I wanted him to go with me to Bonner, where I had a good job, and he could go to work for me. He was a stationary and hoisting engineer.

We came out to Missoula. At that time the Northern Pacific Railroad Company was just about to start construction of the [steel] Marent trestle [to replace the shaky wooden trestle built the year before]. He applied for a position as engineer and they gave him a job running a pump, which was about the only work he was able to do on account of poor health. I was afraid to leave him there, as he was suffering a great deal of pain, and I applied for a job, as I could not afford to lay around and do nothing, and wanted to stay with him until I was sure he was strong enough to get along all right. They were just starting to break

The wooden Marent trestle just after it was completed in 1883. It was replaced by the present steel structure in 1884, erected by Kenneth Ross.

ground for the excavation of the foundation of the two big towers that run from the bottom of the gulch to the top of the bridge, a distance of 226 feet. I was given a job running a wheelbarrow. This, of course, was quite a comedown from sawmill superintendent, but was better than loafing.

We excavated down about 4 or 5 feet below the grass roots and we would drive sounding bars 15 feet ahead of us. We soon discovered that we were going to encounter a big deposit of quicksand. There was no way of determining how deep it went, and of course the more of the solid dirt we removed from the top, the poorer foundation we would have. They filled the entire excavation full of piling almost as thick as they could be driven, sawed them off even with the bottom of the excavation, and put in concrete piers. When they started to build the forms to hold the concrete, the engineer in charge came to me and wanted me to take charge of the forms and the putting in of the concrete. I told him I knew nothing of concrete, and nothing about the forms, thanked him for the job, told him I was not going to stay there, and told him why I was there, on account of my brother, and said that I really was very anxious to get away. "Well," he said, "I have nobody else, so just take charge of it for the present. I will show you, and as a matter of fact, the concrete will be a very simple matter as we mix the cement and sand together, pour it into the form, and then put in the rock."

I took the job under protest, but found with very little instruction that it was no trouble at all to put the forms in the proper manner, and the work became very interesting.

The first form we built was 18 feet square by 3 feet thick. After that got sufficiently hard to stand the immense weight of the next one, we put another form, 16 feet square by 3 feet thick, on which the present stone piers now stand, for the foundation of the steel towers.

After this was completed, a bridge man by the name of Healy came out from Chicago to erect the structure. The chief engineer on this job was a man by the name of Noble, who afterwards was appointed by the Pennsylvania Railroad Company as their chief engineer, which position he held for a great many years, and went down in history as one of the great railroaders of this country.

I had gone to the office to settle up, as I wanted to go back to Bonner. Mr. Healy happened to be in the office, and he said, "I don't want you to quit. I have selected you as one of my raisers—a steel gang. We need eight men, and I have selected you as one of them." I told him I couldn't stay, told him my brother's story, and about my job in the sawmill. He would not take no for an answer. Then I told him that I couldn't go up high—if I went to the top of a house, I would get dizzy-headed and fall off. He said he knew that my head was level enough so I could go as high as any of them, and very much against my will, I consented, and we started the erection of the steel towers.

Of course, it was just as he had said—we went up at stages of 20 feet at a time, and the height made no difference to us. The big steel posts weighed twenty tons, and these were hoisted from the ground till we ran the two big towers up a distance of 100 feet, the other 126 feet being lowered from the top. This bridge was all raised during a winter, and you can imagine what a cold job it was to sweep the snow off the steel that we had to walk on, which was only about 16 inches wide, with no other staging—not a bit of wood—and the steel girds as they now see them in the trestle.

They were anxious to push the work as fast as possible, and Mr. Healy sent to Chicago for some of his favorite men, and of course there was a great deal of speculation as to how we would show up as compared with them. They were supposed to take one tower, and we would take the other. They finally arrived and came out on the job one very cold morning. It was snowing and we were sweeping the snow off our steel work. They climbed the ladder with their brooms and had started to hoist the tools for them to work with, when suddenly they bunched up and held a little council of war, not over five minutes, went to the office, and that evening took their departure for Chicago. We surely were in for it then, as we could not quit, and by this time I think we were a very efficient gang of raisers. However, we went on and raised all of the towers, put in the spans, and the first railroad trains passed over it.

The bridge was very narrow, very little wider than a flat car; in fact, the only way we could get by a flat car would be to hang from one pocket to the other, and of course get a foothold on the end of the tie. One morning I was on one side of a flat car and Mr. Healy, the superintendent, on the other, and we were working our way along to the end of the car when suddenly Mr. Healy happened to step on a cast washer, his foot slipped off, and he went over falling the entire distance of 226 feet. A young man by the name of Billy Holden was fireman of the locomotive that stood on the bridge; he has pulled passenger trains and freight trains ever since he got his first engine, and is still running on the Bitterroot line. I met him the other day. In a very few months he will be seventy years old and be entitled to a pension. I think he saw Mr. Healy when he started to fall. You can imagine how we all felt. He was a very lovable character, one of the most fearless men I ever saw in my life. He had a wife and a little baby. She used to come out on the bridge and seemed to be able to walk a stringer in mid-air and pack the baby without any fear of falling. My brother George, who was running an engine a short distance from where Mr. Healy landed, was the first man to get to him. A number of us came down off the bridge, packed him into a saloon and laid him on a billiard table. His head was badly smashed and his face was badly disfigured, and I and another man, by the name of Steve Taylor, who was one of the eight of the raising gang, started to wash his face, when suddenly we found ourselves all alone, and who walked in but Mrs. Healy and Mr. Noble, the chief engineer, who happened to be there at that time. I think I would have given all my belongings if I could have gotten away. We all loved Mr. and Mrs. Healy, and she came walking up to the table and she said, "Charlie, just speak to me once."

Of course, we were housed at the bottom of the gulch, and there were a lot of professional gamblers, as usual, living off the suckers who would play their game, but there were a few of us wiser ones who played by ourselves, and wouldn't play with the professionals. There was one professional gambler whom we used to play with—he had consumption but was a very fine man—and he played on the square and showed us a great many things about the cards that were a great deal of benefit to a good many of us. We were always glad when he made a winning because this was the only way he had of making a livelihood. We used to play every night for a few hours, and sometimes we had considerable money on the table.

We used to play in a saloon run by Alec Dow and Camille McGowan, and our rooming house was next door to the saloon. As anybody who ever played cards knows, at times you will play in ill luck, and other times you will play in good luck. For a long time I had been playing in ill luck, losing mostly every night, so my luck changed and the usual gang of five or six fellows around a big table were playing a very liberal game with considerable money on the table, or checks rather, which represented money. Hanging around was an old professional gambler by the name of John Harvey who had killed a man in Missouri in early days and had come out to this country and really was a desperate character, always carrying a Colt .44 inside his blouse. I am sure that he never played an honest game in his life. I never would play with him or in the same game, although some of the boys used to let him in, but they had to watch him all the time, as he would put up the cards on them. So this night my good luck was with me and I was winning considerable money when Harvey came along and wanted to get into the game. Of course, I protested, as it meant that I would have to get out of the game, as I would not play with him. He was too hard to watch. My own brother George, who was sitting on my left, favored him coming into the game, and they put it to a vote and he was admitted. To safeguard myself all I could, I made room for him alongside by shoving my chair around, as I would have a better opportunity to watch him, for I only intended to play a short time as I knew there would be crooked work in the game. It soon happened, however, that there were some very good hands out and a pretty good-sized pot. George Ross was the one who finally called me on the last bet and I won the pot, probably of $80 or $100. I am sorry to say that George was very ill-tempered when he lost. He hit the table with his fist after cussing

105

his luck, and my checks fell over onto the floor. Well, I started to gather up my checks and stack them in front of me. About the time I had this completed, I found that John Harvey, who sat to my right, had dealt the cards up and I surely had the right hunch that he put the deck up. I looked at my hand and I found I had three queens. Right away I suspicioned that the job was put up. So I made a medium-sized bet, and they all came in. It got around to John Harvey and he raised me—made a very big raise, so I said, "Old fellow, you're at your same old tricks. You've got 'em stacked. I'm gonna call you, but I promise you you'll never get away with that pot."

By this time I was working up to a fever heat. Of course we drew cards. He hesitated and didn't want to go on with the deal. I drew two cards and got the fourth queen. He drew one card for a blind. I was ready to fight about that time, so I grabbed the cards out of his hand and laid them on the table. He had four kings, and I laid out four queens. I said to him in my rage, "I wish you weren't an old man. I would like to spoil your face for you." He jumped up and said, "Of course, you're a young man, but choose your weapons." Like any fool, crazy kid who was beside himself with rage, I said, "Mine's a gun," and I ran for the bunkhouse.

I had a very nice revolver, a .38 Smith & Wesson, and was really a crack shot with it because I had practiced a great deal. I got the revolver, and came back in the front door where, if Harvey had stood his ground, he could have killed me and nothing would ever have happened to him. My intention was to shoot him full of holes as soon as I got sight of him. But Harvey ran out the back door, leaving his checks on the table. I then turned on my own brother, and I don't think there ever was a brother living that got such a cussing as he got, me saying that I was through gambling with him or any other fellow who squawked when he lost.

After I cooled off and thought it over, in the morning I said to the first person I met on the street, "What will you give me for this gun?" He said, "Two and a half," and I said, "Take the gun. I don't want it." And from that time on I was through packing a gun, because I knew I couldn't trust myself, and if this fellow hadn't been a desperate character and probably had been wanted, he no doubt would have killed me and nothing would have been done to him.

There was a man by the name of Robert Johnston who kept a little grocery store at the mouth of the gulch, and one evening I went down there to buy something. I had on my working clothes, had not been to town to get a haircut for a long time, and I surely must have been a pretty rough-looking boy. I was introduced to a very nice-looking girl by the name of Mary O'Keefe. If there had been a knothole in the floor, I think I could have crawled down through it—I felt so embarrassed. She lived but about two miles from the trestle on the O'Keefe

106

Ranch, and was a daughter of C. C. O'Keefe, better known as the Baron O'Keefe. A little later I wanted to come to Missoula and went down to the ranch to hire a saddle horse. I met Miss O'Keefe and became a little bit better acquainted. A short time afterwards she invited my brother and myself to dinner. She sang for us and played the organ and told us of some of her school experiences in Helena. I surely fell for her with an awful thud. I got to be a very frequent visitor at the O'Keefe home during the winter and we became very good friends.

As you can see by the foregoing story, I left home when I was about fifteen years old, among strangers, always boarding in boarding houses. I had no very close friends and had never received a Christmas present. I was invited to the O'Keefe Ranch for Christmas dinner, and this girl whom I idolized so much stuck a tie-pin in my tie. It was a gold nugget with a diamond setting. The nugget was a peculiarly shaped one that her father had mined in Cedar Creek. Of course, I was taken by surprise and did not know what to say, as I was almost dumbfounded. It gave me an inkling that she must care for me, and the only thing I could say to her, or did say to her, was, "Isn't that nice?"

As I was getting ready to go away, as the job was pretty nearly through—I don't know where I ever got the courage—I asked her how she would like to marry me. She wasn't half as much surprised about it as I thought she might be; I didn't know but what she might faint or something of that kind, but on the contrary, she said, "I would like a little while to think it over, and I want to consult with my mother about it, and I will let you know before you go away." Of course, I told her that it would be some time before I could get married, as I wanted to be sure I could make a livelihood for a wife, but if she felt like waiting for me, it would only please me too well.

Her taking time to consider it, and wishing to consult with her mother, who was one of the best women I ever knew, more than pleased me, as then I knew that she was not going to jump to conclusions anyway. So before leaving to hunt for another job, we had an understanding that she was to wait until I felt safe that I could make good.

I came to Missoula and as I was walking down the street from the depot, a man by the name of Jim Ritchey hailed me and wanted to know if I was the Ross who had run a mill for the Eddy, Hammond company. I told him I was. He said that Marcus Daly had sent him out to get a lumber man to put in two small mills at Bearmouth for the purpose of cutting timbers for a new smelter that they were going to erect at Anaconda. So he employed me.

I went to Bearmouth. In due time the mills arrived, and we put one up Little Bear Gulch, about five miles west of Bearmouth, but across the river from the railroad. The other one we located south of Bearmouth.

We had a very successful operation. We got out some of the biggest timbers in Bear Gulch that had ever been gotten out in the state—some of them 24 inches in diameter by 50 feet long. This took an immense big tree, to square up 24 inches. We operated with oxen entirely, and you can imagine that it took a good many yoke of oxen to get one of these big trees into the mill to be squared up.

Along about the fourth of October, a very severe blizzard set in. The thermometer went down to 30 below zero and froze the water works up. Considerable snow had fallen. We shut down. I took the oxen over to Camas Prairie, as we called it then—now it's called Potomac—and arranged to have them wintered there. They called me to Anaconda and appointed me one of the deputy sheriffs to guard the works. A great many incendiary fires had taken place in smelters in the country and they thought it was an organized gang from Europe to destroy the smelters. So they appointed fifteen of us and no one was allowed in or about the works, either day or night, without a pass.

Logs frozen in the Blackfoot, McNamara's Landing, 1914
UM Mansfield Library

The cold spell in October lasted only a short time and the weather got very warm, raining a good deal of the time. On the twenty-fourth of November, they instructed me to go to Bearmouth and load out some lumber that we had in stock there. I arrived at Bearmouth the night of the twenty-fourth. It was still very warm, but there was a soft snow coming down, very thick. I went to a boarding house a little way from the station. The people's name was Lannon. That snow storm continued for twenty-five days and twenty-five nights. The snow got four feet deep on the level, and it got extremely cold. There had been a drought in the country that summer and hay was very short, and I saw in front of the boarding house as many as 150 head of cattle freeze and starve to death. This was one of the hardest winters that Montana had ever experienced; more than 50 percent of the livestock in the state perished.

So it is needless to say what happened in the spring of the year, when the ice started to break up and go out. The rivers got very, very high, taking out most of the bridges.

I came down to Missoula and was called upon, as soon as I arrived there, to go over to Tom Greenough's house across the Rattlesnake and help to get the family off the knoll where their house stood, as they were marooned.

I went back to Anaconda. When I arrived there, O. J. McConnell, who was a partner of William Thompson, the retail lumberman of Butte, came after me and he wanted me to go to Rock Creek and take out a drive of logs, and as I did not like Anaconda, I resigned my job and went with McConnell and took charge of the log drive. We were very successful in bringing out the drive of logs at Joe Irving's mill, that sat very close to the mouth of the creek at that time.

When the drive was over and with my lumber experience, I decided to try to get into the lumber business for myself, so I purchased a little sawmill from Jeff Lovell, of Butte, which had a capacity of about 25,000 board feet a day. My brother George, being an engineer, went into partnership with me, and we moved our little mill to Evaro. By this time, my brother M. M. was back from California, and joined with us. That made the starter for a sawmill crew.

The Montana Central Railroad was just starting to build from Helena to Butte. The Porter brothers, who afterwards became our biggest railroad contractors in the country, had the contract to build the bridges. I secured a contract to furnish a considerable amount of bridge timbers. We got an outfit together with cattle and horses to do our logging, and started in and were very successful. J. D. Porter, one of the brothers, inspected timbers at our little mill all summer, and paid us $2 a thousand extra for all timbers that we would cut overtime and Sundays.

Our first season's run cleared our outfit, and we had a considerable amount of lumber in the yard, and $14,500 in cash. So you can imagine how happy I was to go to this girl whom I idolized so much and who had waited all this time for me. I told her that I felt safe, that we had a very good start, and that I had built a little house of rough lumber in Evaro at the sawmill, and was ready. So on the twenty-fifth day of April, 1889, we married.

Mrs. Ross had a great collection of gold nuggets and finger rings, some of which were beaten out of pure gold nuggets. These, of course, passed into the possession of my daughter Marjorie.

It is needless to say that I was very happy in our little bungalow at *the sawmill, with my wife and baby daughter, whom we named Marjorie, but Mrs. Ross told me later that the first year of our married life she was in constant dread of my coming home sometime in an ill temper in which I could smash up the furniture. I had told her many times before we got married that I had an ungovernable temper, that I never felt safe, and that I was afraid I might kill someone, as I really was not accountable for my acts when I was in a rage. But the first year passed without any rages. And thirty-one more years passed without any rages. I can say in all truthfulness that in the thirty-two years I lived with her, I never said more than four or five cross words. When we started living together, this wonderful, even-tempered woman whom I admired so much that I would sooner have cut off my right hand than to have offended her in any way, let alone get into one of my tantrums, was the cause of my being able to control my ill temper. I remember the day I got married. I passed three resolutions: that I would not say an unkind word to my partner whom I was taking for life; I would not taste wine, whiskey, or beer for five years; neither would I gamble. Before I got married, I used to gamble a great deal, but have only gambled two or three times from the day I got married until the present time. And I went seven years without ever tasting any kind of intoxicant.*

In the summer of '89, there was a very severe drought here. A lot of the cattlemen did not have hay enough to get their herds through the winter and were obliged to sell. The price of stock cattle was $15 a head, so my brother George and I decided to go over to the Sun River, where the drought did not affect cattle so much and where they had plenty of hay. So we started with our pack outfit up the Blackfoot on the old Indian trail, as there were no wagon roads into the Blackfoot country at that time. In fact, there were very few people living there. We continued our journey up the Blackfoot to Cadotte Pass, which is the top of the main range of the Rockies, and leads over to the Sun River, a distance of about a hundred miles from Missoula. We found the pass and all the mountains on fire, and we had to come back. We came back over the old Nez Perce Indian trail, going by Ovando and past Fish Lake, which is now called Binkos, and crossing the little prairie which is now called Corlet. It was surely a wonderful sight to see on the evening when we came up over the ridge of mountain and looked down into the valley below. There were moose, elk, deer, and mountain goats in the meadow. The trail crossed the prairie just where Morrell's old buildings are, crossed the Clearwater River, and went up over the mountain to the head of the Jocko. Of course, the trail came right down the Jocko Creek to Arlee.

There is quite a good-sized lake, which we called Black Lake because the water was very dark, about half a mile across, right on the top of the mountain. You descend on the other side and go down the hill about a quarter of a mile. Most of the Jocko River comes out of the bottom of the canyon, which is the outlet for this lake.

I have never seen, before or since, the amount of fish you could catch in a few minutes. They would actually come up to within three or four feet of the shore after the hook, and needless to say that they were the finest fish that could be caught due to the fact that the water in this lake was as cold as ice, which made the fish very solid. They ran anywhere from a pound to two and a half pounds. Occasionally you would get a very big one. We caught half a gunnysack full, cleaned them, rolled them in leaves and wet gunnysacks, packed them on our pack horse, and brought them home to Evaro that night in splendid condition.

After riding home, I took the train and went over to a place called Yantic on the line of the Great Northern, some five or six miles west of where Chinook is now located. The Gros Ventre Indian reservation had just been thrown open, and I bought a section of land with 500 tons of hay already in stack from a half-breed. I came back to Missoula, and we bought 350 head of cattle and shipped them over. My brother George went to take charge of the ranch and cattle. We also bought some very fine brood mares, and raised some very fine horses.

My brother George and I dissolved partnership, he taking the ranch and the stock, and I taking the sawmill.

Kenneth Ross's journal does not relate the horror and tragedy of his brother's venture into cattle ranching near Chinook, but letters and old files tell the story.

The white owls from the Arctic came after Christmas. Only the Indians knew what this meant. The arrival of the owls, perched on fence posts and on the roofs of barns, presaged the coming of one of the worst winters in the time of the white man in Montana. It struck with full fury in January 1890. George Ross and his young wife were alone in the cabin on the Gros Ventre reservation and his wife was pregnant. She gave birth to a baby girl that month, but both died within a few days. George was alone with his seven-year-old daughter Mamie in a small cabin on the Montana plains.

The temperature sank to minus 40 degrees, the fierce winds piled the snow around the cabin, and George Ross fought desperately to keep himself and Mamie alive. He was snowbound.

In Missoula, Kenneth Ross became concerned about George. Taking his older brother, Malcolm, he rigged up a pack outfit and headed northeast up the Blackfoot River. In the upper Blackfoot Valley, their horses gave out as they fought the driving wind and the mountainous drifts. They had to turn and make their way back home.

In the spring, they rode out again for Chinook. George and little Mamie had survived, but the bodies of one hundred head of cattle lay piled in the ravines and gullies.

George Ross moved to Idaho and left Montana for good. Kenneth adopted little Mamie in 1890, as soon as he had his own home.

In the fall of '89, Pete Larson and I took a contract from the Northern Pacific Railroad to build the Coeur d'Alene branch from DeSmet to Wallace, Idaho. I took a contract from them to furnish the piling and bridge timbers from DeSmet to St. Regis. At a place called Ferry, our plans called for a pile bridge across a big flat, very near a mile long, and I moved a portable mill to that section in order to furnish the timbers. It was quite an undertaking to take an engine that weighed 24,000 pounds over the hills to Ferry, and get it across the ice. It happened to be that by the time we got down to where we had to make our crossing, there was a big thaw on and the ice was breaking up in places in the river. We got our horses across and realized that we were taking a great many chances in putting the heavy weight of the boiler on this ice, so we got a long rope, and had the horses, of course, on the land. We started across the ice with our heavy load. You can rest assured that we were very anxious from the time we started from the opposite side until our sled landed on our side. We had no sooner landed when the ice broke up, and it was not five minutes until the river was running wide open. There were some happy jigs danced and some hats went up in the air then.

After we got our mill set up and ready to commence operations, at a great deal of expense, the railroad company changed their plans, cutting out the bridge entirely and putting the track around the bench to its present location. This expense, of course, they did not ask me to stand, and resulted in their buying out my entire outfit, paying me a liberal price, and they moved the mill themselves down to Fish Creek to saw out timbers for that bridge.

I bought another mill and set it on the Coeur d'Alene branch about three miles below where Nine Mile Creek empties into the main river. While the mill was there, they called it Ross Spur. I had a very successful run there and made some money, bought a tract of timber on Six Mile Creek, and moved the mill to Huson, where we operated for a number of years.

The most wonderful experience and the closest call that Mrs. Ross and I ever had was fording the river just above the mouth of Nine Mile—a very bad, deep, treacherous ford—as oftentimes the gravel would change in the bottom and make it uncertain. I had gone to Butte to a horse sale of eastern horses that had come in, and I bought a big four-horse team, shipped it to Missoula, and bought a new logging truck. Anybody who is familiar with logging trucks knows that there is so much iron on them that they will sink to the bottom of the river and stay there. I drove the four-horse team and the truck from Missoula to the crossing, Mrs. Ross driving the buggy team

112

Skidding by chute, Greenough, 1928

with our little girl Marjorie, who was then but a baby, and our perilous trip commenced to ford the river. Mrs. Ross sat on the hand bunk of the logging truck, and knowing that the truck would be entirely submerged under the water in the deepest place, she had her feet under some iron braces which would keep her from being swept off. We started across and the horses, being eastern horses and having never been in the water before, started drifting down the river. The leaders could not be headed up, but I managed to get them stopped. It was not until, however, the water was over the logging truck at least two feet, and Mrs. Ross was holding the baby up under her chin to keep the child out of the water. I got the horses stopped, walked out on the pole between the wheelers, unhooked the spreaders, and cut the lead lines, and set the leaders adrift. Fortunately, I got the wheelers to head up river and we finally got across all right. I want to say in all truthfulness that Mrs. Ross was the most nervy person I had ever been in a mixup with. When we landed on the shore, she said, "Well, Mr. Ross, we had a pretty close call, but thank God, we are here."

At this point Kenneth Ross's prosperous career took a setback. In 1892, he suddenly awakened to find that Marcus Daly, A. B. Hammond, and W. A. Clark had swiftly acquired most of the accessible timberland in western Montana. His little sawmill west of Missoula was no longer viable as a business. So when he got an invitation to meet with Marcus Daly, A. B. Hammond, and C. H. McLeod, he was pleased and, most of all, flattered. His ego now surfaced. Here he was, not yet thirty years old, entirely uneducated, sitting down with three titans of industry who were imploring him to assume command of their timber empire—to take charge of a sawmill, a planer, a logging operation, a ranch, and a railway, all owned by Marcus Daly's Anaconda Mining Company. He played hard to get. But was he as hard to get as his journal indicates? After all, the continued profitability of his own little mill was now jeopardized. The temptation to take over a huge organization, with the assurance from Marcus Daly that there would be no interference, must have been strong. And they said they'd pay him more than a United States senator received! No doubt Daly, Hammond, and McLeod wanted him badly. He had made a reputation as a hard driver and as a businessman of integrity.

But, as he sat dictating his journal in 1929, did he not look back through rose-colored glasses and come to believe that he was the indispensable man? Any way you look at it, he traded his independence for a copper collar, as Montanans used to say about Anaconda employees.

In the fall of '92, they sent a messenger from Bonner after me, wanting me to come to Bonner at once. I went there. Marcus Daly, A. B. Hammond, and C. H. McLeod were there. Mr. Daly told me that they had just taken an option for the purchase of the entire plant and timber land, and made a very heavy down payment, and in six months' time they had to make another payment of a half a million. He said that Mr. Hammond had sold him 90,000 acres of timber land, and he didn't know whether Hammond was kidding him or not. He wanted me to come there and have the timber estimated within the six months and let him know whether it was pasture land or timber land that he had bought. I protested and told him that I had my own business that had to be taken care of, and that I was getting along all right and didn't want any job. However, he insisted that I come there, that I was the only one in the country who knew the conditions, and he wanted me to take charge of the company and take over the Blackfoot interests for the Anaconda Mining Company. I made a very strenuous protest not to accept, and I remember him saying that they would pay me more than a United States senator was getting. This did not appeal to me because I was making a good deal more out of my own business than any salary they would be willing to pay. So I told them I would think it over for a couple of days and let them know.

So I had another conference with Mr. Daly and told him that I would go, with the understanding that I was going to run the business and have an organization of my own selection. The Anaconda Company had been in the lumber business at Hamilton and had a great many managers, two of whom I knew to be good

114

men, but through political heelers and bad influence, they practically had made a failure. This, of course, was what I wanted to avoid, and I told him so. His remark was, "I am tired of running a kindergarten school. I have had lumber clerks out of Chicago retail lumber yards to try and run a business in this country, which they can't do, and we know you can run it, and you are going to run it in your own way. There will be no interference from anybody. There will be no handicaps, and above other things there will be no politics mixed up in it."

So I took charge of the office, went to St. Paul and hired a man by the name of Frank Vogle, an expert timber cutter, and brought him to Montana. He organized estimating parties and had the estimating all done in due time. There was an immense amount of mining timbers piled up all over the country, enough to last the Anaconda Company for two years, so a lot of the small mills running had to be shut down and settlements made, so you can imagine that for the first year and a half, it was a big job.

After I had been there about eighteen months, just as winter was coming on, a bill came into the Bonner office and was ordered paid by the auditor of the company at Anaconda. It was for a quarter of a million dollars of fire insurance put on the lumber yard at that time. I thought this was rather a funny procedure—that most successful lumbermen would be cancelling their insurance in the wintertime when there was absolutely no danger of fire. Following this bill in a short time was another bill to be paid, for services rendered, so I immediately resigned.

Mr. Daly, when he heard of it, wired me from New York to come down. So I went down. He was stopping at the Netherlands Hotel, and was sick. I told him why I had quit and he seemed very much put out. He didn't know anything about the bills and they shouldn't have been sent, and he told me to go back. I told him no, I was through.

So it resulted in a very short period of time that they had two or three different managers imported from the east, and the business got in a very bad shape. Mr. Daly was still in poor health and not able to come to Montana, and they sent John R. Toole, who could take charge of the company's interests and run it successfully. Mr. Toole had been associated with Mr. Daly for a great many years, being a mining expert who Mr. Daly sent all over the country examining mining properties, and who was his political manager.

Mr. Toole came to see me and told me that they were really in a bad way and wanted to know if I wouldn't come back and help him straighten matters out.

Along about that time, I had an offer to go to the coast. C. P. Huntington, the railroad magnate, was looking for a man who would start him in the lumber business. So I was offered this *position, and they offered to give me all the stock in the company I wanted and would carry me at 2 percent interest, and give me a salary of $10,000 a year. This did not appeal to me very strongly, however, and I figured that it would take the $10,000 to keep my family, and whatever money was made and accumulated by the lumber company would be tied up, but as the Anaconda company took an option on all of the Northern Pacific timber lands in the state of Montana, I could readily see that I might as well move before my timber supply was entirely cut off.*

I started to sell off my outfit and told Mr. Toole I would go with him for a year and a half, as it would take me that long to dispose of what I had, and I would do the best I could for him.

So in 1900, I went to Bonner and took charge. We found the company's affairs in a horrible condition, and it was just a year and a half after we started in and had everything rounded up, that we got out a statement for the New York office, which pleased them immensely. Mr. Toole, of course, was not a lumber man and evidently had a great deal of faith in my ability to conduct the affairs of the company in a businesslike manner, as he never interfered with my plans. We always talked them over and he always got behind me to carry out my ideas. I never knew there was such a broadminded, honest, Christian man as Mr. John R. Toole. We were associated for sixteen or seventeen years, and in all that time, I never can recall that there was one cross word or unpleasantness that came up between us.

Kenneth Ross's relationships with Marcus Daly were stormy indeed. The bill "for services rendered" meant political services. Such billing was in direct contravention of the commitment Marcus Daly had made. Kenneth resigned, but Daly sent the right man to Bonner when he sent John R. Toole. There were few troubles after this benevolent and understanding man arrived. And there were no more irritating invoices from Butte.

Almost every man who came in contact with John R. Toole idolized him. Kenneth Ross was no exception. But it was a situation ready-made for friction. John R. was no lumberman, yet he would obviously have the last word because of his pipeline to the great moguls of Standard Oil, which now owned the Marcus Daly properties and had created the monstrous Amalgamated Copper Mining Company. "The Company," or "the A.C.M." as it was sometimes called, would touch the lives of every single Montanan—man, woman, and child—for the next sixty years.

John R. recognized that he had an efficient, hard-driving administrator in Kenneth Ross, and he simply gave Ross his head.

There are intriguing overtones of a power play among the titans in the Kenneth Ross journal: E. H. Harriman controlled the Union

*Bonner Mill,
1910, Timbers
center
foreground are
stulls headed for
Butte.*
UM Mansfield Library

Pacific railroad; Jim Hill controlled the Northern Pacific railroad and the Great Northern; the Rockefellers controlled the Milwaukee railroad, a small but profitable line in the Middle West, and William Rockefeller's favorite enterprise. The way things were developing, the Milwaukee simply had to have the ability to forward freight originating on its line to the Pacific Coast; otherwise, it would wither and die on the vine in the Middle West. Harriman and Hill put their heads together and refused to forward freight. Understandably, William Rockefeller became furious. "I'll show 'em," he said. "I'll build my own railroad!"

Thus was born the sixth and last of the great transcontinental railroads. Conceived in a brief fit of anger by the Rockefellers and destined to lead a short, desperate existence, it terminated in hideous cost overruns, three bankruptcies, and final oblivion. Today the Milwaukee's bright yellow cars no longer snake across the Montana plains and its huge box-like electric locomotives no longer sneak up silently on the little boys playing on the tracks in Hellgate Canyon. The reassuring, high-pitched, piercing whistle bespeaking the power and efficiency of the Rockefellers no longer sounds in the night.

John D. Ryan, a bold and clever man, was president of Anaconda. He also was on the Milwaukee Board of Directors and was the first president of the Montana Power Company. He schemed and puzzled out a way to enjoy the best of all three worlds. The Milwaukee would run on electricity, and it would have to buy all of its power from Ryan's infant utility, Montana Power Company. The Mil-

117

waukee would need 800 miles of copper cable. This, of course, would be purchased from Anaconda.

In 1906 John R. Toole was visiting H. H. Rogers, the Standard Oil chief executive, in New York. Rogers offered Toole the contract to build the Milwaukee from Pipestone Pass to the Taft tunnel in western Montana. Toole had built the Butte, Anaconda & Pacific Railroad for Marcus Daly in the 1890s and had railroad construction experience. He signed the contract and returned with it to Bonner. Then he had second thoughts. He didn't feel well enough to undertake such a huge job. He offered the contract to Kenneth Ross, who accepted immediately. Then John D. Ryan appeared on the scene. Ross told him of the deal and said he hoped it would be all right. Ryan replied, "It's not all right. Anaconda needs you right here."

This angered Kenneth Ross, and he demanded an increase in salary. Rogers was advised of this affair, and he told Ryan to give the contract to Winston Brothers, to let John R. Toole stay at home in peace, and give Ross some deals that would make him some money.

Ryan put Ross to work acquiring the right-of-way through Missoula County. The landowners of Missoula County had gotten together to raise prices unconscionably for Milwaukee right-of-way. The Milwaukee had not received a land grant, as the Northern Pacific had, and the situation was serious.

Right-of-way acquisition was not in Ross's line of work but he set at it with characteristic vigor. We know that the Milwaukee was highly irritated about what it had to pay, and the story goes that it moved its shops and division point to Deer Lodge out of anger at Missoula.

In the year 1906 there was only one means by which logs could be delivered to the Bonner sawmill. They had to be floated down the Blackfoot or Clark Fork rivers. Logging railroads had not yet entered the picture and truck hauling was thirty-five years in the future. The problem of delivering logs to the plant loomed larger

Pork for the larder at Seeley Lake logging camp, Anaconda Co., 1908.

with each passing year. The great stands of pine and larch bordering the rivers were about gone. Kenneth Ross—by then an almost legendary "bull of the woods," big, strong, and aggressive—had to solve this problem.

In 1906 the U.S. Forest Service, at the request of President Theodore Roosevelt, designated 160 million board feet of timber at the south end of Seeley Lake for public sale. The timber was mature pine and larch—huge trees. They were located in a high mountain valley, 60 miles northeast of Missoula. The great trees bordered a quiet, jewel-like lake named after the only resident, Jasper Seeley. Anaconda was the high bidder on the sale. It was the first timber sale ever conducted by the Forest Service, a brand new federal agency.

A small stream called the Clearwater flows out of Seeley Lake. Kenneth Ross inspected it and concluded he could drive the great logs down the Clearwater to the Big Blackfoot River, thence to Bonner. He did not reckon with the bureaucracy of the U.S. Forest Service.

In the fall of 1906 Ross started great trains of wagons up the Blackfoot loaded with the accoutrements of a major logging camp. It was a three-day journey. Trees were hacked down to construct a cookhouse, bunkhouses, an office, and a shop. By the first snow, when the temperature dropped to zero, the lumberjacks arrived and logging started. Every morning, these hearty men shouldered their axes and saws and headed for the woods. The great teams of 2,000-pound Belgian and Percheron horses, their nostrils blowing steam, pulled their heavy sleighs through the forest on slender trails made by "swampers." The huge logs were skidded by other horses to the "landing," where they were loaded on the sleighs. The

119

loading was done by the "crosshaul" system. A sleigh pulled up parallel to a "deck" of logs. A cable was wound around a log, then a team on the opposite side of the sleigh hit their collars and rolled the log up on skids to the "bunk" of the sleigh, where it would fall into place. On the sleigh was a man called a "top loader" who used a peavey to roll the logs around to make a compact load. The top loader worked in such fantastic danger that an inspector for the modern-day Occupational Safety and Health Administration would faint just to watch him. A loaded sleigh was frequently 15 feet high. It swayed and slid down to the ice of Seeley Lake. The "skinner" (teamster), also in fantastic danger, sat on top of the load, hurling curses at the horses, which were alternately pulling and braking. Only the frictionless, silent snow enabled these huge loads to slide to the lake where, in the spring, the logs would burst out of the lake and shoot down the river with the melting ice. These lumberjacks had no workman's compensation insurance, no unemployment benefits, no Social Security, no minimum wage, no radio or TV, no whiskey, and no female companionship. They would come down the river in the "drive' in the spring and charge into Missoula like a swarm of hungry locusts.

Larch trees (also called tamaracks) have a butt that is loaded with pitch. It will not float. It is splintery, and any good-size nail driven into a board sawed from the butt will split it. This wood is good only for shakes or shingles. Loggers for generations have "long-butted" the larch; they have simply cut off the lower five feet and left it lying in the woods.

Two-thousand-pound Percherons, Seeley Lake, 1909
UM Mansfield Library

Logging superintendent Bill Brian commenced operations in the usual way—long-butting the larch trees. But the rules had changed; it was now the day of Gifford Pinchot and Theodore Roosevelt, the first conservationists.

The Forest Service ranger, Jim Girard, a small wiry man, came up to inspect the logging. He found a team of sawyers sawing off a long butt. He commanded: "You can't do that. I order you men to stop long-butting that log!"

The sawyers looked up, spat on their hands, and replied: "We don't take orders from you, mister."

They went on with their work.

Girard stumped down to the company office, burst in upon Brian, shouting, "Your men are long-butting tamarack!"

Tamarack log,
Potomac, 1914
UM Mansfield Library

"Well, sure they are. What's wrong with that?"

Girard, his face blood-red with fury, exploded: "You know the Forest Service will never stand for that kind of waste!"

"Waste! What's wrong with you, ranger? Them long butts ain't no good for nothin'!"

By now the two men were shouting nose to nose across the desk; the ranger yelled, "Good for nothin'! Wait till Mr. Gifford Pinchot, Chief of the Forest Service, hears about this. I order you to stop long-butting at once! And from now on, every tree must be cut 18 inches from the ground!"

"Hell! I never heard of no Pinchot. If we don't long-butt those logs, every one of 'em will sink to the bottom of Seeley Lake! And how kin we cut stumps 18 inches off the ground with four feet of snow on the level? Get the hell out of here!"

Brian sat down in rage and picked up a pen to write a letter to

121

Tying down the load on a horse drawn sleigh, Potomac country, 1909

Kenneth Ross. He summoned a horseman and headed him for Bonner with the letter. But that night, Brian addressed the men in the cookhouse: "Boys, you can't cut no more tamarack until we get this deal straightened out."

The sawyers became alert. "Hell, Brian, we're gyppos. We can't make no money if we have to hunt here and there fer pine trees!"

"Yeah, I know, but I sent a letter to old man Ross today, and if I know him, he'll be up here pronto and take care of these goddamn feds!"

"Gyppos!" That was the term for lumberjacks paid by the thousand board feet. The more they cut, the more money they made. The practice is still in use.

The horseman reached Bonner late the next day. He went straight to the porticoed, one-story office and handed the letter to Kenneth Ross. Ross read the letter; his cigar moved rapidly from one side of his mouth to the other and finally ended clenched between his teeth. He called to his assistant, "Go out to the barn and tell Johnny Le Claire that I want my team of bays hitched to a sleigh before daylight tomorrow and tell him to get a good skinner and pick me up at the Margaret Hotel at dawn. I'm goin' to Seeley Lake!"

The next morning, Kenneth Ross heaved himself into the little sleigh, wrapped his great buffalo robe around his legs, jammed on his fur hat, and clamped a cigar in his teeth. The skinner cracked the whip over the bays and the sleigh leaped forward. They made Clearwater that night. This spot, where the Blackfoot and the Clearwater join, had an inn. The next day, they headed straight north across Blanchard Flat, over Sperry Grade, up Cottonwood

122

Creek, and directly down to the Seeley Lake camp. This was the route that Ross called "the tote road." In 1906 there was no road around Salmon Lake.

Ross went straight to Brian's office. Later in the morning, he walked to Jim Girard's office and was closeted there for two hours. He emerged, waved to Brian, and the two sat down together. Ross said, "All right, Brian, here's what I want you to do. You can't long-butt the tamarack and you've got to cut the stumps 18 inches from the ground."

Brian stared at Ross in disbelief. "Mr. Ross, we can't do that. It's just impossible!"

"Now listen, Brian! We've got to send 40,000 board feet per day to keep the mines open in Butte. The only place we can get the timber is right here and, by God, we're going to meet our delivery date, which is next July. I'm sure as hell not going to get the can tied to my tail for failure to deliver. Now, here's what I want you to do: I want you to powder-wedge every tamarack log over 36 inches DBH [diameter breast high]." Ross meant that the men should split the logs by driving a hollow wedge loaded with black powder into the butts and detonating the explosive, which usually blew the logs into two parts end to end. "I know you know how to do that. If you can't powder-wedge 'em, you can notch 'em full length and blow 'em apart with black powder. Them logs are straight grained. They'll split even and they'll float flat side up. The river pigs can ride 'em to Bonner.

"Furthermore, I want you to go down the creek and build three splash dams between here and Salmon Lake. Back up as much water as you can and fill the pools with as many logs as you can. I want those dams blown up one after the other, starting upstream, and I want every log floating in Salmon Lake by the first of May."

"Mr. Ross, how're we gonna get 'em through Salmon Lake?"

"I'll give you instructions on that later."

"Mr. Ross, I'm gonna need a lot more men, and wagons full of black powder."

"All right. I'm goin' to the cookhouse and get a feed; then I'm gonna pull out for Bonner. I can make Billy Boyd's ranch tonight. I want a list of everything you need and I'll send it right up."

"Mr. Ross, how about the sawyers? They ain't gonna make no money if they have to shovel snow away from the butts of them tamaracks."

"All right. I want you to figger a new price for the sawyers and send it to me. If the price per thousand is reasonable, I'll authorize you to pay it."

Kenneth Ross stood up and got ready to leave. Brian said, "Mr. Ross, there just ain't no justice in all this!"

"You're damn right there's no justice in it! I'm findin' out that it's a one-way street when you're dealin' with Uncle Sam."

Then he leaned over Brian, clamped his cigar in his teeth, and said, "But remember! We ain't gonna throw twelve thousand miners out of work in Butte because we couldn't provide stulls [props] and laggin' [two-by-six planks placed above the stulls to support the ceiling of the mine tunnel]. And when this deal is over, the Anaconda company is gonna sue the United States Forest Service and we'll collect every dime of our losses!"

Brian broke into a broad smile. "That's the kind of talk I like to hear, Mr. Ross. You can count on me!"

The little sleigh danced across the meadow where the Double Arrow Ranch is today, and Kenneth Ross pulled the buffalo robe tightly around him. The cold was intense and the sky blazed with stars. The skinner headed up the ridge above Salmon Lake and picked up the tote road. Ross thought of his conversation with John R. Toole, who had remarked, "You know, Ross, that Seeley Lake

Anaconda Co. Ranch, Potomac, 1916
UM Mansfield Library

sale looks risky to me. But you know more about logging than anybody in the country, and if you decide to take it, I'll back you up. We really don't have much choice."

Ross thought grimly that it would be John R. Toole who would take the blame if the Seeley Lake project turned into a fiasco.

Billy Boyd greeted Ross jovially, but it was soon bedtime, and before dawn the sleigh was bouncing across the Boyd meadows. The skinner whipped the bays unmercifully and they pulled into the Margaret Hotel after dark.

Now Kenneth Ross had a job on his hands. Within days, the freight teams were headed up the Blackfoot Valley loaded with lumberjacks, food, black powder, and a variety of equipment. Nothing was stinted; the Forest Service rules would be honored; the commitment to the great mines in Butte would be honored; and, in the background, the contemplated lawsuit simmered.

For it's break the rollways out, my boys,
  and let the big sticks slide!
And file your calks and grease your boots
  and start upon the drive.
A hundred miles of water is the nearest
  way to town;
So tie into the tail of her
  and keep her hustling down.

There's some poor lads will never lift
  a peavey hook again.
Nor hear the trees crack with the frost,
  nor feel a warm spring rain.
'Twas falling timber, rolling logs,
  that handed them their time;
It was their luck to get it so,
  it may be yours or mine.

But break the rollways out, my lads,
  and let the big sticks slide.
For one man killed within the woods,
  ten drowned on the drive.
So make your peace before you take
  the nearest way to town,
While lads that are in heaven,
  watch the drive go down.

Old ballad

Spring of 1907 brought the melting of snow and the cracking of ice to Seeley Lake. The river pigs punched and pulled the great logs to the outlet of the lake and down to the pool behind the first splash dam. Sometimes, they had to lash a butt-heavy tamarack log to a buoyant pine log; then both would float.

The dam was a primitive affair built of logs and timber. When the pool back of the dam was plumb full of logs, high explosives blew out the dam with a terrific explosion.

A horrendous mass of ice, water and logs poured through the breach and roared down the Clearwater to the next splash dam. Behind the logs swarmed dozens of river pigs in narrow, high-prowed mackinaw boats. Some hopped on the flat surface of the big split tamarack logs. The men were doomed to be wet for the next thirty days, but they all yelled lustily as they went bobbing down the stream. They yelled because they were going to town—going to town after six months of unremitting toil, bitter cold, and isolation

125

Baptiste?

Driving the Clearwater, 1908

The Clearwater below Salmon Lake, 1909

from the world.

When they encountered a log jam, they would pile out into two feet, four feet, or six feet of water and attack the logs with peavies. And there were many jams of the big logs on the small Clearwater.

Of all the dangerous enterprises in the old West, none was so dramatic, colorful, or exciting as "bringing in the drive."

As he had done so many times before, Kenneth Ross surveyed the scene from a small hill. This time he didn't like what he saw. Hundreds of big tamarack logs lay stranded, some as far away from the stream bed as 100 yards.

He set his jaw and called to Brian: "Get a dozen teams down here and skid them logs to the stream bed. Next year's drive will take 'em down."

Rollways waiting to receive logs, Seeley Lake, 1908
UM Mansfield Library

"The horses are in bad shape, Mr. Ross, after workin' all winter."

Ross gave Brian a steely look: "I said, get a dozen teams down here! I'll send some more when I get back to Bonner!"

He turned and mounted his big black horse. He rode back to camp thinking about splash dams, extra teams, extra lumberjacks, long-butting and shoveling snow, and calculating the devastating cost.

Brian did his work well. By May 1, 40 million feet of logs lay floating in Salmon Lake. This lake is a narrow, six-mile body of slack water. The river pigs could do little here because the lake was 100 feet deep with an abrupt drop-off. An effort was made to punch and pole the logs from the boats, but every day the wind blew up the lake and the logs floated back to the lake's north end.

Kenneth Ross arrived, took one look across the lake at the mass of quietly floating logs and yelled to Brian: "All right, Brian, you've got to winch 'em through by hand!"

127

"Winch 'em through?"

"You bet; I've done it before in Wisconsin. Here's how to do it."

Ross knelt down and drew a diagram in the dirt. Brian shook his head—then got going.

A giant, hand-turned winch was placed on a flat-bottomed boat called a "bateau." A long string of logs was chained together to form a boom partly enclosing the floating logs. One end of the boom was tied to a tree on one side of the lake, the other to a cable running to the winch on the bateau, which was positioned at the south end of the lake. Rotating the drum winch drew the logs down the lake, but it was so tiring that relays of men had to take turns on the handles.

Gradually the great masses of logs moved southward through the lake and entered a canyon where the Clearwater forced its way with tumbling speed and foaming white water. As the logs burst into the rapids and raced down with bucking violence, the river pigs once again raised their primitive yells and launched their mackinaw boats into the torrent. After building two more splash dams, the men got the logs to the confluence of the Clearwater and the Big Blackfoot rivers. They yelled again when the first logs poured into the heaving rapids of the big river. Now they were home free.

The mill at Bonner had been idle since November for lack of logs. Now Kenneth Ross stood on the dam he had helped build in 1884 and watched as the first logs from Seeley Lake rounded the bend and were hoisted into the mill. Suddenly came the explosive report of the steam "dog" that turned the logs—suddenly came the high-pitched whine of the band saws—then came the thumping of

Driving the Clearwater, Seeley Lake, 1910 UM Mansfield Library

128

Seeley Lake logs at the Bonner Mill, 1908 UM Mansfield Library

planks on rollers—and the bang of mine timbers falling on the conveyors that raced them to the waiting freight cars. Ross turned and walked back to the office. This was his life.

At the end of four years, the Seeley timber was cut out. They were years of herculean effort and runaway expenses. An old logger said, "Ross almost lost his job over that Seeley Lake deal."

And many of the river pigs needed medical attention. Their feet had absorbed so much water that they had contracted "squeak heel": when they walked across the floor barefooted, their feet squeaked with an audible, slushy sound. There was no cure.

The flood of 1908 helped greatly in getting the logs to Bonner, but it caused a huge strain on the dam. The logs all arrived at once, and an enormous pile choked the mouth of the Blackfoot Canyon. Logs blocked the county road, floated around the office and into the yards. Everyone held his breath about the dam. The forty million feet of logs had nothing between them and the Pacific Ocean, but the old dam held.

The lawsuit against the U.S. Forest Service was filed and tried. Anaconda got a small settlement. The camps moved to Potomac and a railroad was used for the first time. The logs were dumped into the Blackfoot at McNamara's Landing. The drive was short and easy.

The moguls were as good as their word about giving Ross a chance to make money. They tipped him off to get-rich-quick deals on the Fritz Heinze mining property (see page 236) and on the formation of Montana Power Company.

When tourists visit the tomb of Lenin in Moscow's Red Square, they are invited to view the tombs of the great Communist leaders imbedded in the fortress walls. Americans are startled to see the bronze tomb marker of one William Haywood, who lies next to the body of Joseph Stalin. Big Bill Haywood was the leader of the I.W.W. He veered into Marxism and died in Russia, the promised land.

The Industrial Workers of the World was the most radical labor union America has ever seen. Indeed, the I.W.W. was more than radical; it was revolutionary. Its enemies jeered that the initials stood for "I won't work." Its tools were violence, sabotage, subversion, and street riots. And it zeroed in on the logging camps of the Pacific Northwest. The deplorable conditions in these Soviet-like work camps provided a fertile ground for them, and at least in logging camps, their campaign produced results.

Logging camps were a difficult field for unions. They were remote, and workers had to depend upon employer-furnished transportation to get to them. The men were hard drinkers without families and interested in next week's paycheck rather than vague promises of better working conditions and higher wages. If a camp became embroiled in a labor dispute, the men often threw up their hands and drifted to another. In attempting to unionize loggers, the I.W.W. had to infiltrate camps. A "Wobbly"—an I.W.W. member—would get a job, and when ensconced at the camp, would start his destructive work.

One of the Wobbly's specialties was sabotage. He would sneak out and drive a railroad spike into a big log. When the speeding band saw in the sawmill struck the spike, the saw would disintegrate into a thousand flying, lethal shards of steel. The Wobbly would loosen the rail plates on the logging railroads so that when the Shay engine chugged by, it would derail, career off into the

*Slide-ass jammer
at Chamberlain
Creek, 1943*
UM Mansfield Library

A smile for the camera on a Sunday afternoon, McNamara's Landing, early 1900s
UM Mansfield Library, Dengler collection

woods, and turn over. The Wobbly's main joy, however, was frightening horses. He would hide in the brush alongside a logging chute, and when a horse came by skidding a log, the Wobbly would rush madly out of the brush at the horse, yelling loudly and flapping a blanket. The poor, panicked beast would bolt, perhaps breaking his harness and injuring the skinner. In the meantime, all the horses behind him would be held up.

Wobblies harassed the crew at the Bonner Mill. They would wait at the gates at quitting time, harangue the workers, and pass out literature. Kenneth Ross seethed. He had started to make improvements in logging camp living conditions, but he would make no improvements under duress. The vicious stalemate went on. All known I.W.W. agitators were blackballed from employment in the woods and mills.

The I.W.W. men erected a tent camp just below the Bonner mill. From here, they would sally forth to the various camps, to public meetings on the streets of Missoula, and first and foremost, to the gates of the sawmill, where they swarmed over the workers coming off shift. At length, Ross had enough. Listen to the words of Hjalmar Karkanen, who witnessed the upshot:

> Your granddad sent a telegram to the Burns Detective Agency in Spokane. These fellows were strikebreakers, big, tough men, and they wore derby hats. They hit the Wobbly camp before daybreak. They carried billy clubs and guns. The Wobblies never knew what hit 'em. The Burns men waded through the camp beatin' up the Wobblies and settin' fire to the shacks. They shot a fellow who was called the "Silver-tongued Orator." He never made another speech. He got shot in the throat. The Wobblies took off in all directions.

On April 4, 1917, the United States declared war on Germany. By April 10, wildcat strikes started to spread all over western

131

Lumberjacks at lunch, Greenough, 1930

Montana. The timing could not have been worse for the I.W.W. An immense wave of patriotism had swept the country. Sabotage, subversion, and strikes revolted the population, and the Wobblies were immediately labeled pro-German. Indeed, a letter to U.S. Senator Henry Myers from Missoula businessmen stated: "They are insulting the flag, belittling the authority of the government and are increasing in numbers. For weeks they have terrorized the lumber camps." Federal troops should be sent at once "to disperse or arrest these . . . traitors." One of the signers of this letter was Kenneth Ross.

But the I.W.W.'s basic goal had some strong support. F. A. Silcox, Regional Forester at Missoula and later Chief U.S. Forester, wrote the Secretary of Labor that 'lumberjack,' 'blanket stiff,' and 'river pig' have been terms of contempt. . . . Little or no effort has been made to liberate the creative energies of the men. They have been treated not quite as good as workhorses."

Burton K. Wheeler, a Quaker and a pacifist, (and soon to be a U.S. senator) refused to use his office as U.S. Attorney to prosecute the Wobblies, and stern, uncompromising U.S. Federal Judge George Bourquin backed Wheeler up.

The Montana National Guard was called out. The Wobblies packed the streets of Missoula "from one side to the other." Some refused to register for the draft. Neither side would negotiate. The

Log jam at Bonner, 1910
UM Mansfield Library

Wobblies countered the charges of disloyalty with charges that the war was a "capitalist plot in which the workingman made all the sacrifices."

The strikes dragged on through the summer, shutting down all logging and milling operations. They had the support of nobody. The people were incensed and disgusted with an organization containing members who refused to register for the draft and who divided capital and labor in a time of national emergency. As the soldiers started embarking for France, intense bitterness was directed at the Wobblies. They were called "yellow curs," and the patriotic American Federation of Labor kept them at a safe distance.

In September the strikes collapsed, and immediately Kenneth Ross did an about-face. On September 15, 1917, he convened a meeting of the Montana Lumberman's Manufacturing Association at the Hotel Florence in Missoula. Wrote Dr. Benjamin Rader, Assistant Professor of History at the University of Montana, in the May, 1967, issue of the *Pacific Historical Review:*

> Kenneth Ross of the Anaconda Company, representing a corporation that had already made substantive improvements, led the demand for the education of cooks, standardization of menus, installation of bathing facilities, steel bunks and springs, and [dear to Ross's heart] reading facilities for the men. The individualistic operators argued until past midnight before capitulating to Ross's persuasive patriotic appeals. To guarantee compliance, the Montana lumbermen appointed a special inspector to visit the camps. They also called upon the University of Montana to furnish standardized menus. . . . The self-imposed discipline of the lumbermen was a unique step in improving the conditions in Montana logging camps.

And at the Pacific Logging Congress, the *Timberman* magazine quoted Ross as writing that, "after all, the lumberjack is human."

So the hard-driving, hard-headed, uneducated man from Nova Scotia played two ennobling roles in this sad affair. He vastly improved the lot of the lumberjack, and he brought labor stability to the Anaconda camps. The mills and woods of the Company would not be unionized for another twenty-four years, when the AFL-CIO finally succeeded in 1941. Contrast this with the violent labor troubles that plagued the Butte mines during this same period.

One today must feel some empathy with the I.W.W. The union struck out with violence and sabotage against the outrage and exploitation being perpetrated upon the lumberjacks. But it inadvertently launched its attacks at the beginning of a World War, a war that was single-mindedly supported by almost the entire popu-

Waiting for the opening of the rock-filled lunch bucket

lation. Thus the I.W.W. came crashing down in defeat, but its work had a lasting effect on the welfare of the men who toiled in the sawmills and the woods.

Kenneth Ross makes no mention of the I.W.W. struggles in his journal. Perhaps his memories of it were painful, but it was without question his finest hour.

In his own view, he reached the pinnacle of his career when John D. Ryan called him to Washington and placed him in command of mobilizing the production of lumber for the burgeoning aircraft industry. In 1918 the structural members of fighter airplanes were made of wood. Ross relished the broad grant of power given him by the War Department; he was in his element, slashing red tape, driving lumbermen and Army brass, using his knowledge of lumber to produce what was required. And all in a noble cause— the destruction of the Kaiser's Germany, and making the world safe for democracy. It was in keeping with the instinct of many nineteenth-century American businessmen that mankind was on the march toward a better and more enlightened world, and all evils that stood in the way would be trampled underfoot.

In 1919 the course of Kenneth Ross's life suddenly pitched

downward. In that year, Mollie O'Keefe Ross, the Irish girl he had met in the little store under the Marent trestle in 1884, died suddenly in Spokane. He was shattered by grief.

And in the fall of that year, the great mill at Bonner burned to the ground.

Gramp (my name for Kenneth Ross) began to ail. First, it was gallbladder trouble, then mysterious sweats, and, most ominously, failing eyesight. He had strange thirsts and swilled huge amounts of Coca Cola and near beer (Prohibition was in force). He went away to various clinics, but the medical profession of the day couldn't come up with an answer. His weight increased dangerously.

During the early '20s, his first love became the construction of his estate at Salmon Lake. The location was magnificent—a heavily timbered peninsula meandering out into the lake.

He first built a lodge, based on a Frank Lloyd Wright plan, on a hill at the end of the point. (Unfortunately, subsequent owners have remodeled this building until today it looks nothing like it did in 1923.) The other buildings, a cookhouse and dining room, and a combination garage, office and bunkhouse, are like logging camp buildings. He hauled hundreds of cubic yards of earth for fill and constructed mammoth plazas extending into the lake. He installed a water system and included inside toilets, an unheard-of luxury for country places in those days. He supervised all the construction work with relish, and my mother, Marjorie Toole, was appalled at the expense. He plodded around in a hat and vest. He now carried a cane and would wave it imperiously at workers, grandchildren, and anyone else nearby.

By 1926, with his eyesight dimming and his physical activity declining, he knew it was time to resign. My brother K. Ross and I went up to Bonner during his last days and visited him in his office. I'll never forget his words: "Yes, boys, it's time for me to get out of here. Mrs. Ross is gone, John R. Toole is gone, there's no more river drives, the men don't work like they used to, we've got a big new, modern mill, there's all kinds of headaches, and women are great flappers, smokin' 'pills' and wearin' skirts above their knees. I guess it's time for me to bow out."

Flappers, pills (cigarettes), and short skirts were the bane of his existence. But these things didn't prevent him from enjoying his retirement party.

The employees at Bonner gave him an Edison phonograph on that occasion. The party was held at his lodge on Salmon Lake. K. Ross and I were there, aged nine and seven. The room was smokefilled; the dancers whirled and jiggled madly in that strange dance called the Charleston. Gramp sat in his big leather chair, pounding his cane on the floor, clapping his hands, and laughing

135

uproariously. Never mind that the flappers and their boyfriends sometimes sneaked outside and took some drags on pills or partook of a shot of bootleg whiskey.

For K. Ross and me, it was pure, unadulterated, joyful excitement. We scampered around among the dancers, pulling on skirts and coattails and climbing on Gramp's knee. For two little kids, it was a hilarious night.

After his retirement, Gramp went to Salmon Lake early in the spring and stayed until late in the fall. He could not drive a car because of his eyesight, and this is when the Cayuse Kid came into our lives. His name was Roy Provoncha—probably "Provencher" in French. He was a short, husky man, with a ready laugh and much patience. Like Charlie Dunham, Slim Madden, and the others, his origins were obscure, but he said he was born in Vermont. He, too, talked of cowboys, lumberjacks, and mining in Alaska. He was kind and steady—good to Gramp, and he seemed to like us kids.

Our dear mother feared for our lives at Salmon Lake. Gramp got saddle horses for K. Ross and me. Mother was afraid to death we'd be hurt on the horses. Gramp therefore fashioned an elaborately safe saddle for K. Ross. Two round poles were fastened at each end to the pommel and cantle of his saddle and buckled on so that they pressed against his legs and he couldn't possibly fall out. This arrangement was a death trap. If his horse had fallen, he would have been pinned under the animal and would have broken his neck. All such safety devices conceived for us had lethal potentialities.

Dave Madsen was a huge bull of a man. He had been an I.W.W. operative in 1917. He lived in a little cabin on Sourdough Island five miles up the lake. Gramp had blackballed him in 1917. One day Gramp and I and the Cayuse Kid were driving down to the Armstrong Ranch for fresh milk. Ahead of us on the road strode a large, broad-shouldered man. Gramp told the Cayuse Kid, "Stop and pick up that man, Roy. He looks like a lumberjack."

When the car stopped, Dave Madden came over and stuck his massive face in the window. Upon recognizing Gramp, he shouted, "Ross!" It was the first time I had ever heard anyone call Gramp by his last name.

Gramp drew back and gave Dave a steely look. Finally he burst out: "Dave Madsen!"

The Cayuse Kid spoke up, "Do you want to let that low-down Wobbly in the car, Mr. Ross?"

Kenneth Ross and Dave Madsen stared at each other for a few seconds with implacable enmity. Finally Gramp's face relaxed and he said, "Yes, Roy. Let him in."

Sourdough
Island
McKay Photo

Dave got into the car. He sat in the back seat with me. He reeked of sweat and tobacco juice. No one spoke until we reached the Armstrong Ranch. The Cayuse Kid got out to get the milk; I stayed in the car. I felt the drama. I knew about Dave Madsen. All was quiet for a few seconds. Then Gramp turned and said, "What're you doing, Dave?"

"Oh, just fishin' and trappin,' Ross."

The ice was broken. They chatted easily about the woods and the old timers, but no mention was made of the I.W.W.

These men had the same origin. Both had spent their lives in the timber and the mills. Both were uneducated, toughened by weather and hard labor on the river, and had survived the terrible hazards of their occupation. But one had become a big boss; the other had spent his life in violent attempts to redress the grievances suffered by his comrades. After a bit, Dave leaned forward.

"Ross," he said. "You know the Anaconda Company owns that island I'm livin' on. I'm just squattin' on it. I'm wonderin' if the Company might sell it so I could settle there."

"How could you pay for it?"

"Well, maybe I could pay for it on time. I ain't got much."

Gramp settled back and was silent for several seconds. Then he turned around.

"Dave, are you figgerin' to go back in the woods and start agitatin' and wreckin' Company property again?"

"No, Ross. I ain't gonna do that. After the strike in '17, the Company camps had better conditions."

"All right, Dave. I think I can get the Company to deed that island to you. It's of no use to them. But, by God, if you ever take to the woods again and cause trouble, the Company will take it back! That'll be in the deed!"

"That's a deal, Ross. I'm too old to do any more agitatin'."

He got out of the car and stuck out his hand to shake. Gramp grasped it firmly. Then Dave said, "I gotta start hoofin' it. I'm headed for Missoula."

137

I watched as the man with the great shoulders strode easily down the road and disappeared around the bend.

He got his deed to Sourdough Island.

In 1928 a rough fish called the squawfish began to invade Salmon Lake. It fed on trout spawn and the trout rapidly became scarce. The Montana Fish and Game Department thereupon commenced one of its many noble efforts to rid the lake of squawfish. One line of attack was to catch as many squawfish as possible in nets. The other was to plant black bass in the lake, the theory being that the swift ferocious bass would kill the sluggish squawfish, while the remaining trout would be quick enough to escape the bass and would begin to multiply.

The bass indeed looked formidable.

They swam rapidly in pairs, close to the surface and darted fiercely at all choice morsels. The squawfish, on the other hand, was one of the most obnoxious creatures ever created. It had a white, soft belly, above which were sickly yellow sides verging into a dirt-colored back with feeble fins that seemed to exhaust themselves after twitching once or twice.

The Fish and Game Department had to hire a man to tend their squawfish nets. It hired Dave Madsen.

Every day Dave would row his decrepit boat out and gather in the nets. The piles of squawfish started to grow on Sourdough Island. It got so you could smell Sourdough Island a mile away.

But Dave Madsen was not a squeamish man. The squawfish didn't offend him. In fact he ate them. He had several tons of nourishing food at his doorstep. Why not eat it?

As we've seen, Dave and Gramp had patched up their differences. Every week or so Gramp would load Ross and me into his boat and we'd head for Sourdough Island. We kids loved these trips except for the stops at Sourdough. The stench was too much for us.

Bonner Mill, 1949
UM Mansfield Library

But Gramp was not a squeamish man either. He didn't mind the stench and, in fact, always partook of Dave's squawfish stew, which bubbled all day long in a large pot on Dave's cookstove. The Cayuse Kid always went along as pilot. He didn't like the stink either and sat morosely in the stern of the boat while Dave and Gramp visited and enjoyed a plate of stew.

One day, Ross and I were wading in the lake in order to put as much distance as possible between ourselves and the stinking piles of fish. Dave Madsen appeared at the door and shouted:

"Come on up, boys!"

We hesitated, but Dave's command was imperious, so we climbed the little hill and entered the cabin. Gramp was sitting at Dave's table with a dishtowel stuck in his shirt for a napkin and an empty plate before him. Ross and I resisted the temptation to hold our noses.

Dave asked: "Say, boys, ain't you hungry?"

He went over to the bubbling pot and spooned a great hunk of yellowish-white squawfish meat up and let it plop back into the pot, saying, "How's that look to ya?"

Uncontrollable nausea hit Ross and me simultaneously. Our hands went to our mouths and we rushed out of the cabin and down the trail, desperately trying to prevent vomiting. We were partially successful.

We looked back. Dave and Gramp were standing in the door laughing uproariously. The trip home was glum.

Dave Madsen was a typical Scandinavian drinker. When he drank he drank as much as possible and became violent. In 1941 he went to Spokane and in the slum area down by the railroad tracks he got into a fight with four sailors and was killed.

Like the Baron O'Keefe he is known better in death than in life.

The bass died out in Salmon Lake. The trout never returned. The squawfish did.

Our grandmother Anna Toole owned a 1915 Packard automobile that she prized until the mid-twenties, when she decided to sell it and buy a more modern vehicle.

Gramp took us up to Seeley Lake to look the Packard over. It was an open touring car, huge and immensely impressive, with isinglass curtains that could be snapped on for protection against the weather. The giant motor had sixteen cylinders, and the air they sucked in made it hiss like some great reptile. The car had no fuel pump, and to push the fuel to the engine before it was started the driver had to pump air into the gas tank, using a little hand pump under the wheel. The engine did not have a self-starter and had to be cranked by hand, but the compression in the cylinders was low and the cranking was quite easy. The car was alleged to be stupendously powerful. The rear wheels were larger than the front, and power was transmitted to them by a chain drive that rattled reassuringly.

Gramp looked it over and liked it. He bought it from Mrs. Toole, and we immediately nicknamed it "the Pack."

Riding in it was utter joy. The back seat was heaped with buffalo robes, and a thick mat covered the floor. It had jump seats, and its long wheelbase smoothed out the bumps on the rough Blackfoot road.

One winter Gramp decided to remodel the Pack. He had the rear of the car's superstructure cut in half, and mounted a weird sort of truck body on it. He used it for hauling wood, garbage, dirt, and rocks. K. Ross and I were bitterly disappointed.

The Blackfoot Valley has always been a kind of Mecca for young, wealthy men from the East. Gramp called them remittance men, meaning that their parents paid them monthly remittances to stay away. Most were spoiled, most were reckless, but most were pleasant and courteous.

These young men loved to drive their Locomobiles, Hupmobiles, Marmons, Stutzes, and Pierce Arrows at breakneck speed down the dangerous narrow road running along Salmon Lake, and frequently they plunged into the lake. No lives were lost, however. These were all open touring cars and all the drivers had to do was swim out of their cars to shore.

It got so that almost every day we'd hear the Cayuse Kid shout at Gramp: "Another remittance man in the lake, Mr. Ross!" Gramp would immediately bestir himself. The Cayuse Kid would rush out and pump up the Pack. Piles of rope, blocks, and hooks would be loaded. Ross and I would jump in the rear and we'd be off on our rescue mission.

We would usually find the hapless remittance man soaked and mournfully gazing into the lake where his car had disappeared. He might be Frank Scully, Bob Ryan, or Jan Boissevain. The poor Cayuse Kid would don his pajama-like, 1920's swim suit and submerge with a hook that he fastened to the axle of the sunken car. The services of the remittance man were not requested, since Gramp considered them all incompetent.

Gramp sorted out seemingly miles of rope, which he hooked to a pulley on a tree, thence to the back axle of the Pack. Ross and I were road guards. The Cayuse Kid came blowing out of the lake and jumped into the Pack. The Kid stepped slowly on the gas and the submerged car rose slowly and unbelievably out of the lake. There was little spinning of the wheels on the Pack. She was heavy in the rear.

Gramp didn't like remittance men, and he left all communica-

140

tion with them to the Cayuse Kid. The submerged car did not always start immediately, and the poor remittance man was sometimes left to his own fate on the road. But sometimes he had to spend the night with us. Gramp did not invite him to sleep in his bridal suite in his House on the Hill; the poor fellow had to sleep with the Cayuse Kid.

Gramp loved these missions and so did we kids. But some of the plungers into Salmon Lake were not so lucky. One poor woman got her skirts wrapped around the steering column of her car and by the time we got there she had perished in the clear, cold waters of the lake.

At the time of his death, Sen. William Andrews Clark was reported to be the richest man in the world. He died in 1925, but before that he built an estate on Salmon Lake only half a mile from Gramp's cabins. He called it Mowitsa. Today it is owned by the Roman Catholic Church.

Mowitsa is, without doubt, one of the most fabulous private estates in Montana. The buildings are built of hand-peeled larch logs and set tastefully down in a grove of huge ponderosa pines. There are ten buildings for guests, along with a large two-story lodge facing the lake. It boasts tennis courts, bowling alleys, a golf driving range, all set among lush, green rolling lawns amid magnificent flower gardens and lawn statuary. About a thousand feet above it, perched on a crag overlooking the lake, is a Japanese teahouse, and on a higher crag an astronomical observatory housing a powerful telescope. The observatory door was never locked, and Ross and I often opened it and peered in wonder at the telescope.

Clark's eldest son Will (W. A. Jr.) was deeply involved in the creation of Mowitsa. He was handed millions before the Senator died, and inherited tens of millions after the old man's death. Will was reportedly a sexual pervert and had many young boys frequenting the place. It was he who dabbled for a few months in astronomy and had the observatory built. He was a violinist and sometimes in the evening we could hear the strains of his playing.

Gramp disliked all the Clarks, first because Gramp was a Daly man and Senator Clark had been the adversary of Marcus Daly in the Wars of the Copper Kings, and second because he objected to Will's personal habits. We were instructed to stay away from Mowitsa after Will took over. This wasn't necessary because Will kept a pack of ferocious Dobermans and German shepherds that he turned loose on all intruders. When Ross and I climbed to the teahouse or the observatory we went up by going around the mountain.

Will had fathered a fresh, engaging, reckless son, Billy (W. A.

Clark III). Billy was wild. He kept a fleet of magnificent limousines in Missoula, all equipped with sirens. Although Will and Billy didn't get along, Billy visited Mowitsa frequently.

When Billy and entourage were approaching Salmon Lake the sirens started to wail. This was a signal to the servants at Mowitsa to launch a fleet of boats and cross the channel to the east side of the lake, where they would pick up Billy, his baggage and his guests.

On these occasions Ross and I went into a high state of excitement. We could look up the lake and see the doors on the boat house fly open and watch the sleek, white inboard launches back slowly out, their motors roaring. Then the wailing of the sirens came closer and closer, and soon roaring down the Salmon Lake hill came one big limousine after another. We ran out to the road. The wailing grew deafening as the cars neared Gramp's gate and soon the limousines, filled with laughing young people, flashed by us in a cloud of dust. By now, up the lake, the launches had landed on the east shore, and the servants were lined up to meet William A. Clark III and his guests.

But sometimes Billy did not choose to cross the lake immediately on arrival. On the east shore were the Clark stables containing blooded horses, and we could see Billy leading his guests away from the boats and toward the barns. The stableman had saddled and bridled the horses; Billy and the others mounted them, and galloped down the road. Once again Ross and I would run out in time to see the riders flashing by—beautiful people on beautiful horses, laughing and shouting, with Billy always in the lead. We could glimpse his black silver-mounted saddle and bridle. After a while they would gallop back again, and Ross and I would hide behind the trees to watch them go by.

This performance infuriated Gramp, and he'd walk up and down flailing his cane: "Them horses aren't shod! It's a goddamn crime to run 'em up and down on that rocky road!"

The Clarks were not of us. Gramp disliked and disapproved of them. For Ross and me, living so near Mowitsa was rather like two French peasant kids living in the shadow of Louis XIV and the Palace of Versailles—intriguing, mystifying, exciting.

Will lost interest in Mowitsa in the late '20s, though he came back there to die in 1934.

At summer's end when the nights started to chill, the Clarks left for California, and Mowitsa reposed peacefully in the hands of its caretaker. The only sound we could hear was the melodious tinkling of the bell on the Clark dairy cow. The sound seemed to float gently down to us.

One day in 1981 I stood beside Ross's bed just a few days before he died. He opened his eyes and said to me, "John, do you remember how exciting the Clarks were?" He paused and went on, "They

142

added a little verve to our lives, didn't they?" And finally, "Do you ever hear the sound of that little cowbell and the way it came wafting down the lake?"

Then the sound of the little bell came back to me, and together with the sight of my dying brother in the bed before me and the passing of the turbulent years of our lives since those days—all this kind of made me want to cry.

Gramp had much trouble with his womenfolk over the houses he built. Three of these houses stand in the 500 block on the north side of Eddy Avenue. They are built "hell for stout," as he put it, and my mother assailed him fiercely over the design.

In 1928 the doctors told Gramp that he had heart trouble and that he must not climb any stairs. His answer was to build elevators. He installed a freight elevator in the old Victorian house at 905 Gerald Avenue in Missoula. At Salmon Lake he constructed a monstrous arrangement consisting of a long catwalk that extended out from the lodge on the hill and terminated in two

Kenneth Ross' home at 905 Gerald in Missoula, 1900. This house was erected by Marcus Daly for the use of his lumber executives. Kenneth Ross later purchased it. Hellgate High School now occupies the site. Author born in this house.

perpendicular shafts. One shaft contained a hanging barrel filled with 250 pounds of rock. The other shaft contained a mine elevator car. When he entered the car from the top, his weight would cause the barrel of rock to rise while he majestically descended in his mine elevator. At the bottom, he would stick a railroad spike through the car's wall into the shaft so as to fix his own car at the bottom with the rock barrel swaying 20 feet in the air above him.

143

One day, he neglected to insert the railroad spike in the shaft wall. Two hundred and fifty pounds of rock came crashing down. He was spilled to the ground as his own car shot up, and a great roar went up as splintered boards, boulders, and nails spilled all over him. We all rushed out, but he was unhurt.

After this debacle, he constructed a railroad. He laid two parallel lines of rails along a graded road. He brought in two mine cars from Butte. The first served as his own vehicle, and upon it he placed an easy chair. In the car on the opposite track, he placed a barrel loaded with 250 pounds of rock. The two cars were hooked together by a cable running through a pulley at the top of the hill, the idea being that when he entered his own car at the top, his great weight would carry him serenely down while the rock-filled car rolled up the parallel track. This contraption didn't work well. There was too much friction, and when he wanted to come up, I had to winch him up the hill, and when he went down, I had to push him.

In retrospect, the elevator projects seem utterly bizarre, but now I know that they were a great diversion for him. He'd plan them during the winters on large pieces of drafting paper, and during the summers he would direct the work with imperious waves of his cane. He loved to build things—anything. He wasn't worried about his heart—sometimes he would trudge fearlessly up the hill.

He often went to California to a "sanitarium" to treat his ailments. One year he took Howard, his son Kenneth Ross II, and myself along. He was absolutely uninhibited. He would walk into a hotel lobby and let out a war whoop announcing that he was the warden of the penitentiary in Montana and that he was hauling two horse thieves—pointing to Howard and Kenneth—back to that institution. Because of the loud whoop and his immense size, the bellhops and clerks would blanch and come running. He would then burst into loud laughter. Sometimes he would play the superintendent of the insane asylum in Montana, and point to Kenneth and Howard as escaped inmates. Kenneth and Howard took all this in good grace—but plotted to get even.

Gramp always patronized Standard Oil service stations, presumably because Standard Oil had once controlled Anaconda. When we pulled into a Standard station, he would stick his head out the window and ask: "Is John D. Rockefeller around?"

The amazed attendant would, of course, shake his head and Gramp would roar with belly laughs. One day, Howard and Kenneth got to the attendant before we pulled in. They told him, "We're taking a crazy man back to the insane asylum in Montana. When we pull in, watch him—he's dangerous!"

Sure enough, Gramp rolled down the window and asked the Rockefeller question. The frightened attendant went into a panic, ran into the station, bolted the door, and fled out the rear. Gramp turned to Kenneth bewildered and asked: "Say, what the hell was the matter with that fella?"

Gramp built a big boat for navigation on Salmon Lake, such as our visits to Dave Madsen. It was 24 feet long and flat-bottomed. It was named "The Scow." He and the Cayuse Kid would cruise up the lake, propelled by a two-horsepower engine. Maximum speed was three miles per hour. Gramp sat in an arm chair and sleepily trolled for rainbow trout. Gramp liked to gaze out over the lake gesticulating at the "deadheads"—the great tamarack logs which hung, butt down, with their tops breaking the lake's surface, remnants of the log-drive at Seeley Lake twenty years before.

In 1931, Gramp instructed me to accompany a crew up the lake to cut firewood. We felled three big tamaracks into the lake and towed them back to Gramp's point behind The Scow. I thought the work marvelous and exhilarating, and when we got home, I was wet from head to foot. Gramp laughed and said to me, "All wet, eh, John? Well, don't worry. I was wet for thirty days at a time when I was a river pig!"

When I got up to the house, my mother said, "Good Lord, John! You're soaking! Get into these dry clothes immediately!"

But those voices from the past were speaking to me, and this time their message of endurance of hardship came in loud and clear. I refused to change clothes. My mother stamped her foot and chased me around the house. I crawled under a bed.

"John, what's the matter with you?"

I replied indignantly, "Gramp says he was wet for thirty days when he was a river pig. That's what I want to be when I grow up, a river pig!"

"A what?"

"A river pig. They're the men who drive the rivers, and I won't change my clothes!"

She stamped out, and I shivered under the bed as long as I could stand it. The voices, particularly when they came directly from Gramp, were powerful.

Harriet Rankin Sedman was Dean of Women at the University of Montana. She and Gramp struck up a close friendship. He was interested in education because he had none. Hattie, as she was known, visited us frequently, and University of Montana affairs were always discussed. Hattie was worried about the institution, and he listened and counciled her at length. I can remember his reassuring her, "Hattie, the University has been in trouble since it was founded. It will be in trouble long after we're gone."

Gramp built Hattie a house in Missoula. An immediate clash came up over the design. Gramp wanted a house that would be hell for stout, which meant that the house would look like a logging camp cookhouse. But Hattie held out for good design. The resulting gracious, small house still stands on the corner of Eddy and Helen streets, just opposite Gramp's three earlier hell-for-stout houses.

In 1929 Gramp was very well off financially. He had acquired a business block in downtown Missoula, had built numerous rental homes, and had acquired a large block of Anaconda Copper Mining Company stock, then worth $90 per share.

To Gramp, Anaconda was a monolith, an indestructible rock which would spew out profits until the end of time. He knew. He had walked with the great men who founded the company and who had conducted its affairs. It was powerful, ruthless, and its accomplishments justified the means it used.

In late 1929 Anaconda stock began an ominous decline. Gramp didn't worry at first. It was just an adjustment. Then the declining became a plummeting. He couldn't believe his eyes at first. The brokers advised him to hold on. Anaconda, rich and powerful Anaconda, simply could not go much lower.

By now he was bedridden much of the time. It got so that I had to call Rochester & Company, the local brokerage firm, to get the price of Anaconda stock just as soon as I got home from school. One memorable day, I reported the price to him: $10 per share. He seemed visibly agitated.

"What's the matter, Gramp?"

His humor had not left him.

"John, I just got kicked by a copper boot!"

Then his tenants couldn't pay their rents. He couldn't pay his taxes. The big house went uninsured. During 1933 everything started to skid. Gramp retreated into slumber. He took no pills. He just went to sleep. It was his way of saying, "Stop the world. I want to get off."

In 1926 Anaconda had granted him a $500 monthly pension. Despite the Company's beleaguered state, it kept the pension coming. And then there was Howard. His law practice was beginning to make a contribution to the family business. Every night he would bound up the stairs to read the paper to Gramp, who was, by now, almost blind.

Gramp had his last summer at Salmon Lake in 1933. He slept most of the time. When I went there from the Circle W Ranch in September, he and his son Kenneth Ross II were there alone.

Dave Madsen came rowing down the lake one day. As he pulled his boat ashore he asked, "How's the old man doing?"

"He's dying, Dave," Kenneth replied.

"Why don't you go up and slit the old bastard's throat?"

I was shocked.

They brought up a combination hearse and ambulance and they loaded him in. He said, "They haven't got me yet, Johnny boy!"

In a week the Bull O' the Woods was dead, at the age of seventy.

146

His death certificate showed that he was a victim of a tumor on his pituitary gland, a condition that had been bedeviling him for a decade. A few days after Gramp's death, Billy Clark killed himself in his own airplane near Jerome, Arizona.

The funeral was held in Gramp's great old house on Gerald Avenue. It was hot and the house was filled with sweating loggers and lumberjacks. Dad brought Ross, my other brother Bruce, and me in to see Gramp in his open casket. His stomach protruded high over the rim and I became terribly troubled about how they would ever close the lid. I asked Howard about it. He replied that that was the undertaker's job.

Three of Gramp's brothers, George, Malcolm, and Eliakim, all clothed in black, stood somberly and, with their typically-Scottish dour demeanor, glowered about the room. After the service started, George Ross went to sleep and talked loudly of past days on the cattle ranch at Chinook. My mother jabbed him several times with a hat pin. He came to life with a start and a snort, then relapsed into slumber.

They played "Rock of Ages," and the casket was slowly carried out by big lumberjacks to the waiting hearse. I asked Dad why they played that song, and he said, "Because Gramp was like a rock." And it was true. Gramp was like a rock.

Kenneth Ross

147

5   1935: Optimism and Disaster

5   *1935: Optimism and Disaster*

Naturally I had to return to Douglas Creek in 1935. I felt inextricably bound to the place. I was desperately anxious to see it succeed.

All was different this year. Howard had attracted some more investors, people from Spokane. They were highway construction men, well-financed and confident. They would operate the place with their know-how and pay the Toole brothers a royalty of ten percent of all the gold they mined. One of the men was Paddy O'Brien, a genial Irishman; another was a distinguished-looking gent named March; the last was the real money-bags, a Spokane capitalist named Hopkins. They were experienced dirt-moving men, but alas, they were not gold miners. They had been highly impressed with the optimistic report made the year before by the mining engineer Nick Sheridan.

The key man in the operation was Harry Wirt, the superintendent. Harry was a genial, bluff, burly man. I liked him.

There were no half measures for these men. They would build nine miles of road to the diggin's, routing it to Douglas Creek from the Blackfoot side of the Garnet Range. No more tortuous climbs up Bear and Deep gulches, no more transshipping of the freight at the Top O'Deep, and no more frightful descents of the mountain with horses and burros. No more hauling of water with a yoke; a new cookhouse would be built down by the creek.

151

And the equipment! A giant 60 Caterpillar bulldozer, huge trucks, pickups, and to top it off, an immense boom drag line with a structural steel boom, mounted on tracks. No more gin poles and looping cables attached to a bottomless bucket.

The jumping-off place was Charlie Peterson's ranch on Douglas Creek just as it debouched from the mountain into the prairie around Helmville. It was a magnificent place, situated in a little green valley. Above and below it were countless beaver dams, where lurked huge trout. From the ridge above the house was a heavenly view of the upper Blackfoot Valley.

Charlie was a sheep rancher. He had a network of corrals, sheds, and barns, and the bleating of sheep was terrible.

I was shown a bunkhouse in which to sleep. They were shearing the sheep and castrating the male lambs. Powerful men with black tousled hair were doing the work. They had electric shears; the wool came off in huge bands as the men wrestled with the animals. Another group was castrating lambs. They would grasp a bleating lamb by the hind legs, bury their faces in the wool between the hind legs, bite down on the tiny testicles, sever the cords, raise their heads, spit out the bloody little organs, and go on to the next lamb. When they came in for lunch, their faces were smeared with blood and wool, which they scrubbed off noisily in a wash basin. This was the traditional method of castrating sheep. Instruments have been invented since 1935, but the biting method is still being used on some Montana sheep ranches.

Appalled at this barbarism, I asked Charlie, "Why don't they cut off the lambs' balls with a knife?"

"Oh," he replied, "a knife makes 'em bleed too much. You've got to bruise 'em off."

The road-building crew was already about two miles up the creek. I had my Model T Ford and the familiar apprehension came over me about the possibility of steep grades ahead. I didn't have to drive far. An impossibly steep stretch of newly built road sloped up to the north and out of the Douglas Creek valley. I approached it desperately at full speed, but the motor quit half way up. Then the familiar routine: I turned the Ford around and crazily tried backing up the hill time and time again. I backed down, shut the motor off, and got out dispiritedly. Just then I heard a man laughing. It was Harry Wirt sitting at the controls of the great 60 Cat at the top of the hill.

"Come on, Johnny! Hook this cable to your axle and I'll haul you up."

This pleased me. I thought maybe this would be the worst hill on the road. The Cat effortlessly pulled me and the Ford up the hill and into the road-building camp. A cook tent had been put up. Mrs. Wirt was the cook. She was a good one, and a pleasant lady. I had to sleep under one of the big trucks. Porcupines roamed around me all night. I knew I must lie still. I wanted no mess of quills in my face. It rained torrents, and rivulets of water turned my blanket into a sodden mass.

The next day I saw the Cat at work. A letter to my mother records my impression:

> Mom, you ought to see the big bulldozer! Why, in one swipe it will move as much dirt as twenty teams of horses all pulling slips! And it knocks down big trees five or six at a time! It just uproots them!

Two days after I reached the road-building camp, Harry Wirt gave me my instructions:

"Johnny, I want you to hike up to the diggin's and stay there. This is the month fer claim-jumpers, and I want you to take your rifle and watch out fer 'em. Split all the wood you can and start clearing the right of way for the road. You'll find blazes on the trees. You'll have to pack your own grub in and when you run out hike down here for some more. We'll have the road punched through in three weeks."

Before I left, I watched my last double-jack operation. The Cat had hit a rock reef which defied even that monstrous machine. As I watched the supple, rhythmic swinging of the drillers, I didn't realize that I would never see such an operation again. Pneumatic drills would appear in another year and hand drilling would disappear forever.

My pack was immense—full of grub, clothes, and, of course, the guitar, accordion, and Dad's 30:40 Krag.

I labored up the trail, stopping frequently to blow. Behind me the boom of the explosives and the roar of the bulldozer gradually receded.

Douglas Creek was overflowing its banks. Everything was green. Ducks flapped away from the beaver ponds, and a deer with its white tail flashing bounded ahead of me. It was all so marvelous, and after I'd hiked two or three miles, I could no longer hear the roar of the bulldozer.

I was unsettled about the new road. This little valley would all be changed when the machine got here, and this gave me a pang. I tussled with myself about the whole business. This beautiful little valley, unfolding before me, had been here for thousands of years, but in just a few days, it would be irretrievably changed by the great forces following me. Last year we had struggled with the environment; this year we would conquer it. Last year we had left few marks; this year we would mark it with great permanent slashes, and automobiles would be able to reach the Douglas mine. This seemed kind of like a sacrilege to me. I came to realize that I

153

loved Douglas Creek, not for its gold, but for its remoteness, its inaccessibility, and its beauty. I realized that I did not regard the Top O'Deep as an irksome, impossible barricade, but as some kind of glorious, magnificent mountain to be scaled and descended, then left alone. The Top O'Deep would be terribly vulnerable to the machines I had left behind. This really worried me.

And then I thought: Somebody will bring modern machinery into Douglas someday and reap its hoped-for wealth. Why not Howard and Brice Toole, who had sacrificed so much time and money in their attempts to exploit it? Harry Wirt's money and machinery were the only way to do it. And maybe, I thought hopefully, there are other little valleys in other places that will never be destroyed.

Those voices, coming across the years, were very confusing on that day.

I reached the diggin's just as the sun was setting. All was still except for the gurgle of the creek. It seemed very lonely. I toiled up to the old cookhouse. Everything was in good shape and I built a fire. I stepped out on the porch, and the great mountain of alpine fir seemed to block out the sky; but stars blazed above it, and all was silence. It seemed to be the silence of eternity, but then I thought: where man intrudes, there is no eternal silence. He must have noise and roads and machines, and he has no time for quiet little valleys and great lush mountains beneath blazing stars.

The next three weeks I spent in solitude, but kept busy. I split wood, went down the road to clear right-of-way, and dug test holes looking for gold. I never found much.

In 1934-1935, small groups of cattle from the ranches down the creek roamed the hills around the Douglas mine. I was not careful about closing the door to the cookhouse. One late afternoon I came home and found a huge Hereford bull in the kitchen. He had turned over chairs and tables and covered the place with manure. How was I going to get him out?

I slipped in the door and tried to get around in back of him, but to my alarm he was more interested in me than in the open door. He looked at me, lowered his head and horns, and pawed the floor with his hoof. This scared the daylights out of me and I beat it for the door. In the meantime he got thirsty, turned over a five-gallon can of water, flipped his tail in it, and switched an indescribable mess of water and manure all over the kitchen. I *had* to get him out!

After several attempts to slip in the door, I spotted the small rear window. Ahah! I'd climb through the window and attack him from behind. The window was tiny and I made noise removing the glass panes; but he didn't seem to notice. He just faced the front door with head lowered, waiting for my appearance. I fell from the window with a crash. Then, banging on a frying pan with a spoon, I dashed at his hindquarters with a crazed, furious rush, yelling like mad. He took one look around and lumbered out the door. And I got busy on one of the biggest and most unpleasant cleanup jobs of my life.

A few days later, as I was getting out of bed, I almost put my feet down on the back of a porcupine. That open door again! There was a .22 caliber rifle in the house. I used it to stalk pack rats. But I did not want to shoot a porcupine, so I just tried to keep the door closed.

One day I hiked to the Top O'Deep. Several blue grouse exploded ahead of me; a golden eagle circled high above, and the place was magnificent with silence and beauty.

Bilk Gulch was one of the rich gulches that radiated out of the Top. Someone had placed a crude sign that read:

BILK GULCH
Largest Nugget Ever Found in Garnet Range
Found Here
32 ounces

Multiplied by the 1935 price, the value was $1,120. In 1981, it would have been $19,200, except that nowadays the price is doubled for collector's nuggets—hence $38,400. The nugget was found in 1897. There are no such nuggets left in any stream beds in the country, but the fabulous finds of the past continue to draw miners to the hills in vast numbers. Bilk Gulch was a tributary of Weasel Gulch, which was a tributary of Douglas. It was easy to imagine those great hunks of gold being washed down slowly, ever so slowly, through the eons, until they came to rest in Douglas Creek. I remember Dick Herzer waving his arms around at the mountains and talking enthusiastically: "You see, that gold came down right here and got held up on that blue lime reef. That reef's bedrock. It caught the gold. That's where we'll find it."

Dick acted on his own theory and sank a timbered shaft until he hit the blue lime reef 90 feet down. He got some gold too. But today's miners have one overwhelming disadvantage: They simply won't subject themselves to the harsh labor and the extreme danger involved in sinking a 90-foot shaft by hand in mid-winter. They would never undertake it, let alone possess the determination to drive it down to the blue lime, come what may. They would have to find a machine, and the machine that would do what Dick Herzer did doesn't exist.

One morning I stepped out on the porch. I drank in the freshness, the silence, the beauty. Suddenly, I heard a loud *boom*. There was no question; it was dynamite. Harry Wirt was blasting out solid rock. He was getting closer. I was filled with dread at what was happening to our country and at the same time with wonder at the speed with which the road was being built. I thought: I must get down there. I need grub anyway.

I found that they had advanced to Charlie Bonham's claims, a serene little meadow laced with beaver dams. At this spot they had to build the road right down the creek bed. Frank, the operator of the big bulldozer, eased the great machine into the water, nosed it into a beaver dam, stepped on the gas, and completely wrecked the dam, pushing the little sticks and mud up on the bank in a huge pile. The terrorized beaver fled their little house of sticks, swimming upstream, but their pond quickly went dry, and they found themselves on dry land running about helplessly. This casual destruction appalled me, but I found a big arm around my shoulder. It was Harry Wirt's.

"Well, hi, John. Any claim-jumpers?"

I hadn't thought much about claim-jumpers, but I was glad to see Harry. He was a good guy.

"Come on over and get somethin' to eat. You know, at the rate we're going, we'll be with you at the Douglas mine in a week!"

He was brimming with enthusiasm. But I was an old Douglas miner by then, and I realized he was dangerously late. It was almost the first of July and the creek was already dropping. Water! The lack of it was the curse of every placer mine in the Garnet Range.

I started hiking back up but stopped to watch the bulldozer roaring and uprooting lodgepole pines. Behind the 'dozer came a line of Harry's trucks and pickups.

Every day now I could hear the ever-increasing roar of the dozer's engine. Harry Wirt was getting close. The ecology of Douglas Creek was being altered, more profoundly, perhaps, than it was when the last glacial ice retreated northward. Then one day the dozer burst out of the trees into the little clearing where stood the log cabin I'd built in '34. And right behind came my dad, Howard Toole, in a Buick sedan with my two brothers, K. Ross and Bruce, in the back seat. When Dad stepped out of the car, I noticed that gray, drawn look on his face. The mysterious disease that would claim his life ten years later at the age of fifty-five was already working on him; but I didn't think much about it as I greeted him joyfully. No man was ever more beloved by his sons, indeed by everyone who knew him, than was this man.

I immediately took Ross and Bruce in tow and ran all around the diggin's showing them the sights. Harry Wirt wasted no time. The great dragline that had "walked" the entire distance on its own tracks was immediately headed for a platform on the sidehill. From there it would reach out to grab huge buckets full of dirt and move them to the washing plant, a huge, revolving steel cylinder perforated with holes. The dirt would be dumped on a grizzly—a sloping platform made of railway iron—and poured into the cylinder, which was called a trommel. The fine material would fall out of

156

the holes in the trommel and into rows of sluice boxes. It all looked marvelous and efficient to me. When the apparatus was set up and operating, Harry Wirt said to me, "You see, John, we're going to mine the same stretch you fellows mined last year. The only difference is, you boys had a bucket with no bottom in it, and you lost most of your gold out the bottom of the bucket! Ha! Ha! Wait till you see what we get out of this piece of ground where you guys worked last year. You're gonna wish you had used a different bucket!"

I felt kind of mortified and turned away, thinking of Brice Toole and his dedicated little band of workers in '34.

I performed much of the same work as I had last year, but there was one procedure that mystified me. On every clean-up, Harry Wirt called me over and asked me to check the quantity of gold poured into the bottles, heft it in my hand, and approximate the weight. Also, I noticed that they made a big deal over my wages. Harry would deliver the check to me—$100 every month. This was a hell of a good deal, I thought. I didn't understand what all these strange procedures meant until I examined the Douglas Creek files thirty years later. In June 1935, Howard had written Jewett Orth, an investor who still held a small interest in Douglas Creek:

Dear Jewett:
    I don't think you have to worry about our getting our 10 percent royalty from Harry Wirt. I have sent my son, John, up to the mine with instructions to check on all the clean-ups. He is very young but large for his age. I trust him implicitly, in fact, I trust him more than anyone I know.

But Howard had never told me I was supposed to check on the clean-ups. Even though he trusted Harry Wirt, he had told him I would be there to check on the clean-ups. At the same time, he didn't want to make a spy out of me. So I never knew why Harry was so self-conscious and elaborate about showing me what he did.

About mid-summer, a kid named Hopkins was sent up to work with us. He was the son of the Hopkins in Spokane who was bank-rolling Harry Wirt. He wasn't much older than I, but he was a hell of a lot smarter. He was deep into the intellectual ferment of the 1930s. He had brought with him books by Sinclair Lewis, H. L. Mencken, F. Scott Fitzgerald, and John Maynard Keynes, and he made me read them. I didn't like these books. I couldn't understand Keynes for sour apples. Sinclair Lewis's *Babbit* reminded me of an old real estate man in Missoula. Every year he gave the local hospital $10,000, then bragged about it, waving his cigar all the while. But what the hell? If it hadn't been for the old guy, the hospital would have been $10,000 poorer.

157

Mencken, I felt, was a sarcastic iconoclast who made fun of a lot of things I believed in. Fitzgerald was a frivolous playboy.

"Hoppie," as he was called, made a great to-do about these characters. I couldn't see much in any of them. We argued every night, but because of his superior education and brains, he always won.

Harry Wirt's machinery worked steadily through July. I didn't pay much attention to the clean-ups. Then, predictably, the water dropped to a point where the washing plant could operate only intermittently. Harry promptly had another dam built, this time in the creek just below the machine. With the big dozer, it took two hours to build a structure like the one that took three days to build the year before with a team and slip. Then Harry brought in a pump and placed it in the pool above his new dam and pumped the waste water back into the washing plant for reuse.

"We'll lick this water problem, John," he said confidently.

But it was not to be. The pump rapidly drained the pool, and for half an hour at a time, as the pond slowly refilled, the men sat around idle. Harry watched grimly, his jaw thrust out, his hands on his hips.

It was about this time that Harry started to deteriorate physically. He lost weight; his face became drawn. The fading water in the creek was an enemy with which his burly, aggressive nature could not cope. One Saturday he announced loudly, "Come on, boys! We're all going to the dance at Gold Creek! Knock off at four. The party's gonna be on me!"

Harry Wirt had a panel delivery truck called a "Star." It was a rickety, undependable vehicle, but we all got in and headed for Gold Creek. The dance hall was just off the highway. They had a jazz band, and we danced until dawn. On our return, the Star quit just as we reached the mouth of Douglas Creek canyon. The mine's mechanic labored over it, but without result. Harry said, "Come on, boys. We'll hoof it up to John's Ford and drive it to the diggin's."

I objected, "She'll never pull the grades, Mr. Wirt!"

"Oh, yes, she will! You'll see!"

Harry loaded my Ford with men, some riding on the running boards. When we hit a steep pitch, Harry would holler: "Step on it, John." The boys would pile out and Harry would yell: "Everybody push!"

Every man put his shoulder to the car. There was a helluva lot of grunting and blowing, but we topped each steep pitch and I drove the Ford proudly into the Douglas Creek claim. Never in my wildest dreams had I thought such an event would occur.

Harry's operation had become stop-and-go: a case of idle machinery for lack of a few miner's inches of water. Mining experts were brought in for consultation. I noticed that they all left shaking their heads. One day, Harry said to me, "You know what we're going to do, John? We're going to move up to where Herzer got all that gold out of those little holes."

The "little holes" were "vertical shafts" to Dick Herzer and Chuck Cook in past winters. They represented the harsh labor of excavating the dirt by hand, a bucket at a time. Harry's big dozer and dragline tore into the ground around them and made a wasteland, but the results were negligible. Harry scratched his head.

Dick Herzer had spent a lifetime nosing for gold. Instinctively he knew where to dig his little holes. And they all produced rich finds. With Dick, it was an art, not a science. Harry was a road builder. He knew nothing of such an art. Harry did not need heavy machinery; he needed Dick Herzer and a few hardworking men with strong backs and weak minds. The little holes were rich indeed, but Dick had gotten most, if not all, of their wealth with a bucket, a wheelbarrow, and a willing helper.

It was time for me to go back home and to school. I said goodbye to Harry Wirt, who was sitting on the bank staring at his big dragline. He looked worn, totally lacking the ebullience he had possessed in June. I felt sorry for him.

I noticed that the big dozer had contemptuously pushed Brice Toole's bottomless bucket into a hole. It had also unceremoniously upended Marvin McDonald's big dragline engine and swept it out of the way.

I had agreed to play for one more dance at Garnet. I had left my car at Deep Gulch, so to reach the town I had to drive down to the highway and up Bear Gulch. The China Grade up to Garnet was one more steep pitch I couldn't pull; I left the Ford at the bottom and hiked up. On my way down in the morning, I met Lars Ness coming up in a Model A coupe. He stopped and stuck his head out the window.

"Watch out for my wife down the road, kid. She passed out and I put her down by the side of the road. I laid some big rocks on the down side of her so she wouldn't roll into the gulch."

I hiked on down and, sure enough, there was Mrs. Ness slumbering peacefully on the roadside.

Except for a few brief visits, I never returned to Douglas Creek. Small groups of miners worked there during summers for several years.

The last miner wrote to Howard in October 1941:

Dear Mr. Toole:
I hope you kin read this. It's startin to snow and the wind is blowing something fierce. I am diggin' a shaft right under your kid's cabin. Hope he don't mind.

I haven't hit much gold, but I know if you could see the ground I'm workin' in, you'd know I am close to rich gold.

Mr. Toole, could you send me a little money for a grubstake so I could keep goin' fer a while this fall? I know it would be a good deal for both of us.

And the books showed:
GROSS RECEIPTS
| Brice Toole Operation | 1934 | $12,250.00 |
| Harry Wirt Operation | 1935 | $ 5,500.00 |

6   Westward to Daylight

Mathew Dunn

162

6   Westward to Daylight

You simply cannot put yourself in the place of Matt Dunn. The hardships of his boyhood are almost incomprehensible to me. But for the people of Matt Dunn's generation such trials were commonplace, and met simply with whatever means came to hand. No one thought of asking the government for assistance. Freedom was a fierce flame blowing through the land, and that meant freedom to move about, freedom to engage in commerce, and the freedom of every man to die in the attempt to move forward and upward.

Now read this.

William Dunn was a potato farmer who lived in horrible poverty in Ireland. There was some spark in him that told him he must get out, that he must never let himself and his family be gripped in the vise of a land so poor that once you started the routine of farming the potato you could not get your head above water and you were trapped, trapped so firmly that you could not even buy a ticket on a sailing vessel.

In 1842 William Dunn and his wife, the former Bridget Fogarty, escaped the trap and sailed for Quebec in the New World. The first of their seven children was born that year. Nothing is known of their life in Canada. In 1851 William Dunn moved west to Racine,

Wisconsin. Farming was his life, and he was looking for a better farm.

Bridget cared for the children and did her farm chores, and her body began to weaken under the strain. She died in 1854, leaving the young ones with William. He tended the farm and the children, and that became too much for him. He died in 1862.

Did it ever occur to this family to complain? To ask for charity? To expect government aid? To blame their lot in life on others? Of course not. Probably the only solace they sought and received was that given them by the Roman Catholic Church.

The result of this kind of life in the America of the nineteenth century was to produce a nation of incredibly self-reliant people, a degree of self-reliance that we cannot even comprehend.

Mathew Dunn was born on November 15, 1850, and when William Dunn died, Matt was eleven years old. He literally was thrust out into an uncaring world. He had some brothers and sisters, but there was little they could do for him; they had emergencies in their own lives.

Matt was a strong kid, and somehow he got a job doing chores on the nearby farm of one James Crawford. Arrangements were made so that Matt could attend school, providing he performed his chores in the early morning and until dark after school was out. For seven years Matt worked in this way and never received a day off. He accepted his life because his job carried with it something prized above all others in America. He could go to school.

But adolescence brings rebellion in all the young. When he was eighteen years old, he asked Mr. Crawford for a day off to attend a picnic. His request was peremptorily refused, and Matt Dunn got mad. One privilege available to him in nineteenth century America was that of quitting, and this he did.

He walked off the Crawford farm and got another farm job at $14 per month. Then he heard about the lumberjacks in northern Michigan and went to work in the woods. We know now what these jobs were like. But he stayed with it; his wages were better and he saved every cent he could.

Matt had an older brother, Tom, who had gone west and had driven the first herd of cattle into Sun River in the early 1870s. Matt decided to join Tom and on April 10, 1874, arrived in Helena by stagecoach. His world had been much circumscribed in Wisconsin and Michigan. You can imagine his feelings when he broke out of the hills just north of Bowman's Corners and saw before him the great, broad, green valley of the Sun. The valley was dotted with herds of buffalo, over which the warriors of the Blackfeet Tribe asserted ownership. Down the valley a few miles were the stockade and watchtowers of the U.S. Army's Fort Shaw.

Matt went to work for Tom Dunn as a ranchman, which is a

formal way of saying that he became a cowboy. Now, as he breathed the air of this free and open country, the shackles that had bound him to a poor Wisconsin farm became only a bad memory.

He soon acquired his own herd of cattle, and like Kenneth Ross and John R. Toole across the mountains from him, he began to make money. The frontier was now rewarding a man of boldness, courage, and enterprise. He let his cattle roam with the herds of others; he had a brand, and had hired a "rep," a cowboy who helped round up his cattle in the fall and made sure that all of the herd was accounted for.

Now he could count as peers such potentates as Granville Stuart, Pierre Wibaux, Conrad Kohrs, T. C. Power, W. G. Conrad, the Marquis de Mores, and Robert Coburn. In 1882 Matt Dunn, virtually a serf in the Middle West fourteen years before, bought four hundred head of cattle in Blackfoot, Idaho, and trailed them to Fort McLeod, Alberta. He formed a partnership with Robert Ford, and they obtained a contract with the Canadian government to supply beef to the Indians. There were long, hard rides over the vast reaches of Alberta from one Indian encampment to another, but the Indians were glad to get the cattle, for their buffalo were being slaughtered. This was a profitable contract for Matt Dunn.

Any early settler in the Sun River Valley had to reckon with the tall, fierce Blackfeet warriors, but Matt Dunn's relationships with them were good.

Grass. Montana was the nation's great grassland. Its grass, sometimes called buffalo grass or bunch grass, was nutritious the year round. Whether green in the spring or brown in the fall, it was far superior to the marsh grass of Oregon or the dry mesquite of Texas. And that is why the great herds of cattle converged on Miles City on the Yellowstone River. Every cowman in the West wanted to see the Yellowstone, and from Miles City he could ship his cattle to the East on the newly completed Northern Pacific Railroad. But they had to reckon with the winters. Many a cowboy left Montana for happier climes after one year.

In 1883 or 1884 Matt Dunn went to Texas, purchased a large herd and headed it north on the Chisholm Trail, thus participating in one of the most storied, romantic episodes in American history. It would be written about endlessly; it would generate an entirely new repertoire of music and verse; it would be the subject of a new literature and a thousand movie and television shows. But Matt was doubtless unaware of all this as he rode behind his cattle. The enterprise was financially risky and physically demanding. Thousands of cattle could be lost in a river crossing or a stampede. He drove his herd clear on into Alberta.

Collingwood, Ontario, is straight east across Lake Huron from northern Michigan. While he was in the logging camps of Michigan, Matt must have visited Collingwood. It was an important town, a central lake shipping point for the burgeoning shipping trade on the Great Lakes. And it was in Collingwood that he had met his future bride, Barbara Elizabeth Brown. In 1885 he went to Collingwood and claimed her.

The orphaned boy who had been turned loose in the world at the age of eleven had come a long way. He could afford to take his bride on a long honeymoon. They toured the western states. One gets the impression that he looked for good business propositions in every state, but he ended up in Calgary, Alberta, with every intention of making it his home.

Louis Riel was a half-breed Cree Indian. He was slender and handsome. He had received a good education in eastern Canada. He was fiery and emotional, and he had taken upon himself the amelioration of the plight of the many thousand half-breeds who wandered around the plains of Canada and at times ventured into Montana and North Dakota. These unfortunate people were called Metis. Louis Riel himself lived for a time near Lewistown. He had also hidden from the authorities in the Missouri breaks, and he was seen frequently in Fort Benton. Riel was always discouraged about the debauchery of his people by the white Canadians; he speculated that Fort Benton might provide a healthier and more moral place than Canada, but he found it as bad or worse.

The Metis were neither noble red men nor domineering white men. They could claim no heritage of race, tribe, or nationality. The land was stripped of game, but none of it was available even to farm, white men having grabbed it. The Metis had to endure a harsh climate. They were basically a peaceable people, but under the strident oratory of Riel, they arose and a new nation was in the making on the western Canadian plains. The government at Ottawa did not extend its power westward with much force. The Metis rode hither and yon and preyed upon the white settlers. The Royal Canadian Mounted Police was in its infancy, and its few hundred officers fought the Metis with a detachment of citizen volunteers. In the Plains provinces there was chaos. Finally, Ottawa dispatched a regiment of indifferent troops.

The Chamber of Commerce of St. Paul, Minnesota, scenting a chance for the United States to capture western Canada, beat the drums for annexation and America's Manifest Destiny seemed about to take another long leap. But President Ulysses S. Grant had sent his spies into Canada, and he learned the true situation on the Plains. He put his foot down hard. There would be no American invasion of Canada.

166

Louis Riel was a strange revolutionary. At times he would call a halt to the fighting, sit down with his enemies and plead for the justice due his people; then he'd ride back to the sporadic battles on the Plains.

He was bound to lose. He led a passive, phlegmatic people. They loved him and fought bravely, but his mercurial temperament and his intense emotionalism were too overwhelming to them. He was finally captured and taken to Regina, Saskatchewan, for trial. The charge was high treason, and the defense entered a plea of insanity. Dressed in a black suit, white shirt, and black cravat, Riel rejected this plea and made a speech to the court. His words were intense, articulate, and inspirational; he defended himself brilliantly in both English and French.

Nevertheless, he was found guilty. His appeal dragged through several layers of Canadian and English courts until it reached Queen Victoria. She denied clemency.

On the day of sentencing, Regina filled with bedraggled Metis, who stood in the cold wind all day. All available armed forces converged on the city. Riel was sentenced to death, and a great visceral moan escaped the lips of a thousand Metis. If they could not fight for Louis, they could at least express their love.

He was hanged a few days later and a Catholic priest was heard to say: "Louis Riel dies a saint."

The waves of the Riel rebellion washed dangerously near the cities of Edmonton and Calgary in the province of Alberta. Communication was cut off between the two cities because no one dared to carry the mail. Matt Dunn rode off to Winnipeg and negotiated a contract with the Canadian government as a dispatch bearer. He brought the contract back to Calgary. He bought twelve fast and sturdy horses and hired four riders.

It was 220 miles between the two cities, but his horses and riders were never attacked. He loved the excitement of this work, and his profits were $100 per day. It was free enterprise at its highest and best. Only a man who had the daring, the organizational ability and the willingness to take great risks in advancing his own fortune could carry this off.

Mathew Dunn moved his family from Calgary to Great Falls in 1888. The Great Northern Railroad had only just been completed to Great Falls and Senator Paris Gibson, the founder of the city, met Mr. and Mrs. Dunn and their baby daughter, Edith, upon their arrival. The depot was a boxcar and the city consisted of a few wooden buildings straggling across the prairie.

As Mrs. Dunn stepped from the train holding her baby, Senator Gibson came forward and said enthusiastically:

"Welcome to Great Falls, Mrs. Dunn! You've come to God's country!"

*Barbara Dunn and
granddaughter Barbara Keith*

Mrs. Dunn looked around, felt the strong blast of the northern wind, and the endless plains stretching in all directions and thought: "Good Lord! Where is it?"

Despite the city's barrenness, Matt Dunn proceeded to take an interest in it, starting by acquiring real estate there. On Central Avenue, he constructed a building that became known as the Dunn Block; it is now owned by the American Legion. Later, with his brother-in-law, H. P. Brown, he built the Dunn-Brown block on the south side of Central Avenue in the 300 block. You can see the words Dunn-Brown in bold letters near the top of the facade. Another of his buildings went up on First Avenue North.

In Great Falls, he decided to get into politics. He was a Democrat of the "progressive" type. But the Democratic party wasn't quite progressive enough for him. He ran for the Great Falls City Council on the Populist ticket. This was the year of the great silver coinage dispute and all the Democrats were swept out of office. Silver coinage was a matter that concerned every Montanan. Practically all state and local offices went to Populists, including Dunn, and Republicans.

Matt Dunn's desire to serve on the City Council of Great Falls was prompted by his desire to see the city own its own water works, and he succeeded.

Due west of Lewistown by highway is the little town of Utica, on the headwaters of the Judith River. Utica lies in the middle of the country where Charlie Russell worked and painted when he first came to Montana. It is also the country of Jake Hoover, the mountain man and trapper with whom Russell rode and hunted in the early 1880s.

Matt Dunn had now branched out into mining. One day, while prospecting in the Little Belt Mountains on the headwaters of the

Judith, he chanced upon Hoover. The trapper took Matt back into the mountains and showed him a mine that proved to be different from any other in Montana. On a small stream, Hoover showed Matt a spot where he could dig up magnificent blue sapphires of varying hues. Thus was discovered the famous mine of Yogo Gulch, the richest sapphire mine in the United States.

Dunn formed a partnership of himself and four others, one of whom was W. W. Hobson, after whom the town of Hobson is named. They did the necessary development work and then put the mine up for sale. A famous buyer came along, the London Sapphire Syndicate. Needless to say, the partners came out very well on this sale. Once again, the frontier had rewarded enterprise and initiative.

Barbara Dunn

Matt Dunn then interested himself in a mine known as the Blackjack, near Basin, between Butte and Helena. It was a gold, silver, zinc, and copper property. The books of account from this mine are available, and from them it appears that this mine made big profits for a time, but nothing is known of its discovery or ultimate disposition.

I first met Mrs. Mathew Dunn in 1939 when she was in her

169

mid-seventies. She was always meticulously dressed, and her pure white hair was carefully tended. She was a buoyant person with a hearty laugh and an intense interest in the people surrounding her. One would never know that her life had been beset by tragedy. Her husband had died in 1915. Her only son, Harry, had been tragically killed in a gun accident in 1919. Her vivacious and beautiful daughter, Edith, had died of a brain tumor in 1935, and the Dunn family, like the other families in this narrative, had seen the fortune left them by Mathew Dunn swept away in the Great Depression.

These were shattering blows, shattering enough to make a recluse out of some people. But Grandma Dunn had an innate *joie de vivre*, and it gradually returned. I remember her as being an uttery delightful lady.

The Dunns were well-fixed until the bad times came. Then Matt Dunn's property in downtown Great Falls was mortgaged, and they were forced to sell one building and concentrate the mortgage on another. They retained the Dunn Block, and among their tenants were the Alcazar Theater and the Spray Cafe. The Dunn ladies—Mrs. Dunn and daughters Edith and Josephine—took to marching down to the Spray Cafe for dinner in the evening, thus collecting a portion of the rent in the form of a meal.

The Alcazar Theater played silent movies, and for a brief period when it could not be rented, the older daughter, Edith, undertook to manage it. In those days silent movies were enlivened by an organist who varied the emotional pitch of the music to fit the emotional intensity of the scene on the screen.

Josephine Dunn, the younger daughter, had taken training in the organ, and she was assigned this exacting task. However, Josephine found that playing the organ over and over for the same movie was somewhat boring, and she let her music lapse into dull repetition of the same tunes, neglecting the continued emotional heights expected by succeeding audiences.

Grandma Dunn frequently attended the movies to see how things were going. When Jo's playing did not come up to her expectations, she would grasp an usher firmly by the hand and say in a barely restrained whisper:

"Go down and tell Jo to play something else besides that same old chestnut." After six weeks, the Dunn sisters' bold experiment succeeded, and the theater was rented to professionals on a permanent basis.

The beautiful and vicacious Edith found a job as woman's editor of the Great Falls *Tribune*, but after nine years at work she loved, times got so bad that the *Tribune* could no longer afford her. Life grew grim for the Dunn family. But they were always high-spirited and could see the humor in everything.

Edith Dunn Keith

And they had happy memories. Grandma had always been nervy
about doing exactly as she pleased. During their early married life,
Matt Dunn bought a "wheel"—a bicycle. It was designed for use by
men. Ladies had wheels of a different kind to accommodate skirts;
ladies' wheels had no crossbar in the middle of the frame. Mrs.
Dunn wanted a wheel, but her husband considered them inappropriate for women.

One day when Matt Dunn was out of town, she took his men's
wheel downtown and traded it in on a ladies' wheel for herself.
Matt Dunn returned in a few days and, astonished at this transac-
tion, said, "Barbara, you have the damnedest nerve of any woman I
ever saw!"

In the fall of 1922 the Dunn women moved to La Jolla, California, for the winter. Hiring a chauffeur for their Buick sedan, an
open touring car typical of the 1920s, they went in style down the
coast. In the spring, they decided to drive back to Montana without
a chauffeur.

Josephine had a boyfriend in Rock Springs, Wyoming, and it
occurred to her that it would be a good idea to go home by that
route, so she could say "hello."

After consulting such road maps as existed in that day, the ladies
found that, indeed, there was a road that would take them through

171

Mathew Dunn and Josephine, San Diego, 1910

Rock Springs. So Mrs. Dunn, Edith , Josephine, and little Barbara (Edith's daughter and later my wife) climbed into the Buick and headed north. The car was powered by a six-cylinder, valve-in-head engine, generating 140 horsepower. It had mechanical brakes, on the rear wheels only. The steering wheel (no power, of course) had to be wrenched mightily on every curve. Narrow rubber tires (the famous balloon tires of the '30s were still a decade away) made for a rough ride. The car was completely open to the weather, so that the amenity of a heater was not feasible. It had no fuel pump, no oil pump, no water pump, and no oil filter. But you could dim the lights, and it had a windshield wiper that the driver could operate manually while he grasped the steering wheel with his other hand.

To reach Rock Springs, the ladies had to cross the deserts of southern California , the entire length of Nevada from south to north, and the panhandle of Utah, ending up on the high Wyoming plains. The roads were nothing more than two parallel ruts across the desert, and the traffic was virtually nil. In 1923, people didn't use that route between Montana and southern California. If the ladies were to have a breakdown (and there were many breakdowns in 1923) their situation would be dire.

They tooled across the southern California desert and reached Las Vegas, which was nothing more than a depot and a few shacks beside the railroad. Then they headed north in a general way, guiding themselves by the North Star. In the vast, uninhabited desert between Las Vegas and Ely, they drove on into the night. They found no settlement in which they could stay. Then, on a hill on a distant horizon, they saw a large multi-storied house, ablaze with light from every window. The Dunn family headed for it gratefully. But as they drew near, every light in the house went out. The big mansion sat ominously silhouetted against the blue-black sky. After a hurried consultation the ladies decided to execute a withdrawal and proceed north by a different route. It is not recorded where they spent that night, but as to the multi-storied house, Grandma said matter-of-factly, "Probably just bootleggers."

At Wells, Nevada, they turned east, crossed the Bonneville Salt Flats, and met a highway, which, while not improved, carried more traffic and ultimately took them to Rock Springs. It is not known whether Josephine found her boyfriend or not.

They headed north up the Ham's Fork of the Snake River, crossed the Continental Divide at Monida, and reached Great Falls. When Grandma told me about this trip, I was appalled, but she didn't think it any big deal.

One time, when Grandma was in her eighties, I drove to Helena to pick her up and bring her to Missoula for a visit. It was bitter cold, a raging blizzard was sweeping down from Canada, and the visibility at McDonald Pass was zero.

Grandma was completely unperturbed about the weather. She settled back in her seat to enjoy the ride. For my part, I was greatly disturbed about the weather. I could see myself in the ditch on McDonald Pass with an octogenarian lady on my hands.

As we proceeded up the pass, I noticed numerous cars in the ditch and great trucks spinning out on the ice. The road lacked gravel for traction, and my car skidded dangerously from one side to the other. I could see virtually nothing ahead because of the blowing snow. Grandma, apparently oblivious of the danger, chatted pleasantly.

Finally I concluded that we must return to Helena and I veered into a wide spot on the highway to turn around. Grandma looked at me and questioned me sharply, "What are you doing?"

"Grandma, we'll never get over the pass tonight. I'm going to turn around and go back to Helena."

"Nonsense, complete nonsense," she said severely. "We started out for Missoula and that's exactly where we're going. Now pull out on the highway and get a move on. This storm doesn't amount to anything!"

So I did as instructed and we made it.

Grandma Dunn took the roaring '20s in style. She visited her daughter Josephine, who was studying music in Chicago. When she returned to Great Falls, lo and behold, she was smoking cigarettes and wearing her hair in a bob. This caused a few raised eyebrows among her many brothers and sisters, and it particularly shocked her brother, George, whom she visited in Havre on her return trip from Chicago. He said:

"I have never smoked. The only time I ever smoked a cigar was when someone gave it to me."

Grandma said vehemently: "Well George, I wouldn't be such a darned old tightwad!"

The tragedies and ill health in Grandma's family would knock her flat for a while, but after each blow she would rebound. Her view was always outward, directed at the people around her. She did not brood, but sometimes when she reflected on her own life she would say philosophically, "It makes you wonder what it's all about."

But she wasted little time in wondering. She lived to be ninety-two and is buried in the Great Falls cemetery. When she died, the last of the second generation passed from my life.

As for Matt Dunn, after the turn of the century he eased off. He became a director of the Great Falls National Bank; he continued

173

The Dunn family (left to right): Harry Dunn, Edith Dunn Keith, Mathew Dunn, Barbara Brown Dunn, Josephine Dunn Dye

to interest himself in the Blackjack Mine; and it was at this time that the final negotiations with the London Sapphire Syndicate were consummated.

Of the few photos of him that are available, one shows a big broad-shouldered man with a direct gaze, wearing a broad-brimmed hat. At some point during his dangerous years on the Plains, he had lost an eye. He had a glass eye which he could pop in and out. The kids who witnessed this performance were astonished.

Like every other member of the second generation, Mathew Dunn was attracted by California. He bought a home in Fresno and later one in San Diego. In his last years he spent much of his time in San Diego. His daughter Edith graduated from Mills College; daughter Josephine attended Monticello and the Bishop's School in La Jolla; son Harry graduated from Stanford.

On his way from Great Falls to San Diego in 1915, Mathew Dunn died suddenly in Helena. He is buried in the Great Falls cemetery, where one can look out on the rolling prairies and the flat-topped buttes of the great land that grudgingly yielded to him freedom to control his own destiny and a fortune beyond his wildest dreams.

174

Helen Fitzgerald Sanders, the daughter of Wilbur Fisk Sanders, in her *History of Montana*, has this to say of him:

Mathew Dunn knew nothing but sorrow and unkindness from his earliest childhood until, master of his own fate, he broke the only home ties that he had ever known. Friendless, penniless and alone, he set forth, not knowing the meaning of fear or failure. Through all of his hardships, he never lowered his standards of integrity or honor. He built for himself a competence that must be measured by pounds of sterling and gold, but more than that, he has built him a character measurable only in the hearts of those he has loved with his true Irish tenderness, or aided with his native generosity.

7 1936: Big Logs and Silent Men

Don MacKenzie

7   *1936: Big Logs and Silent Men*

In the 1930s the big logging camps of the Anaconda Company were wondrous places.

First, there were the men. They were lithe and sinewy. They wore black pants stagged off well above the ankles, and loggers' boots with a pincushion of tiny sharp caulks (pronounced "corks"), which tore wooden floors to shreds. All wore suspenders; most wore checked shirts and nondescript black hats.

In the evening, the teamsters, who were called "skinners," came into camp behind teams of great, beautiful, 2,000-pound horses: Belgians, Percherons or Clydesdales. They headed for the barn, and I could peek in and see the harnesses being removed, the hay being forked into the manger, and when it was cold great clouds of steam rising from the horses' backs. Every skinner would give his big animals an affectionate pat on the rump as he left the barn.

Just after five, the strange little locomotive called a Shay would give a confident little toot on its whistle as it approached the camp, pulling several flat cars loaded with lumberjacks. The drive wheels of this intriguing locomotive were turned by a complicated set of gears. Instead of the majestic blast of steam of the big main-line locomotives that we all remember, the Shay gave off a kind of desperate little panting as it hurried over an incredibly untidy track snaking across the land on ties set close together but entirely unburied.

Before the train stopped, the lumberjacks piled off and headed for the bunkhouse. They seemed so great and strong to me, with their gleaming double-bitted axes sharp as razors, and their long crosscut saws springing lightly at their shoulders.

In the bunkhouse they changed their shoes and socks, and at 6 p.m., Joe Kingham, the chief cook, took a steel bar and rattled it around in a hanging triangle of steel, making a fearful racket.

The men streamed out of the bunkhouses and headed for the cookhouse to refuel their bodies, which had expended so much energy at labor in the forests. The cookhouse was the most important facility in the camp. Its tables sagged under huge platters of roast beef, potatoes, vegetables, cake, pies, and sugar cookies. The men attacked this appetizing pile voraciously. They stuffed themselves with unbelievable quantities of food, swung their feet over the bench, and strode out of the cookhouse and back to the bunkhouse.

From the time they got off the train until they went to bed, these men never uttered a word. The meal, in particular, was eaten in absolute silence.

Gramp often drove down to the camps and sat in his car watching. This had been his life for almost fifty years. The only time the silence was broken was when an old lumberjack would come out to reach in his car and shake his hand. I always asked Gramp: "Why don't the men ever say anything to each other?" He would reply, "I guess it's just in the nature of the beast."

In 1936 the Douglas Creek mine was about finished, although a few men were working there on a royalty basis. But there was no job for me. By now, I was crazy to work in the Anaconda camps. I was eighteen and had traded my Model T Ford in on a Model A.

I told Howard of my desire. One night he came home and said, "John, Don MacKenzie's in town and he's staying at the Shapard Hotel. If you want a job, you better go down and see him."

I beat it downtown in a fierce Hellgate blizzard. Don was sitting in the lobby reading a newspaper. Don MacKenzie was a formidable man, a tall, rangy Scot, born in the old country. He had iron-gray hair, a huge hawklike nose, and a strong Scottish burr. I approached him with some trepidation.

"Mr. MacKenzie, I was wondering—if I come up to the camp in June, when school is out, if you'd give me a job."

Don looked me over from head to toe with his penetrating eyes. Finally he said: "Oh, I don't know, young fellow. I can hire good, experienced hands these days. There's a lot of good men out of work."

Then my words came rushing out of me, and I told him about all the experience I had had in mines and ranches.

He looked me over with a level gaze and said: "Say, aren't you the grandson of Kenneth Ross?"

I nodded an eager affirmative.

"Well, all right, come on up in June and I'll see if I can't find something for you."

I raced home through the raging blizzard in a state of absolute joy.

June came, and I was off in my Model A. I wanted to experience the joy of driving it into Douglas Creek, so I headed up steep pitches of the long canyon. The Ford growled up the hills without strain. To me, the Model A. was the greatest thing on wheels.

A man named Sprinkle had a crew working there. I thought he was well named. I figured that he would need plenty of sprinkle when the water started dropping in July. These men were hard-working and sober about their prospects, but they definitely had gold fever.

I turned back and went to Woodworth, a magnificent little green valley surrounded by huge ponderosa pines and in 1936 site of the Anaconda lumber camps. It was with a pang that I realized that these magnificent trees would soon go.

In these summer days, my life was tightly circumscribed. Woodworth was only ten miles from Seeley Lake, where Gramp had had his tussle with Ranger Girard thirty years before. I could see Blacktail Mountain just above the Circle W Ranch, where Charlie Dunham had guided me to my shot at the whitetail buck three years before. To the south I could pick out the ridge that overhangs Douglas Creek. The Blackfoot Valley was a wondrous land; it had everything in the world for a kid to do, all set in haunting beauty.

I walked into the camp office. The floors were in splinters and the place had an ineffable smell of wood. Don MacKenzie was there leaning against a counter. He looked at me and I could see that he did not recognize me.

"I'm John Toole, Mr. MacKenzie. Do you remember that you promised me a job last winter when you were in Missoula at the Shapard Hotel?"

He looked at me again with that cold level gaze and finally said: "That I did now. I remember. You are the grandson of Kenneth Ross. Well, all right, you can go to work piling ties. Report to Fred Larson at the steel gang in the morning."

So far, so good. Piling ties. Well, at least that didn't require any brainwork. I was never any good at anything that required brains. I reported to Fred Larson. Fred had a reputation as a slave driver. He looked me over and asked:

"Who sent *you* up here?"

"Don MacKenzie."

"Are you a 'candy kid'?"

He terminated this abbreviated conversation. I asked myself: "What's a candy kid?" I suppose he meant something like "sissy."

In the morning, I got on the train and dangled my feet over the side. The little locomotive wheezed, and the wheels clicked over the rails. It was a beautiful June morning; the sky was radiant; the bushes were bursting with color. I looked around at my fellow lumberjacks; not a man was speaking a word. The train stopped; a lean and lanky man with a bushy mustache motioned with a gesture of his head for me to dismount. We stood by the tracks and he said: "Kid, you're my partner, follow me." We took off through the woods without saying a word. After a while we reached a spot where some ties, flattened on two sides, were strewn about. Silently he handed me a tool called a picaroon. It had an axe on one side and a sharp pick on the other. The ties were too heavy to carry, so you sank the pick in one end and dragged the tie over to a pile and hoisted it to the top. My partner never said a word until noon, when he announced that it was "quittin' time." We hiked over to Cottonwood Creek, where a bunch of lumberjacks were silently sitting around eating their lunches. I looked forward to lunch. The lunch buckets, I knew, contained marvelous slabs of roast beef sandwiches, cake, and steaming coffee. I sat down among the men and opened my bucket. It was full of rocks.

Sawyers at Woodworth, 1936   UM Mansfield Library

I looked at it in bewilderment and dismay and raised my head to look at the other men. They were watching me in silence. Finally, the chuckles came, and with them came a rain of sandwiches and cake. One man even handed me a cup of coffee. Jeezes, I thought, I hope this breaks the ice. And it did, though not completely.

Working near us was a giant of a man who was felling the trees and hewing out the ties. He worked feverishly because he was being paid ten cents per tie. He was a Czech, or a Jugoslav—some kind of eastern European, all of whom were designated by the lumberjacks as "bohunks." He was pleasant to me, always waving and smiling. I thought, hell, this is one guy I can probably communicate with, so I went up to him to engage him in conversation, but he smiled and laughed and signalled to me that he didn't understand English. God, the only nice guy in the camp, and he can't understand English!

Piling the ties was rigorous and demanding work, so I was pleased when Larson told me that he was going to release me to foreman Joe Grace, who was starting a "rag camp" to get out stulls (mine timbers), about 13 miles south of headquarters. In the morning I was on the train to the new camp, where I had the same partner.

We piled off at the rag camp, so called because in earlier days timber crews lived in tents. Our bunkhouses consisted of three Company-made box cars; the cookhouse was in a fourth. A special siding had been built.

The view from the rag camp was stupendous. The Blackfoot Valley billowed out to the east; in the close foreground were the great hay meadows of Billy Boyd, and the camp was set down in the midst of a grove of large ponderosa pines. On the first weekend, I moved my Model A to Boyd's home ranch.

Joe Grace

Al Henderson, my partner—I had finally elicited his name—and I were put to work falling tamarack trees to be made into stulls for the Butte mines. We had, of course, no chain saws, only razor-sharp crosscuts and double-bitted axes. I had had a little experience in falling trees, but not much. My first effort at performing this work with Henderson brought forth the only emotion I ever saw him show. When we tied into our first trees, a series of monosyllabic words, uttered in a monotone, came out of him in a controlled irascibility:

"Pull, don't push. Yeah."

"Don't jerk. Yeah."

"More water. Yeah."

"Dumb kid, you got the saw pinched."

"She's fallin.' Get the hell out. Yeah."

Every lumberjack is instructed to holler "timber!" when a tree

183

starts to fall. Al muttered the word under his breath. You couldn't hear him six feet away. When the tree lay on the ground he'd invariably say: "You put 'er in the wrong place, kid, yeah." Each of us carried a half-pint whiskey bottle, one filled with kerosene to lubricate the saw for pine, the other with water to lubricate it for tamarack.

By 1936 crawler-type tractors had taken over the job of skidding the logs, cut 32 feet long, to the landing, as the loading point on the railroad was called. But horses were still used to distribute the logs, now cut to 16 feet, alongside the cars. Then the eloquently named "slide-ass jammer," a steam-operated winch that could slide itself from car to car, pulled the logs aboard.

In the evening after supper, the lumberjacks went about various tasks. The sawyers who were cutting the big logs were gyppos, paid by the thousand board feet produced. They would go out to the landing and inspect the ends of the various logs to be sure that their particular mark was still visible on the logs they had cut during the day. Al and I were working for wages of 47½ cents per hour; we didn't have to inspect our logs. The Company provided numerous foot-operated grindstones and files; the men set to work sharpening their axes and saws for the following day.

Every night, each man washed his socks and hung them in the bunk car to dry. Entering the bunk car was like entering a steam bath. The humidity was 100 percent, not conducive to sleep. The dripping socks hung down only six inches from my face. Bunks were double- or triple-tiered, and almost on the dot at 9:30, an absolutely horrendous chorus of snores started. Had I not been exhausted, I would not have slept a wink. The clanging of steel on steel roused us at 6 a.m. Our pay didn't start until we hit the work site, often half a mile away.

My dialogue with Al Henderson remained almost non-existent. Occasionally, there would be an exchange like this:

"You Kenneth Ross's grandson, yup?"

"Got your job here through pull. Yup?"

I never did advertise the fact that Kenneth Ross had been my grandfather, but the word got around.

One day I left my watch in the bunkhouse. I said:

"Al, what time is it?"

He pulled a big gold pocket watch out of his pocket, looked at it and put it back.

"Well, Al," I asked, "What time *is* it?"

He replied: "I bought this watch for my own use."

About the only thing I enjoyed at the camp was the beauty of our surroundings. Everything else was grim. The weekends were short; we worked a forty-eight-hour week.

On Saturday nights, I hiked across the Boyd meadow to my Ford, and headed for the Circle W Ranch. Needless to say, the atmosphere there was an improvement over the camp.

I had gotten together a little hillbilly band. In addition to myself, there was the drummer, Ken Demmons; the guitarist, Henry Turner; on the mandolin, Hank Pennypacker; and the banjo player, Warren Skillicorn. We played for some dances at Ovando, others at Seeley Lake and Helmville. But there was one at Salmon Lake that topped all the others.

When W. A. Clark, Jr., died, the great estate on Salmon Lake, called Mowitsa, was sold to Al Wertheimer, a member of a gambling ring. Somehow he ended up in my dad's office for his routine legal work. Howard handled his deeds, contracts and other matters. His headquarters were in Detroit; he headed a nefarious outfit called the Purple Gang. Dad was never called on to handle any illegal activities for him.

He was a tough guy, but he was friendly and also rich. He liked the people in Montana and had many festive parties at Mowitsa. He cultivated the big shots from Anaconda, and one night he arranged for our band, which was variously called "Demmons and his Demons" or "Toole and his Tooters," to provide the music. Present at this affair were: Carlos Ryan, the son of John D. Ryan; Gay Kelly, the daughter of Dan Kelly; Ed McGlone, the superintendent of the Butte mines; their various wives; and a galaxy of W. A. Clark's granddaughters, legitimate and otherwise. Al Wertheimer had a wife named Thelma, a hard-looking gal but extremely pleasant.

The party became exuberant, and Howard got intoxicated, the first time I ever saw this happen. He had an immense *joie de vivre*, a marvelous capacity for a good time, and he would dance around the floor, bumping other couples with his rear end. He also did a god-awful dance called the monkey dance, in which he imitated a baboon, and he danced this solo terpsichorean exhibition with complete abandon. I was utterly shocked to witness this behavior on the part of my dignified and respected father.

Carlos Ryan asked me to play a song that I didn't know and declined to attempt. He became angry, grabbed Henry Turner's guitar, swung it above my head, and brought it crashing down on my skull, splintering it to pieces. Strangely, I was not injured, the dancers swirled on as though nothing had happened, and only Henry Turner grieved over his loss. Then Carlos settled down, dug out a $100 bill, and handed it to Henry with instructions to buy a new guitar. The sight of these huge bills circulating around made my eyes bug out.

The party came to an end and Al Wertheimer bade the band goodbye at the front door. He handed each of us a $50 bill for services rendered. I had never seen a $50 bill before.

On the porch was a carton of imported champagne. As we filed out, one of my fellow musicians spotted it and slipped a bottle under his jacket. When I saw this I roundly berated him for this ungracious act and told him to take it back, but he replied:

"Hell, John, these people will never miss it. They're rolling in money." So much for that.

Then back to the camps, and the unceasing labor in the woods for 47½ cents an hour.

Joe Grace, the foreman at our rag camp, had a reputation as a drinking man; his face was always slightly florid. In the summer of 1936, Congress passed a bonus bill for veterans of World War I. Roosevelt vetoed it, but Congress passed it over his veto. Joe Grace received a huge sum, $1,800; he disappeared for several days and returned in a grumpy mood.

One day, Al Henderson went on sick call, so I went into the woods alone. Working by myself, I wasn't particularly diligent. I sat down on a stump to have a cigarette. I saw brush moving, heard twigs breaking, saw branches parting, and then found myself looking at the face of the worst imaginable man to confront an employee who was goofing off. It was Joe Grace.

He walked over and fixed me with a stern, penetrating look:

"Now look here, John. There's a lot of men out of work in this country and here you are, lucky enough to have a job, and I catch you sitting on your ass and smoking a cigarette. Now you listen to me. If I ever catch you doing this again, I'll tie the can to your tail and send you down the road, and I don't care who you are. Do you understand?"

The "I don't care who you are" was an obvious reference to my connection with Kenneth Ross. I stammered something to the effect that I'd never do it again, and he turned and left. I felt chastened and uncomfortable. I thought: "This goddamn camp. I can't wait until summer's over."

There was one man at Woodworth who was unfailingly friendly. He always smiled at me and spoke to me cheerfully. This man was Don MacKenzie's alter ego, Cassius W. McEwen. He was one of the two Macs, and in military terminology he was a "G1" and a "G4" wrapped in one. McEwen was in charge of supply, personnel, and finance. He was a short, stocky man, and he spent most of his time at a desk in the office. He was an old friend of Gramp's.

In 1936 the Anaconda Company offered a group life insurance program, a voluntary fringe benefit with a payroll-deduction plan. McEwen came down to the rag camp and the crew gathered in the cook car to hear his presentation. I didn't know much about life insurance and somehow didn't think it applied to me, but I figured that if Mac recommended it, it must be a good deal, so I signed up. I

186

was pleased to do it because it seemed to please him. For many of those lumberjacks it was important; there was always somebody getting killed.

Unbeknownst to Mac, many of the men to whom he sold insurance made him their beneficiary. They were single men, without relatives. Mac got some richly deserved nest eggs. He was dumbfounded.

Al Henderson resolutely refused to tell me anything about himself or his life. I concluded that I would have to probe him with guesses, because he refused to answer any inquiry which required an answer beyond "Yup" and "Nope."

"You came out here from Wisconsin, eh, Al?"

"Yup."

"You came in 1910, eh?" Another old lumberjack named Joe Jenkins, similarly reticent, had told me that he and Al had arrived in 1910.

"Yup."

"The Company's river drive on the Clearwater was rough work, eh?"

"Yup."

"Was W. A. Clark better to work for than the Anaconda Company?"

"Nope."

"Can a lumberjack afford a wife and family when he works in the woods all the time?"

"Nope."

"Al, were you a Wobbly?"

This time, no "Yup" or "Nope." He straightened up from his axe work on a small tree and told me with a trace of irritation:

"Here, kid, take this bottle down to camp and fill it with kerosene." End of conversation. But I got a rough profile of his life.

On August 20 I decided to quit my job. I wanted more pleasant surroundings and people around me who would communicate. I

"You want a book, huh? Didn't know you could read." Al Henderson, retired lumberjack, lived in one end of the library car and took care of its contents.
UM Mansfield Library

went up to headquarters camp and thanked Don MacKenzie for the job. Then I went back to the rag camp, said goodbye to a taciturn Joe Grace, and hiked up to the spot where Al Henderson was working alone. I had found out that nobody in camp would consent to work with Al; he was a misanthropist. He was alone, rhythmically swinging his axe on a small tree. I said: "I've quit my job, Al. I've come to say good-bye."

No answer.

I went on. "Are you sorry to see me leave, Al?"

"Nope."

That was about what I expected.

It was a relief to get back to the Circle W Ranch, where interesting and congenial people were all about. The ranch had quite a number of guests that summer, and the Weisel family was concerned about seeing that they had a good time. The Weisels conceived the idea of taking them on a pack trip to Garnet, to show them a bona-fide ghost town. This fell right in with my plans; I wanted to go back to Garnet anyway.

John Weisel and I went ahead in my Model A to find a good camping place for the outfit. We took an old mining road that starts from the top of Greenough Hill and winds along the ridge, past the ghost town of Coloma and down into Garnet. It was a horrible road, designed for horse-drawn vehicles only. Solid granite teeth studded the road's surface, and unless the driver used extreme care, he would tear out the bowels of the car. But the Model A made it, and John and I found a level flat just above town, where the party could camp.

Garnet was beginning a new relapse into a long sleep. Upon our entry into town, Mr. Davey came out in the street and greeted us, but the throngs of miners had diminished; the mines had proved to be poorer than anticipated, and jobs were more plentiful in the country. Nevertheless, I rounded up some musicians for a dance, and in a couple of days the Weisel pack string and guests arrived.

There was the usual exploration of old buildings, the fruitless efforts involved in panning for gold, and "oh'ing" and "ah'ing" over Mr. Davey's inventory. In 1936 this inventory was Garnet's most intriguing attraction.

You could pour coffee beans into his coffee grinder with a cast iron spoon and grind your own cup of coffee. You could then heat it on Mr. Davey's kerosene stove. There were large jars of sticky red, white, and blue candy, which had come down from the 1890s, and looked it. You could buy a stick of candy, but a moment's inspection would convince any customer that to eat it would be deadly.

Mr. Davey had raised his prices unconscionably, because his supply of merchandise was obviously finite. Indeed, he had locked some items in glass cabinets, which were adorned with richly scrolled mahogany. These items were not for sale. The guests marveled at high-button shoes; purple velvet, off-the-shoulder, formal dresses with plunging necklines, beautiful wasp-waisted bodices and handmade lace shirtwaists; derby hats; and silver-mounted walking canes.

In the back of the store were the practical items needed by the miners of the day—shovels, picks, rope, magnets, drill steel, carbide lights, sledges and axes. But though he was happy to deal with miners, Mr. Davey enjoyed most of all people like the Weisel guests, who appreciated and marveled at his ancient inventory. Few purchases were made; a feeling was shared by all that Mr. Davey didn't really want to sell his museum pieces. Everything was covered with a thick layer of dust, which plumed out into the store when a garment was held up for inspection.

Then there was the hotel. It was operated by Mr. Davey, though not owned by him. If you wanted a room, you paid in advance and he would give you a key. The hotel was wallpapered with designs of huge flowers with varied colors. A peek into a room would show you a filigreed steel cot and a brightly colored down quilt. If you ventured to sit on the bed, a cloud of dust sprang up and enveloped the room, and you had to flee. The plumbing consisted of a heavy ceramic bowl, a pitcher, and a thundermug. There was a parlor and dining room on the ground floor, but they had been abandoned to the mountain rats. I've often wondered how Mr. Davey kept the drunks out of his hotel; maybe they were just asphyxiated and hauled out.

F. A. Davey was a man who had obviously been exposed to the finer things of life in his native England. Even forty years in Garnet couldn't disguise this. He sported a flowing, white mustache and had a shock of thick, well-combed, white hair. He might have been a butler in an English country estate; his English was flawless.

The activity around Garnet had slowed a good deal. The Nancy Hanks mine was closed and the Dandy mine had reduced its crew. But a new breed had started to arrive, the loggers. Little did I know then how these people would change the landscape. Nevertheless, their vigor and capacity for a good time equaled that of the miners. The news of our dance spread rapidly, and Lars Ness's bar was thumping on Saturday night. The Weisel guests seemed to be having a great time, and the old dance hall was swaying. But a dance in Garnet could be guaranteed to provide a shock, and this was no exception.

Some characters—miners, loggers, or somebody—got together several sticks of dynamite, some caps, and some fuse. They hooked these components together in the middle of the main street, lit the

189

fuse, then beat it for cover. The dynamite exploded with a horrendous explosion. It's a wonder that no one was killed. The noise caused consternation in the dance hall. The band came to a bleating stop, women screamed, and the men rushed for the door. In the silence, horse laughs were heard from behind some of the old buildings. When it became apparent that it was a prank, the dance resumed. People got pretty well liquored up, and in the following days the explosion became an inexhaustible subject of conversation.

In the morning, the Weisel guests mounted their horses to return to the Circle W. I decided to stay in Garnet; I had about three weeks before school opened (college, now), but I wanted a job and I asked Mr. Davey where he thought I could get one. He said:

"Well, young man, I think that will be quite difficult. The placer mines are all closed because the waters have disappeared in the little brooks. The hard rock mines have been discharging many of their employees."

Then he looked at me quizzically: "However, young man, I think I might be able to provide you with employment here in the store for a short time."

This overjoyed me. I had visions of waiting on his customers, and I thought that would be very pleasant. Then he said:

"Come into my kitchen."

In his kitchen, he pumped a large pitcher of water and poured it into the sink. The water just stayed there. He went on:

"Now you will observe, young man, that the water is prevented from draining out of the sink. This has occurred before, and is an indication to me that there is an obstruction in the piping that prevents the free movement of the water as it descends from the sink to the drainage outfall. I have reason to believe that the obstruction is located at the outfall of the drain, which is situated in the street in front of the store at a depth of approximately six feet.

"Now if you would care to excavate an opening in the street so as to locate the outfall, free the obstruction from the drain, and place several large stones around the end of the pipe so that the drainage can proceed unimpaired, I will be glad to pay you the sum of $10.

"Now in the event that you may be repelled in this undertaking by the possibility that the drain might contain sanitary sewerage, I can put your mind at ease. If you will look out the window, you will see that I have my own toilet facilities out there and they are in no way connected to the drain in question."

I looked out the window and saw Mr. Davey's private outside privy.

"Now how does that strike you, young man?" he asked, beaming.

Jeezes, I thought, if there's anything I don't want to do, it's spend

190

the waning days of a beautiful summer digging a goddamn sewer in the main street of Garnet!

"Well, uh, er, Mr. Davey, I've never done much pick and shovel work."

"Now young man," he replied. "It takes no skill whatsoever to work with a pick and shovel. I'm sure you'll get along swimmingly. Why don't you start in the morning? I'll arrange for you to stay with William Liberty." Old Billy Liberty was a nice old prospector who was spending his declining years in Garnet. He was a good cook, but he snored like hell.

The main street of Garnet was compacted almost to concrete by generations of placer miners and the action of water. It took me two days to dig down and expose the end of Mr. Davey's pipe. The pipe was sealed tight with cement-like sand. Mr. Davey came out for a look:

"Aha, my boy!" he said, delightedly. "Your labors have been rewarded. The cause of the blockage is apparent. You may now free the pipe of this onerous material and replace the earth that formerly occupied this aperture in the street. Please remember that the excavated earth must be replaced in the hole and the site of your excavation must be cleared of debris so as not to endanger the welfare of such vehicular traffic as may wish to visit our community."

I felt like glaring at him, but I didn't.

I put several large boulders around the end of the pipe, backfilled the hole, raked up the excess material and went in to report to Mr. Davey. He joyfully poured several large pitchers of water down the drain, and I was scared to death he'd plug it up again before I could get out of town. He turned and said:

"Excellent job, young man, excellent job. Here is your $10 bill." Then he chuckled and said: "I shall be glad to recommend you to His Majesty King Edward the Eighth."

I bade him goodbye and got out of town fast before he could think of another job.

My mother now had a cabin at Seeley Lake, and I drove up there to spend the last week of the summer with her. She had been depressed ever since the death of her father, Kenneth Ross, but she was beginning to come out of it. My cousin, Jack Clifton, and I put a new roof on her cabin, and I read the new novel *Gone With the Wind*.

I was going to college, but I didn't want to go to college. I wanted to spend my life in the Blackfoot Valley. To do that, I had to make a living.

First I thought of ranching, but I didn't like horses and I didn't like cows, so I ruled that out. Then I thought of mining, but I'd never seen a successful mine in the Blackfoot yet. My experiences at Douglas Creek, while educational, were not inspirational. I hit upon logging.

Below McNamara's Landing on the Blackfoot, I had often looked longingly at a small stand—about two million feet—of ponderosa pine. It was on the south side of the river and inaccessible by road. The harvesting of this stand became an obsession with me. I would log it in a way that would not hurt the country and would use all the old tried-and-true logging methods. The trees were located close to the river, only eight miles from Bonner. A river drive down the Blackfoot would be easy.

Finally, I steeled my nerve and went to see W. C. Lubrecht at Bonner, the man who had taken Gramp's place. He was most cordial; he asked me to sit down and inquired what he could do for me. I began:

"Mr. Lubrecht, I would like to talk to you about the stand of pine the Company owns across the river from the highway and about eight miles from here." He nodded. I gulped and went on:

"I would like to log this stand of timber for the company. Here is my plan."

He looked at me as though I were daft but I plunged ahead.

"I would plan to horse-log that timber. I could easily swim the teams across the river. I would deck the logs beside the river and skid all the logs on the snow. I figure I would need two sawyers, two skinners, a swamper, a cook, and a bull cook [cook's helper]. I would have to build a small camp across the river this fall."

"I would leave the woods in good shape, burn all the brush, and leave the immature trees for second growth. We could figure out a fair price per thousand and you wouldn't have to pay me anything until I delivered my logs to the mill."

I could see that he was stupefied but he and I both knew he owed his job to Gramp, so he was very courteous.

"John," he said, "how old are you?"

"Eighteen, sir."

"Well, uh, er, humph." He rubbed his chin. "Such a contract would take considerable start-up money. Will your dad give it to you?"

"No, sir. He can't afford it. I'm planning to borrow it from the First National Bank."

"Have you talked to the bank?"

"No, sir, not yet."

"Well now, John, aren't you awfully young to be starting out as a gyppo logger?"

"I can do it, sir! I worked for Don MacKenzie all summer."

"I see. But John, you know, we don't drive the river any more. It's too dangerous, and we get bad log jams when we drive the river."

"But, sir, this is only two million feet, and the river is free

192

transportation, sir."

"Well, we just don't do it any more. Some day we'll build a bridge across the river there, or we'll build a road down the mountain from the other side."

"I could do it a lot cheaper, sir."

"No, John, I'm sorry, but we just don't do it that way any more. Now you go home and talk to your father. He'll give you good advice. Go to college this fall and get a good education, and if you want to work in the woods some time, we'll think about you."

He shook my hand heartily, and I left his office feeling both dejected and amazed.

My suggestion that the logs be skidded by horses and floated down the river was regarded as quaint. It wasn't. A logging boss for a big company told me recently:

"Your proposal, made in the year 1936, was eminently sound. It made sense, but Anaconda was very inflexible and without imagination or innovation. They should have taken you up. But you had a helluva hurdle—that bank loan!"

I went back to Seeley Lake. Some boys from the Sigma Chi social fraternity came up, picked me up, and spent the drive to Missoula touting their organization. I registered at the University of Montana to get an "education."

8   Miner, Copper, and Kings

8   Miner, Copper, and Kings

My grandfather John R. Toole was not like the other men in this book.

He was contemplative, self-effacing, even secretive. He left a huge library of the classics and history. He had studied mathematics and metallurgy. He had a firm grounding in the humanities and the arts. Yet though he apparently taught school for a time I can find no sign that he was a college graduate or even that he attended college.

He could be affable, and he liked people, but mostly he walked in the shadows. He enjoyed working and associating with the great movers and doers of his time, yet he never seemed to have a craving to be a mover and doer himself.

His milieu was the hurly-burly world of mining and politics. He served continuously in elective office from Deer Lodge County from 1886 to 1902. His constituency was the men who were employed in the Anaconda smelter, and they seemed to love him much as Montanans love Mike Mansfield today. Like most Montana politicians of the day, he was a Democrat.

He became the trusted political and financial adviser to fellow Democrat Marcus Daly, founder and owner of Anaconda Copper, and he was Daly's surrogate in the Montana legislature, the Constitutional Convention of 1889 and the Anaconda City Council. He was also a self-made mining engineer, and he investigated mines

197

for Daly all over North America. He was not a construction man, but for Daly he undertook such major jobs as building the Butte, Anaconda & Pacific railroad and the 13-mile wooden flume from Silver Lake to Daly's early smelter.

By the time of Daly's death this close association had made "John R." (as he was widely known) a wealthy man, and he found himself the principle owner and president of the Daly Bank & Trust Co., the institution Daly used to finance his wars with William A. Clark and the expansion of the Daly mines and smelters.

Two years before Daly's death his great Butte mines and Anaconda smelter were sold to the Rockefellers' Standard Oil Company, which asked John R. to stay on. But with Daly gone, John R. had no compelling reason to remain in Anaconda, so he moved to Missoula and built an imposing ante-bellum, colonnaded mansion, which stands to this day.

It was there that he died, still on the Rockefeller payroll, and it was there that he burned every shred of written material about his past, as if to foil future historians.

When my generation of Tooles was growing up, a photograph of a bald, bespectacled, inscrutable man hung from a wall in every Toole home. If any of us showed enough curiosity to ask the identity of the man, we were always told: "Oh. That's Grandpa Toole. A wonderful man, a great man." That was enough. It was a little like the pictures of George Washington that hung in every schoolroom in those days.

After several months of digging into the life of this enigmatic man, I finally elicited what I think is a fairly accurate picture of him and his times. It is a picture of an insignificant-looking man, dressed in a rumpled black suit, at the center of a knot of cigar-smoking garrulous politicians in the lobby of the Helena Hotel during the 1890s. He is speaking little but observing much, and when the crowd adjourns to the bar, he adjourns to his room on the second floor, because he does not touch a drop of liquor.

And for the rest of the evening, while the politicians make merry in the bar below, John R. Toole makes merry on his flute in his room above. Yes, the flute. He was an accomplished player of that instrument.

The story begins in the little town of Weston, Aroostook County, Maine, on March 21, 1850. My grandfather was one of six children born to William O'Toole and Honora Ryan O'Toole. Some time later, the family moved to Madison, Wisconsin. There John Ryan O'Toole (in later life he dropped the "O'," perhaps because he thought it sounded shanty-Irish) got a sound three-R's education. At the age of twenty-five, he went west and engaged in mining in

Utah. In 1879 he went to Idaho and took some sort of managerial position at the famous Bonanza Mine near Challis. In that year Challis was one of the most remote mining camps in the West. In 1981 it became a booming mining camp again, and it is still one of the most remote camps in the West. The nearest railroad is almost 150 miles away, at Idaho Falls. The camp is 200 miles south of Missoula.

Challis is surrounded by a massive jumble of peaks and high desert valleys. Around it curls the "River of No Return," the Salmon River of Idaho. Only U.S. Highway 93 connects Challis to the rest of the world. It is high, lonesome, and awesomely beautiful.

In the late 1870s the country was invaded by those models of avarice, the seekers of gold. In a gulch about eight miles upstream from Challis, they made a rich find. It was called Bay Horse Gulch, and the minerals it contained were not gold, but silver, lead, zinc, and tungsten. The Ramshorn Mining & Smelting Company was formed to work the property; a town was built and named Bay Horse. The U.S. Post Office did not approve of the name, and refused to deliver mail to any such place. The city fathers, therefore, changed the name to Aetna, after a city of classical antiquity. This made Bay Horse respectable.

Ramshorn Mining built a smelter to reduce ore by the old process of super-heating. A vein of coal was discovered nearby. The coal fire had to be supplemented with wood to aid the oxidation process, and here John R. Toole appears on the scene.

He first went to work in the Badger Mine, in the famous Bonanza mining district. Within a short time he became superintendent of that mine. Then the ore played out and he moved a few miles down the river to Bay Horse. He took a contract to provide wood fuel for the Ramshorn Smelter, and built a flume three miles up into the mountain where timber was located. Logs of small diameter were tossed into a stream of water and raced down in a violently bobbing current to the smelter.

He had his problems. Once the flume was washed out, and another time a large part of it was destroyed by fire. He lived in Bay Horse, but since that benighted community was only eight miles up the river from Challis, he frequently went to Challis for a taste of civilization, and it was there in 1881 that he met Anna Hardenbrook—the same Annie Hardenbrook who as a baby had peeked out from under the canvas to see the covered wagon submerged in the North Platte River in 1865. Annie was now a blooming eighteen years old, and John R. Toole fell for her with a thud.

Alan ("Doc") Hardenbrook, Anna's physician father, was a restless and frustrated man. The high point of his career had come in 1864 and 1865 when he captained wagon trains across the plains. He first tried mining in Montana, but met with no success. Then he started a freight line from Salt Lake City to Virginia City. In Salt Lake City he made the error of allowing himself to become involved in a dispute with the Mormons. He barely escaped with his hide. If one wanted to do business in or around Salt Lake City, one simply did not trifle with the Mormons. When the Bonanza area of Idaho sprang to life, he moved his wife and daughter to Challis, where he set up a pharmacy and doctor's office next to a saloon that he found to be a convenient accessory to his practice.

John R. was determined to have Anna for a wife, and his courtship was strenuously supported by Anna's mother. Thula Hardenbrook saw in him the kind of man she wanted for a son-in-law. If Anna was dilatory about answering John R.'s letters, Thula took pen in hand and answered them herself. John R. and Anna were married in 1882, and in 1883 Anna gave birth to a girl who was named Honora (later shortened to Nora), after the wife of William O'Toole.

John R. considered Bay Horse (elevation 9,600 feet) to be a repulsive place, with its saloons, bawdy houses, and prostitutes, and he wouldn't consider bringing his wife and baby to such a den of iniquity. So while he worked there he poured out letters to Anna.

Many of them have survived and they are memorable. A clerk in a printing shop who was photographing these letters for me took it upon herself to read them. She asked me: "Mr. Toole, why aren't there any men like that today?" Everyone who has read them seems to have some kind of a reaction of wonderment. The letters are eloquent in their love for his wife and baby, but there is more. There are expressions of faith and firm affirmation of his belief that all would be well if everyone adhered to high standards of kindness, honesty, and morality. All is expressed with a grace and dignity seldom found in the writings of human beings a century later. John R. made occasional spelling and grammatical errors, but his penmanship was perfect.

Doc Hardenbrook had come to the conclusion that he didn't like Idaho and wanted to return to Montana. It was in the days when "Your wish is my command," so Thula, Anna, and baby Honora prepared to return to Anaconda and the Deer Lodge Valley. John R.'s letters hint that he rather wanted to stay where he was, but naturally he would follow his wife and baby. Besides, he truly liked Doc and Mrs. Hardenbrook. So he remained in Idaho only long enough to wind up his affairs. Just before the Hardenbrooks left, he was offered the general superintendency of the Ramshorn Mining & Smelting Company, but he told the owners that he was leaving for Montana. The Ramshorn was becoming a significant mine; before its ore was depleted, it would produce minerals worth $34 million. But that was small potatoes compared to the monstrous mine that awaited John R. in Montana.

The Hardenbrooks left Challis on a cold December day in 1883, headed for Anaconda. This city was only about 125 miles northeast of Challis, but three immense mountain ranges barred the way and no roads yet scaled them. They went by wagon 120 miles south to Idaho Falls, boarded a Utah Northern train, and traveled 200 miles north to Anaconda. John R.'s letters to Anna now traveled this circuitous route.

In June, 1884, six months after Anna's departure, he wrote:

> I could get this contract for another year here, so as to make some money out of it, I think; and they have also offered me every inducement to take an interest in the store here, but I have thought it over well and come to the conclusion that I don't want any of it.... Another thing, and that is, if possible, I want to live near our folks [the Hardenbrooks] always. I know well the value of money, but you know, I take the position that it comes too dear when procured at the sacrifice of friends, relatives and all else. Your father and mother have passed the noontime of their lives. They have nothing half so dear as their children and why should we deny them that comfort? From a selfish standpoint, I want to live near them because I enjoy it myself.... Of course, in leaving hear and going to a new place, I may labor under some disadvantages, for I've had experience enough in the world to know that it takes a good while to get acquainted and established in any place, but while I have good health, I'll get along all right, for I can go to work at *something* in Deer Lodge County, Montana.

He made trips to Montana in 1883 and 1884 to visit little Nora, as well as Anna and the Hardenbrooks, but he didn't waste time while there. He met S. T. Hauser, a most important man in Montana. Hauser was a millionaire miner and banker who would later become territorial governor. John R. investigated a mine 30 miles south of Butte and had the ore assayed by Meader, of Meaderville fame. But he had a contract for wood at the Ramshorn Mining & Smelting Company, and he could not leave Idaho until this contract had been satisfied. He was also now involved in supplying coal to the Ramshorn smelter.

Anna Hardenbrook Toole

John R. finally joined his wife, child, and the Hardenbrooks in Anaconda in 1884. The City Directory for 1889 shows his address as 31 Montana Avenue in Carroll, a working-class suburb of Anaconda, located near the smelter.

In the Anaconda City Directory for 1885, he is listed as a timekeeper in Marcus Daly's smelter. Obviously, at this juncture he was not one of Marcus Daly's "lieutenants." Daly did not put such men to work as timekeepers. Nevertheless, this Anaconda job was an ideal springboard for the political career that John now took up. He probably learned the name and family status of every

Carroll, Montana, an industrial suburb of Anaconda, where John and Anna Toole lived when they first came to Montana

man in the smelter, so that by 1886 he felt sufficiently confident to run for the Territorial Legislature, and he got elected. His constituency was the hard-bitten body of smeltermen—Democrats all, union members all. They would elect him five times to the legislative halls, though he was never a bombastic speaker and always preferred to work in the background.

I have always had the impression that John R. was a reluctant politician. His reflective turn of mind and his interest in matters of the intellect somehow never seemed to be in concert with my concept of an extroverted, hurly-burly politician. The fact is, however, that politics was ingrained in him. On September 12, 1884, he wrote to Anna from Bay Horse, where he was still stuck with his wood contract:

I'm giving some attention to County politics. I don't expect to be here for election but before I say goodbye to Custer County, Idaho, I propose to show Shoup and Company that we can run this county just as we please. [Shoup later became the first governor of Idaho. His grandson, Richard, moved to Missoula about twenty years ago and became mayor. He then ran for Congress and served two terms in Congress from the Western District. The Shoups were always a strong Republican family. A little town on the River of No Return is named for them.] We had our Democratic primary meeting the other night and I got every vote in Bay Horse for delegate to the Convention. I have five proxies besides my own vote. Will [John R.'s younger brother] is one of the delegates from Bonanza and will have five or six proxies besides, so that I think he and I will come pretty near controlling the convention and nominating just who we want to. Our Convention will be on the 28th inst. The Republicans held theirs and Jim Porter, who was a candidate for assessor and collector, got badly beaten. Shoup worked against him and said that he would stand in with the Mining Companies if he was elected. . . . I don't think I shall ever again take as much interest in local politics

202

as I am doing here, for there is no money in it, but as a parting reminder I propose to show that myself and friends can 'rule the roost here' and we propose to do it.

John R. Toole was quite active in the 1887 session of the Territorial Legislature. An inspection of the *House Journal* gives one the impression that he was in effect the Democratic Floor Leader, although that position was not officially created until many years later. He was Chairman of the Committee on Territorial Affairs, although the *Journal* does not indicate just what the committee was supposed to do. He sponsored a bill to donate funds to John X. Biedler, the ferocious, man-eating Vigilante, whose undaunted courage helped rid the state of outlaws in the 1860s. Always an opponent of booze, he pushed a bill to make the cost of liquor licenses high.

In the Legislature, the much revered Wilbur Fisk Sanders, a Republican, came over and congratulated John R., as did many other members. And no doubt he attracted the attention of Marcus Daly.

But it now seems probable that the man who was responsible for finally getting the two together was Doc Hardenbrook. Doc knew everyone in Deer Lodge County. He now had a promising young son-in-law who was an experienced miner and an eager politician. The partnership was logical and Doc arranged the introduction.

On February 22, 1889, Pres. Grover Cleveland signed the Omnibus Bill, an enabling act that would admit Montana to statehood after it drew up a proper Constitution. On July 4, 1889, the Constitutional Convention began deliberations, and John R. Toole was a delegate representing Deer Lodge County.

John R. Toole, 1890

In 1889 the Anaconda City Directory shows John R. as a "buyer." Buyer of what? We don't know. In 1890 he was shown as a partner in Toole & Walsh, Harness Makers, with an address at 105 Main Street. The Tri-County Historical Society shows that a house of ill repute occupied the upper floor of this two-story building. John R. was a most upright man; one wonders how he coped with this situation. Toole & Walsh existed until 1898, but John R. was becoming a man of affairs; Walsh probably ran the harness business.

By 1889 John R. was firmly in league with Marcus Daly and the stage was set for the paradoxical drama of his life: his role as an upright, self-respecting, religious man who found it possible to do some distasteful work for the benefit of the famous and sometimes infamous Copper Kings of Montana. He chiefly served his employer, Marcus Daly, but in the Constitutional Convention of 1889, where the interests of W. A. Clark and F. Augustus Heinze were parallel with those of Daly, his actions helped all three of the kings. Specifically, John R. wrote a clause for the Montana State Constitution that markedly assisted the entire burgeoning mining industry. This was the soon-to-be-famous "net proceeds tax," which became a cause celebre in Montana politics.

When the Constitutional Convention met in Helena in 1889, it essentially faced two choices in regard to mine taxation. The first was an ad valorem tax—a tax on the property in proportion to its value. The second was a net proceeds tax—in effect an income tax, based on what the mine earned. The severance tax that is the basis for most mine taxation today had not yet come into use. The Copper Kings favored the net proceeds tax, and John R. had a hand in writing it. The wording was short and simple: "The annual net proceeds of all mines and mining claims shall be taxed as provided by law." This was the gist of what other states had enacted and successfully applied. In Montana the tax subsequently had its teeth removed in the Legislature, which wrote an implementation law giving the copper interests countless loopholes to crawl through and avoid reasonable payments.

In a speech John R. lambasted motions in favor of the ad valorem tax:

I suppose the motive in introducing those two sections [the ad valorem measure] was to get at the proposition of taxing mining property. I trust it is not necessary for me to take up much time in discussing this substitute, because there are some very appropriate reasons why it should not prevail. I apprehend, sir, that the gentleman who offered this resolution, or this section, and others who may support it, are not perhaps aware of what the condition of the mining interests in this Territory or coming state is or may be. I apprehend that they are not aware, perhaps, that it is an utter impossibility to tax mines and assess them at any value that can be agreed upon by any two persons as to what they are worth. I want to state for the information of the gentleman and others, that my business, so far as I have had a business here, is in that line to a certain extent. I want to state that there are not two men in the same line of business, whether they may be assessors, mining experts or professors of mineralogy, that can come anywhere near agreeing on the value of mining property. Even the world-famed mines, such as the Granite Mountain and the Anaconda, and mines of that class, which perhaps those gentlemen imagine can be assessed upon a proper valuation, I desire to say that I believe it to be a fact that there are no two assessors in this Territory, each one basing a judgment upon his knowledge of those mines, that can come within a million dollars of each other as to what they are worth. There are other phases of this question, too. There are a great many poor men who are making their living in this line of business, and it is a fact that they oftentimes have a property that they may

204

value at $10,000, $20,000, or $50,000, and that might be assessed at that valuation, and nine times out of ten, it is a safe assertion to make, that they are not worth 50 cents. And further than that, there is another and very potent reason, and that is this, that I am satisfied it will defeat this constitution if placed before the people, because the people in the mining counties and people who understand the situation would think it worked a hardship to a large class of people, in fact, the people upon whom the Territory is dependent for its very sustenance. The provision as provided for by the report of this committee is the same that is in force in all the constitutions of the different states where mining is carried on to any extent. In Nevada, Colorado, California and in the state of Dakota; and I want to assert again that there is no question in my mind that if this matter should be incorporated, this section would defeat the ratification of the constitution in this Territory. I trust it will not be necessary for me to go into further details to show up this matter, because I believe it is apparent to the members of this convention who are familiar with mining in all its phases, and who hail from the counties where the mining interests prevail to a great extent. For that reason, I will not take up any more of the time of the convention, believing it is needless for me to do so and believing that this amendment as offered will not be supported by the vote of this convention.

John R.'s net proceeds provision was commendably brief. Constitutions should not contain administrative minutiae that are locked into the document for all time to come. They should convey only clear constitutional intent and leave the implementation to the Legislature. The evil of the net proceeds tax lay in the acts of the Legislature implementing the tax. For example, it permitted a mining company to write off all investments in plant and equipment in one year. This is the modern concept of accelerated depreciation with a vengeance. The tax was paid not to the state but to the mining counties, with Silver Bow the main recipient. It was computed by the county assessor, who was given power to examine the company's books, but in fact never did so. He just accepted the figures supplied him by the company. The average Silver Bow County assessor wouldn't know what he was looking at anyway. Whatever taxes the mining companies deigned to pay usually just disappeared. Apparently the corruption in Butte was so massive that little reached the county, city, or school district.

Nevertheless, the net proceeds tax throve. Among its backers, a decade after its enactment, was no less a figure than the governor, Joseph K. Toole—no kin, curiously, to John R. The Toole who was governor and John R. Toole have been confused in the minds of Montanans for almost a century. Both were workers in the Democratic Party, both were delegates to the Constitutional Convention, both were legislators. But Joe was something a good deal

205

In 1912, Anna Toole informed her husband that he had an appointment to have his photograph taken. He dressed, settled into a book and forgot the appointment. When the photographer came, he rushed out to the patio and set his derby hat firmly on his head. At the last minute, someone placed granddaughter Thula Clifton on his lap. He grasped her firmly, stared grimly at the camera, the bulb was squeezed and this photo is the result. A typical Toole family performance.

more. He was elected governor three times, in 1890, 1900, and 1904. Joe was a big, bluff man, a good politician and a likeable fellow. But by 1900 he had fallen into the tender embraces of W. A. Clark and F. Augustus Heinze (Marcus Daly having died). He pronounced the net proceeds tax "wise and salutary," and stated that this provision was "responsible for the development of great properties in the state." He had no choice. The two remaining Copper Kings would expect no less.

But if the tax throve, it was by 1902 an open scandal. Said Wilbur Fisk Sanders, with muffled outrage:

> Claiming for the founders of our commonwealth all that is their due, it were too much to affirm that they were not subject to the infirmities of human nature and made no mistakes. With the courage which was a conspicuous trait in their character to assist in a hazardous, hopeful infant industry, they took upon themselves a portion of its burdens by absolving it from its share of taxation. When thus delivered, the interest and amount was small but it has now grown to colossal proportions and is one of our chiefest and remunerative resources. But the [tax] advantage has not been relinquished, and what in its nature was designed to be temporary, by the adroitness of greed has now become woven in the Constitution.

Outrage did not daunt the Kings. The tax was still in effect in 1918 when a scholarly economist named Louis Levine joined the faculty of the University of Montana and wrote a treatise called

206

"The Taxation of Mines in Montana." The work was a mild analysis of the net proceeds tax and why it failed to produce revenue from mines equal to that in other states. The innocuous little pamphlet so angered Anaconda Copper that it swung a mailed fist and got Levine fired. This crude act forever haunted Anaconda, and it helped to bring to the university's professors permanent tenure and academic freedom. In 1924, under the leadership of Gov. Joe Dixon, the net proceeds tax was repealed and the severance tax was fastened onto Anaconda.

The story is disgraceful enough, but less so in its context. "Conflict of interest" was unknown in 1889. Delegates to the Constitutional Convention openly represented various "interests," of which the cattle and mining interests led the field. Delegates were expected to come down on the side of their particular interest. Mining was the largest industry in the state and the largest employer. Every county in western Montana had mines large and small, and delegates from these counties did not hesitate to support a provision that benefited such a large constituency.

It was not said of John R. Toole that he was in bad company in lining up on the side of W. A. Clark. When Clark got up on the floor and declared, "I am here representing the great mining interests of the state," no one thought ill of him. And so far as John R. went, everyone knew that he represented Marcus Daly. Daly was the most popular man in the state. Far from regarding Daly as an adversary, his miners figured that if Marcus Daly wanted something it would automatically be good for them too.

Probably the Taxation Committee of the convention connived to pass a tax that would lend itself to manipulation by the big mines. No one will ever know. But if the delegates connived, I can find no evidence that John R. was one of the connivers.

Besides expecting the Constitutional Convention to provide for low taxes on mines, Marcus Daly hoped that the delegates would fulfill another goal, and John R. set about to promote it. Rising from his seat one day, he said:

I have a proposition that I wish to state in relation to this capitol question and I have concluded that this is as opportune a time as I will get. I want to say in the first place that I came here, and my constituents came here, willing to abide by the decision of this convention wherever they may see fit to locate the state capitol, and also willing to accept the verdict of the people whenever it goes before them at an election. I want to present this thing to the members of the convention in a business light. I want to present it in the shape of urging as one of the claims we would put forth in favor of our city of Anaconda, and as a matter of economy to the state, that I have this proposition here to make to this convention, and I am

207

ready to back it up. If it is the will of the members of this convention, and their verdict, to temporarily locate the capitol at our city, we will agree to furnish to the state, until such time as the vote of the people shall decide where the permanent location of the capitol shall be, a temporary capital, quarters for state officers' accommodations, etc., and a building for the legislature to meet in. I do not make this in any spirit of buncombe. I am serious and earnest, and ready to back it up in any way that this convention may see fit to require. I think it will make a matter of five or ten thousand dollars to the state, and economy is something that has been dwelt upon here a good deal in our deliberations so far, and as a matter it seems to me it ought to be taken into serious consideration by every member of this convention. It is a matter of five or ten thousand dollars a year to the state over any other proposition that has yet been made. I make this in all candor and seriousness and place it before the convention now for their deliberation and judgment and verdict.

The offer to build public buildings for the state government in Anaconda must have given the young John R. Toole a sense of power, though the delegates no doubt were aware that the offer really came from Marcus Daly, who loved his little city. In 1889 Anaconda was a pleasant and inviting town. A pretty stream curled through it. Trees throve and green grass waved in the breeze. The huge piles of black slag, the monstrous smelter, and the great stack were far in the future. Now Anaconda is ugly, and it's just as well that the capitol was not located there.

About five miles north of Three Forks, on a barren hill, lie the remains of some wooden shacks and caved-in mine shafts. It is a dismal windblown place, and it is all that is left of Copper City, Montana.

Under this site is a vein of exceedingly rich copper—but only one vein, and it tapers to nothing a few feet below the surface. Marcus Daly seemed to be able to smell copper, and when he was prospecting one day in the summer of 1889 he found this vein. His natural enthusiasm mounted quickly; he filed claims and, returning to Butte, started to make plans to develop another great copper mine. This time he would plan a city and its surroundings that would avoid the mistakes made at Butte and Anaconda.

He sent a peremptory telegram to John R. Toole, who was busy at the Constitutional Convention in Helena. The wire told John R. to meet Daly in Three Forks at once—and to bring a tape measure, a checkbook, and some old clothes. John R. did as he was told, and brought Doc Hardenbrook as well. Joining Daly, the three laid out sites for a smelter and a city to be formed of broad, tree-shaded boulevards running like the spokes of a wheel. Daly departed, and John R. sent Doc out to round up the owners of the future city. Once they were assembled, John R. produced his checkbook. There was little haggling. John R. offered large sums, and the owners, taken by surprise, readily signed deeds that had been prepared in Helena. Paying out $95,000, John R. got title to the whole site in his own name, then went to the courthouse and deeded the property to James Ben Ali Haggin, the shadowy, enormously rich Lebanese investor in San Francisco who was among those who bankrolled Marcus Daly.

Copper City was launched. Father-in-law and son-in-law lay down on the green grass to wait for the train back to Helena. John R. looked at Doc and made a mental note to find a good job for the old man when Copper City opened up. John R. was always kind and considerate to Doc, often sending him little checks so that he could go out and perhaps find himself a mine of his own.

Doc could never seem to settle in one place or accomplish much, though he had good credentials. Born in Mount Gilead, Ohio, in 1831, he got a medical degree from Monmouth College in Monmouth, Illinois. He served as a country doctor in Illinois. He led his first wagon train to Montana in 1864, and the next year returned and brought his family.

He went into practice as a doctor, but doctors did not do well in the Montana of the 1860s. They could not effectively treat patients for the disorders common to the frontier—cholera, pneumonia, typhoid, tuberculosis, silicosis. Lacking sepsis, they could not even successfully treat wounds or compound fractures. Many doctors went into mining or sawmilling to supplement their income, as did Doc. He was also a druggist and a freighter. Later he was superintendent of schools in Deer Lodge County.

The train arrived. John R. and Doc got aboard reluctantly. Lying in the sun and tall grass at Three Forks had been a sublime little interlude away from the hurly-burly of the Constitutional Convention. That night, from Helena, John R. sent Anna a letter that is the only historically verifiable mention of bribery in that conclave.

Oh! How I hate to come back here and start in on this old capitol question again. It was so pleasant and grassy down at Three Forks that I just wanted to stay there, but just as soon as I get back here, the lobbying commences and one and then another comes to me, and wants to know if we had not better offer this fellow or that, a thousand or three thousand dollars for his vote. I despise such business and hope that it will be settled tomorrow or next day sure. A number of Anaconda people came in this evening and I just stole away from them long enough to write you this letter.

In the last years of his life, Doc got a house in the Rattlesnake Valley north of Missoula, and dozed in the sun in the front door with his cup of grog and his memories of the Oregon Trail and the

*Alan Hardenbrook with
great granddaughter Thula
Clifton*

days of '64 and '65. In 1916, after the death of John R. Toole, Doc
moved in with Anna at 1005 Gerald Avenue, in Missoula. He died
in 1919.

No sooner had the Constitutional Convention adjourned than a
session of the Legislature was called. Montana now had a new
Constitution, ratified by the voters. To the immense satisfaction of
its citizens, Montana had become the forty-first state in the Union.
The people eagerly looked forward to an act of supreme
importance—the selection of two United States senators. Before
1913 senators were chosen by the state Legislature.

The Republican party was in the ascendancy. It controlled the
Presidency and both houses of Congress. It was therefore necessary
that every loyal and electible Democrat file for the Legislature in
an attempt to send two Democrats to the U.S. Senate. John R. Toole
filed and was elected.

The election produced a deadlock. There were eight Republican
senators and eight Democrats. In the senate a tie vote could be
broken by the lieutenant governor, who presided over that body,
but one of the Republican senators was sick and the lieutenant
governor refused to break the tie in the Democrats' favor. Repeated
attempts were made to organize the two bodies, but they failed.
There was an equal deadlock in the House.

After much partisan bickering, the House Democrats moved out

210

of the capitol (the old Territorial Legislature building, now Lewis and Clark County Courthouse) and set up their own "House" in an adjacent building. The Republicans succeeded in organizing the Senate only to have it deadlock, causing the Senate Democrats to walk out and set up shop in still another building. The great new state of Montana was not getting off to an auspicious start.

For ninety days, the partisans jousted. People took party loyalty seriously in those days. At length the Democrats sent W. A. Clark and Martin Maginnis to Washington and the Republicans sent Wilbur Fisk Sanders and T. C. Power. No state had ever before sent four U.S. senators to Washington.

Levi P. Morton, the Vice President of the United States and President of the Senate, thereupon called Republican Pres. Benjamin Harrison on the new-fangled gadget called the telephone.

"Mr. President, do you know what the new state of Montana did?"

"No, what?"

"They sent four senators back here."

"What! Four senators?"

"Yes, sir. The two parties in the legislature deadlocked and each party sent two senators."

"Well, I'll be damned," said the President. "You know what to do with the two Democrats, don't you?"

"Send 'em home!"

"That's right!"

The President hung up the phone and W. A. Clark, soon to be the world's richest man, wended his way disconsolately back to Helena.

John R. Toole had run again for the 1891 Legislature and once again was handily re-elected. He was nominated for speaker but immediately removed his name as a nominee. He was beginning the self-effacement that would make him the shadowy figure in the titanic battles to come. Joseph K. Toole was elected governor; his determined effort to seek the limelight paralleled that of his namesake to avoid it.

Mining was John R. Toole's all-consuming interest, and during the years 1894 to 1898 he undertook long journeys on behalf of Marcus Daly and Anaconda to inspect mining properties. His trip to Mexico brings into this story the great Greene Cananea mine just south of the Arizona boundary in Sonora.

The Cananea mine had existed for centuries. The earliest Spanish explorers mined copper there, and in the 1890s an American cattleman and adventurer named William C. Greene promoted and parlayed it into a producing property. Greene was a plunger. He arranged for substantial financial support in Wall Street, but

211

he quickly found that the operation of a large mine, a smelter, and a concentrator was beyond his ability and his line of credit was cut off.

H. H. Rogers of Standard Oil had known of the existence of the Cananea mine for several years prior to 1906, and in that year Rogers and Anaconda president John D. Ryan stepped in, paid off Greene's debts and formed the Greene Cananea Consolidated Copper Company. Greene was given a block of stock, and returned to the work he loved best, the operation of his 500,000-acre cattle ranch in Sonora, stocked with forty thousand head of cattle.

John R. Toole visited the Cananea in the 1890s and probably made the report on it to Rogers and Ryan that led to their buying it. The mine was eventually turned over to Anaconda. Then John R. journeyed south to Mexico City and came back to Montana with a collection of Mayan figurines and Mexican pottery.

When he returned, he was interviewed by a reporter from the *Anacona Standard*. "Mr. Toole is not known as much of a talker, but if one succeeds in drawing him out, he proves to be one of the most fascinating conversationalists around," said the *Standard*. The story went on to tell of John R.'s adventures with Mexican robbers and of the hostility of the people.

After reading of John R.'s experiences at Cananea, I was overcome with curiosity, so I journeyed there in the spring of 1983. I was not permitted to take my American rented car into Mexico, so I hired an ancient Mexican car with bald tires, broken windows, and a coughing engine.

Cananea is only about 80 miles south of the Arizona border. It is reached by a fractured asphalt road that leads across immense savannahs of waist-high, billowing grass, the vast prairies upon which Colonel Greene grazed his huge herds. After a time I saw a great mountain looming ahead, and beneath it Cananea. The mine and smelter are just above the town, and the tall stacks were spewing out the arsenic-laden smoke that has killed the grass for miles around. So far as air-pollution abatement is concerned, Cananea has not reached the level of Anaconda in 1920. In that year Anaconda Copper built the famous high stack above its smelter and learned how to trap arsenic emissions.

Cananea is an ugly place, but it does have two motels. I speak no Spanish, but quickly the message was communicated to me in the better of the two that they would not cater to a gringo. At the poorer motel I undertook a bribe, and a room was provided. I was lulled to sleep by the pulsating, vibrating roar of the smelter. But at about 4 a.m. I was awakened by a big pack of semi-wild dogs swirling around the motel. I got cold in bed and opened a bureau drawer in hope of finding a blanket. Instead I found the drawer packed with garbage—cigarette butts, banana peels, sanitary napkins, and

Kleenex. In the morning I visited a local bookstore, to discover that it was stacked with Marxist literature. Above the books, huge photos of the grim faces of Marx and Lenin glared down at me. me.

I headed my Mexican limousine toward Douglas, Arizona. When I looked back I was struck by the similarity of Cananea and Anaconda—except that Cananea vibrates with life, while the hand of death rests on Anaconda. The Anaconda Minerals Company no longer owns the Cananea mine. Fifty-one percent of it is in the hands of the Mexican government, and if Anaconda keeps people there I did not see any.

John R. later went to Alaska. The history of the great mine at Cordova is not available to us, but it appears that he visited that place. Cordova was one of the jewels in the diadem of the Kennecott Copper Company. John R. is said to have regretted that he did not acquire this mine for Anaconda.

In the years 1894 to 1898, John R. was by no means associated with Marcus Daly in all his activities. He owned a lead mine at Melrose, and he searched the country over for attractive mining property. He visited Baker City, Oregon; Omaha; Denver; Billings (where he liked the climate); Livingston (where the wind was blowing just as it blows today); Missoula; and Bear Lake, British Columbia. On the journey into British Columbia he took Doc with him. They went via Bonner's Ferry, Idaho, and the Kootenai River. Then John alone made a 120-mile horseback ride into the wilderness. Poor Doc! He wanted to make the trip so much. But probably John R. thought Doc should not go because of his health.

The letters to Anna streamed home. He was never happy away from her. Anna had a beautiful singing voice. He importunes her constantly to keep practicing her voice so that she can sing for him when he gets home. But she had their five children to care for— Nora, born in 1883; Thula, 1885; Allan, 1887; Howard, 1890; and Brice, 1893.

Marcus Daly was obtaining the coal for his smelter from a place called Cinnabar south of Livingston; another source for coal was the mines at Red Lodge. John R. made several trips to these properties.

Another time, he went to Missoula to inspect a mine described as 125 miles away, via Stevensville and Corvallis. This puts the mine either in the Big Hole Basin or in Idaho near the mouth of the North Fork of the Salmon River.

He visited Virginia City and called it a "torpid old town." He had a mine at Red Bluff on the Jefferson River. While he was in this country he tried several times to visit Sarah Raymond Herndon, the diarist of Doc's wagon train, but could not find her.

213

When he wrote of the two political parties, the name Republican was written with a small "r," the name Democrat with a huge "D."

He never failed to go to church when away from home and, if he could, he attended talks by the itinerant lecturers who passed through the country in those days.

In one letter from Helena he wrote: "'Tis said that the society ladies of this metropolis are among the most accomplished and entertaining anywhere. Should I be so fortunate as to meet any of them, I will view them with a 'cricket's eye' and give you my opinion. However, I have no inclination and don't think I will have any spare time to devote to the cultivation of the 'Creme de la Creme' of this burg. Am more than satisfied with what I possess in that line myself."

From the Rodgers Hotel ("Wm. Kennedy, Prop.") in Missoula he reported that he saw "the benevolent face of Bro. Stanley. He looks much thinner and more care worn than he used to be, and it struck me that perhaps the cares and duties of married life weighed heavily, or perhaps his ideal is shattered, and instead of the airy form of his fantastic fancy, he finds, after all, only a mortal of common clay for a conjugal mate. Selah!"

He engaged in industrial espionage in Denver: "The mission that I am now in is a delicate one and it will be a difficult job for any one to get the information that my company requires of me.

"I understand that the refineries [smelters] here guard some of

John R. Toole and family (back row, left to right) Brice, Nora, Allan, Thula, Howard (front row) John R., John R. Jr., Anna

their secrets very jealously and admit no one to try and get at the bottom of things. I may have to hire out as a laborer for a week or two, but then they might not give me a job, but then, you know, I'm pretty smooth and guess I can get most of what I want."

After spending a day at an assayer's office he wrote: "I think Chemistry must be a very fascinating subject. To take a common looking piece of iron ore and, during the process of analysis, find what beautiful colored liquids of green, pink, and red are evolved. To combine the two invisible gases of hydrogen and oxygen in a glass retort and produce water; to convert silver into crystals that look like common salt, and then change back again to the pure metal. 'Tis all so interesting that I don't wonder that the alchemists of old sought to find the secret whereby they might convert the baser metals into gold and silver."

Another: "I have been brushing up on my trigonometry and surveying and my head is so full of sines and cosines that I must get away from it and get this letter to you."

And from Virginia City: "This place seems to have the mark of age and decay. Some of the old-timers make me think of the Salmon Eaters [Indians]. They stand around and look at me with a sort of wondering stare, and I sometimes hear them whisper that a representative of the great Anaconda Co. is in town looking for mines to buy and every fellow that has a prospect comes around and wants an introduction and asks me to look at his claim. Some of them have been here 20 years staying with prospects that aren't worth a hundred dollars. I can't help but feel sorry for them."

In 1894 Toole was Marcus Daly's chief lieutenant in one of the wildest battles in Montana's political history.

William Andrews Clark, now a bitter enemy of Marcus Daly, scented a chance to even the score against him. Knowing that Daly wanted Anaconda to become the permanent capital of the state, Clark decided to lead and finance a campaign to locate the permanent capital in Helena. By a constitutional fiat, the matter had to be decided by popular vote.

Before the election, Clark's paper, the *Butte Miner*, and Daly's sheet, the *Anaconda Standard*, bombarded each other with a ceaseless flow of insults and invective. The populace became aroused. Daly sent a wire to Kenneth Ross in Bonner: "Tuesday, the people will decide on the location of the permanent capital. Give all your crews the day off on that day and provide each man with a silver dollar. Tell every man to go to the polls and vote for Anaconda for state capital." (Ross did as he was told, and then, as he usually did when something made him angry, he resigned.)

Clark won the battle for Helena, and on election night the atmosphere there was like a Roman holiday. Clark was pulled

215

through the city in an open carriage drawn by Helena's leading citizens. He relished the adulation and smiled broadly at the fireworks, the brass band, and the shouting crowd. He ordered free drinks for the entire city.

Losing the election was a bad blow for Marcus Daly, for he was a spirited and gallant figure who liked to win. He cared nothing for ostentatious display of personal wealth. But he burst with pride for his city of Anaconda; for his Montana Hotel there, which for Montana was lavish and grand; for his railroad; for his ranch; and for his race horses.

His personal tastes were simple. He lived in his hotel in Anaconda, and when he visited Butte, he stayed in a miner's bunk-house. He enjoyed the rough company of miners and smeltermen, and he was constantly with them in saloons, in underground mines, or in their homes. No working man felt ill at ease when in the company of Marcus Daly.

However, he once had to face the threat of a strike.

The Butte Miner's Union called on him and asked for a big wage increase and a voice in working conditions. His miners were already the highest paid in the country. His response to the demands:

"Well, fellows, I can't pay you that much but this is a free country. You've got every right to strike. I've been on strike myself.

"Here's what I'll do. If you go out on strike, there'll be a lot of suffering among your families. When that time comes, call on me. Not one miner's wife or child will go hungry in the city of Butte. I'll pay for the groceries personally and see that they're delivered." Then he winked and said, "Remember, there won't be a cent for beer!"

Then he got a little tougher. "As to your other demands, I'm the boss of this outfit, and I don't intend to divide my responsibilities with anybody. Now you boys go home and talk this over with your women folks."

Talk to the women folks indeed! The miners got an earful: Remember when you were sick and Mr. Daly sent you that check? Remember when you got hurt and Mr. Daly kept your wages going until you went back to work? Remember when Kathleen died and he bought your ticket so you could go to her funeral?

There was no strike.

Was it any wonder that John R. Toole was drawn to this expansive man with his rare mixture of humor, sagacity and vision? In John R.'s letters there are only a few references to Mr. D., as he called him, but the devotion and respect shine through.

Daly's failure to make Anaconda Montana's capital led him to lose interest in his city. Thenceforward he spent most of his time on his baronial estate at Hamilton.

In 1898 W. A. Clark made the supreme effort of his insatiable

216

Marcus Daly   *W. A. Clark*

quest to become a United States senator. He had lost out in the 1891 deadlock fiasco, and he had lost again in 1893 when his bribery became too flagrant. Daly had helped defeat him both times, and Clark was consumed with bitterness against Daly. "This time," said Clark's son Charlie, "we'll send the old man to the Senate or the poorhouse." By then Marcus Daly was lying ill in the Sherry-Netherlands Hotel in New York. But James Ben Ali Haggin, the great, brooding moneybags behind Daly, responded: "So long as I have any interest in the mines in Montana, I shall never permit W. A. Clark to serve in the United States Senate."

William Andrews Clark was a diminutive man. He had long hair, a carefully trimmed mustache and a full, flowing beard. From behind this foliage, two cold, glittering eyes gazed out upon the world. He was an amoral man, a sagacious man, and a man possessed of utter determination. And he was a man of great physical courage.

Born in 1839, he was a young man in Iowa when the Civil War broke out. He joined the Confederate army and served for a short time. Somehow, he got out of his service and headed straight for Colorado. He didn't quit the Confederate cause because of cowardice. It was just that the cause didn't offer any profit, and he was incapable of being moved by the great ideals that surrounded the war. He mined for a time in Colorado, and made careful notes on mining in general. Then he heard about Bannack, Montana, and landed there in the spring of 1863. Mining in Colorado Gulch, west of Bannack, he did quite well. But Clark's nose for a dollar was unerring. It didn't take long for him to conclude that selling essential goods to miners was more certain and more lucrative than joining the throng who were struggling in the gulches.

The mammoth gold strikes at Alder Gulch and Virginia City

took place shortly after Clark arrived in Montana. With his profits from Colorado Gulch, he gathered together a string of pack animals, loaded them in Bannack with such items as flour, sugar, bacon, salt, whiskey, nails, tools, and tobacco, and headed for Virginia City—alone.

This 80-mile journey was dangerous. Bands of Blackfeet, Sioux, Bannock, and Cheyenne Indians preyed on white travelers. The country was overrun with the bandits known as road agents. They had killed and robbed more than one hundred miners. Clark put his rifle across his knees and kept his piercing eyes on every gulch, rock, and patch of brush. He made it. He pitched his tent, spread out his wares on a plank, kept his weapons at the ready, and quickly sold his merchandise to the Alder Gulch miners at a 300 percent profit. His horses were not loaded when he headed back for Bannack, but his saddle bags contained a commodity more to his liking —buckskin pouches of raw gold.

Clark was a sitting duck for the murderous bands of road agents, but he didn't follow the well-known road between Bannack and Virginia City. He guided his horses into remote canyons, through deep forests, out onto lonely, windswept ridges, and pulled into Bannack at dusk. People didn't pay much attention to the solitary, taciturn, little man when he climbed off his horse, and after dark he squirreled away his bags of gold in a safe hiding place.

This was Clark's life for three years. Sometimes he jollied with the road agents in the honky-tonks of Bannack and Virginia City. They would have killed him for $5, but he never gave them a chance. When the Vigilantes of Montana were formed to hunt down and hang the road agents, Clark took no part in the effort, for there was no money in it.

He made several trips to Salt Lake City and returned with goods in a wagon. When a sudden shortage of tobacco hit the mining camps, he journeyed to Boise and returned with a wagonload of the stuff.

In 1866 miners made a rich strike in the Garnet Range on Elk Creek, just below the Top O'Deep. Clark hurried there, brought his goods up Bear Gulch and Deep Gulch, and crossed the little meadow at the top. One wonders if he appreciated the wild flowers or the view. Unlikely.

In that same year, Bear Gulch roared to life, and Clark was there, hawking his goods on a raw plank to the miners in wild and primitive Beartown. I went up to Beartown a few summers ago. It turned out to be a grove of giant cottonwoods, their leaves fluttering listlessly on a hot summer day. No matter how I tried, I could not recreate the swarming miners and the little, beady-eyed man behind his plank. No photographs were ever taken of Beartown. It sprang to obstreperous life, then died leaving no trace. Only the tales survive.

In 1864 a rich strike of placer gold was discovered on Silver Bow Creek, 40 miles south of Deer Lodge. The mines produced well for several years, but then they petered out, and by the time W. A. Clark visited Butte in 1872, most of the miners had departed. A few, however, had stayed because they were intrigued by reefs of hardrock silver and copper ore. One had sunk a deep shaft.

Clark had come a long way. He had started a bank in Deer Lodge and married a startling brunette named Katherine Stauffer. From his Colorado experience, Clark knew that the big money was in hard-rock mining, not in scrabbling for nuggets in a stream bed. He looked over the outcroppings of ore at Butte, and the realization came to him that here was something special, something big. He promptly gathered up some ore samples, filed some claims, and with his wife and two children headed east for New York City, where he enrolled as a student in the School of Mines at Columbia University.

His ore samples proved to be what he had thought they were: fabulously rich chunks of silver and copper. After a year at Columbia, he went back to Silver Bow Creek.

Bill Farlin was an easy-going prospector, but he liked money as well as the next fellow. In Clark's absence, he had discovered a fabulously rich silver lode at Butte, called the Travona. Freighting ore out of Butte was virtually impossible because the nearest railroad was at Salt Lake City. So Bill Farlin got a loan of $35,000 from W. A. Clark's bank to build a mill to treat his ore. Clark took a mortgage on Farlin's silver lode to secure the loan on the smelter. Farlin couldn't make the payments on his loan, so Clark foreclosed on the rich silver lode. Clark promised Farlin that he would operate the mine and smelter efficiently and would use the proceeds to pay off Farlin's note. But somehow the mine didn't do too well under Clark, and the rich silver mine passed to his ownership. Bill Farlin could hardly understand what had happened to him. And W. A. Clark was launched on a career, the ruthlessness of which would make him the world's richest man. The Travona, after Clark became owner, produced fabulously.

Clark built a smelter, the Centennial, and started making enormous profits. But while he was attending Columbia University, a new personality had arrived in Butte. He was a big, hearty Irishman, open hearted and generous, although he possessed the same keen nose for a dollar as Clark. Marcus Daly had powerful backers: George Hearst, James Ben Ali Haggin, and Lloyd Tevis, San Francisco capitalists. Daly and Clark were as different as a grizzly bear and a rattlesnake. Daly started the Anaconda mine and drove its shaft 300 feet to a veritable bonanza of copper. The two men watched each other warily.

219

Needing greater smelting capacity, Clark succeeded in persuading some Colorado money men to form the Colorado and Montana Smelting Company. Clark naturally wanted to be included as a stockholder in the new company, but the Colorado men made some inquiries about him and heard him called a "juggernaut"; they declined to include him as an owner but did agree to process his ore. Later on, they offered him 20 percent of the stock because they heard that Clark was about to build his own smelter. They heard correctly. Clark did so and took all his ore-processing business away from Colorado and Montana, but still owned 20 percent of its stock, which paid him handsomely when the company was liquidated. He had eliminated a competitor, and now smelted his own ore for nothing. No one dared trifle with this predatory man.

In 1877 Clark was appointed a major of volunteers, with a battalion of troops raised in Deer Lodge and Butte to intercept Chief Joseph and his Nez Perce Tribe. By the time Clark arrived, the Indians were already in retreat from the U.S. Army after the Battle of the Big Hole. But Clark was proud of his foray in later years, and talked exhaustively about it.

In 1878, after instructing his minions in Butte to keep an eye on Daly, Clark toured Europe with his family. He learned French, took lessons in elocution, and sought opportunities to speak in public wherever he could. His dress became fastidious. Politics was on his mind, and the U.S. Senate began to loom large in his plans for the future. Back in Montana, Marcus Daly was making the Butte Hill the richest piece of real estate in the world and proudly building his city of Anaconda.

In 1884 Clark was elected president of Montana's first Constitutional Convention and presided ably, showing a sharp knowledge of parliamentary procedure and a willingness to discipline delegates who were out of order. He and Daly, also a delegate, had an amicable relationship. But it was all for naught. Montana's petition for statehood became bogged down in partisanship at the national level, and the petition was denied.

In 1888 Clark ran for territorial delegate to Congress. He should have won. Montana was strongly Democratic, and Clark and Daly had a stranglehold on the Democratic party in the state. But to his dismay, Clark found Daly opposing him, and he was defeated by Thomas Carter, a Republican. The little man's flame of hatred for Daly sprang brightly to life after this affair.

Then came the ridiculous episode in which Clark was elected by the Democrats in 1890 and journeyed to Washington, only to be sent home. He tried again in 1893, and for the first time scattered some money around. Rumors of bribery raced through the state. Marcus Daly opposed him and the Legislature turned thumbs down on him. This was a bitter blow, because the Democrats, under

Grover Cleveland, controlled the Congress, and Clark would have been seated.

Clark's victory over Daly in his struggle to win the state capital for Helena in 1894 whetted his appetite, and by 1898, the year in which Montana again chose a Legislature that would elect a U.S. senator, he was ready again.

John R. Toole did not wish to run in 1898 for the Legislature, and no one will ever know whether Daly importuned him to run or if he considered it his obligation to do so, but run he did and, as usual, was elected handily.

No event in the history of American politics has so assaulted and tested the moral standards of human beings as did the 1899 session of the Montana Legislature. If W. A. Clark had been playing on a larger stage, he would have been another Napoleon, another Hitler. The power of his ambition, when brought to bear on ordinary men, produced such aberrant behavior that many of the guilty went home shaking their heads as to how they were ever induced to commit felonies of such magnitude. Some sobbed on the House floor, some threatened, some laughed. Clark himself suffered a Hitler-like convulsion before it was over. On January 19 he was found in his hotel room doubled up, trembling and vomiting. One man, Sen. Fred Whiteside, played a role like that of Gary Cooper in *High Noon*.

Clark did much of his work before the session and even before the election. His principal lieutenants were attorney John B. Wellcome of Anaconda, attorney Walter Bickford of Missoula, A. B. Cooke of Helena, and his own son, the pale and flabby Charlie Clark. These men were provided with huge amounts of currency, mainly in $1,000 bills. Clark apparently set a limit of $15,000 per legislator, unless he himself authorized more.

In some cases, methods other than direct payments of currency were used. Clark agents scoured the state buying mortgages of legislators who were in arrears on their payments. The agents would advise the mortgagee that if he would vote for Clark for the senate, Clark would declare the mortgage satisfied; if the mortgagee voted for someone else, the mortgage would be foreclosed and his property seized.

The results of the legislative election of 1898 that would choose the U.S. senator as its first order of business in January 1899 were deceptive. Marcus Daly and John R. Toole inspected the list of legislators and found that the Legislature would be anti-Clark. Clark was already suspect because of his attempts to bribe the Legislature of 1893. Now he faced a hostile Legislature in 1899. Daly concluded that Clark could never make it, so after the election he went to New York, leaving John R. in Anaconda to hold the fort.

John R. was naive indeed. It was understood that the Daly forces would pay no bribes, but John R. seemed to lean over backward to avoid them. For example, Sen. D. G. Warner from Jefferson County had gone to John R. before the election and asked for a donation of $2,000 to his campaign. This was a perfectly legal request and it would have been perfectly legal to grant it, but John R. turned the senator down, saying that such a donation would only hurt the senator in Jefferson County because it would be termed "Anaconda boodle." Sen. Warner then went to Charlie Clark, who promptly handed over the money; thus an anti-Clark vote was lost to the Daly forces.

On November 8, election clerks at Precinct Number 8 on the hill in Butte were just completing tallying the vote. Suddenly two masked men broke down the door and charged into the room. Election clerk John J. Daly (no kin to Marcus) jumped the intruders and was shot dead. Another clerk, Dennis O'Leary, caught a bullet and was seriously wounded. A third plopped his body on the ballot box; the invaders lost their nerve and fled. The precinct was right on the Butte hill. It was composed 100 percent of miners. When the box was opened, it was found to contain 302 votes for the Daly-supported candidate and only 17 for Clark's man. The attackers were never apprehended.

Clark was badly disappointed at the outcome of the 1898 election. It appeared that a majority of the members were not disposed to support Clark, so the little man concluded that his only choice now was a bribery campaign of monstrous proportions. Clark believed implicitly that "every man has his price," and he knew that with the cash available to him he could buy his way into the U.S. Senate.

Everybody in the state had heard Charlie Clark's remark: "This time we'll send the old man to the Senate or the poorhouse." But W. A. Clark took an even more dire view. This time it would be the Senate or the state penitentiary. As the opening day of the session approached, every member was tense.

C. P. Connolly, in his book *The Devil Learns to Vote*, describes the atmosphere in Helena as the session opened:

Hundreds of school children might be seen wearing Clark badges. The man who stood out against bribes found that his old friends stood aloof from him. He became conscious of a lack of sympathy, of a curious isolation on the streets and at his club. He found himself marooned on the cold eminence of moral rectitude.

The purchase of votes was talked about almost as freely as the weather. The morning salutation of everyone was: "What's the price of votes today?"

A warm wave of prosperity swept over the city. Struggling professional men stepped into positions commanding large salaries; with many of the lawyers, it was the usual chicken today and feathers tomorrow, and they remembered the adage of the old lawyer who said, "First get on, then get honor, then get honest." Grocers became bankers; railroad employees became mine operators, clerks and bookkeepers wore diamonds and bought wine. Rolls of greenbacks were thrown over hotel transoms in members' rooms. A woman who let lodgings discovered, as she was making the beds one morning, ten one thousand dollar bills under the mattress.

When I was going to Missoula County High School, I knew a girl named Janet Stiff. She was a beauteous blonde, admired by everyone. She liked to go out with athletes, and I didn't appeal to her. She married Squeak Robinson, a handsome football player who was the son of the Milwaukee conductor who had welcomed John Coleman and me when we made our journeys to the Circle W Ranch to hunt. She was the granddaughter of H. C. Stiff.

Grandfather Stiff was well-named. He was a rough, tough old curmudgeon whose moral standards were high and well-defined. He was Speaker of the House, and Clark wanted his vote in the worst way. Clark's man Walter Bickford outlined to Stiff a complex plan that would enrich him substantially. The next day A. B. Cooke, another Clark operative, called on Stiff in his office in the capitol and offered him $20,000 if he would cast his vote for Clark. Stiff replied, "If Clark wants my vote, he can afford to pay me $50,000." Cooke gulped, saying, "Well, for a sum like that, I'd have to talk to Mr. Clark personally." Stiff said nothing, and Cooke went on, "When can I meet you?"

"Tomorrow night at eight o'clock in this office."

Cooke trotted out. At the appointed hour and place, Cooke appeared. The office was locked and there was no one inside, but there was an insulting note addressed to Cooke on the office door.

Old man Stiff was baiting Clark, but Clark didn't know it. Stiff had a written record of all the propositions made him by the Clark forces, a record that would later help unseat Clark when shown to a senate committee in Washington.

In the first few days of the session, Clark appeared occasionally in the thronged lobby of the Helena Hotel, but he found that he was being badgered so much that he finally went to his room and met people only by appointment. When a legislator called on him personally and simply asked for a bribe, Clark would reply genially: "Well, I don't get into that sort of thing myself, but if you will contact my son, Charlie, I am sure he can arrange something."

A few days before the session opened, John R. Toole heard a knock on his door in the Helena Hotel and greeted Sen. Fred Whiteside of Flathead County. They chatted amiably for a few

223

minutes, then Whiteside leaned over and spoke:

"You know, Mr. Toole, I was wondering, uh, if you men would be interested, er, in making a little, uh, financial arrangement of some kind with me, uh, if I would cast a little vote for Mr. Conrad [W. G. Conrad, a Great Falls merchant and banker who was running against Clark] so as to help him out a wee bit?"

John R. had known Whiteside in the past and the thought came to him that Fred Whiteside was not acting like Fred Whiteside.

"Well, Senator, I'm assuming that when you mention a little financial arrangement, you're referring to money that Mr. Daly would make available to pay senators to vote against W. A. Clark for the U.S. Senate. I'm very sorry to say that Mr. Daly has no money that could be used in that way, nor do any of us who are associated with him have any money for that purpose. We happen to think that Mr. W. G. Conrad is better qualified for the U.S. Senate than any man in Montana. Don't you agree?"

"Oh, yes, Mr. Toole," Whiteside replied. "But I've been thinking that Mr. Conrad would be even more qualified, uh, er, if he could arrange for Mr. Daly to send some funds out here so he could, uh, so he could support his friends. You know what I mean, don't you, Mr. Toole?"

John R. smiled as Whiteside backed out the door. Whiteside's dramatic ability had been put to its severest test. He had puzzled John R. Toole. But Whiteside's motives were honorable, if somewhat sneaky. He was seeking bribes from any source in order to expose them later. Indomitably, he went down the hall and knocked on the door of W. G. Conrad, who threw him out.

Meanwhile, Charlie Clark was tussling with Senator Warner of Jefferson County and one of Warner's friends. Charlie spotted the friend in the lobby of the Helena Hotel and said to him in an irritated tone:

"Your old bastard of a senator wants $15,000!"

"What do you mean, $15,000?"

Charlie said, "That's right. And the hell of it is, I've got to give it to him, too!"

W. A. Clark was elected United States Senator from Montana after eighteen ballots. The total vote shown below does not always tally, because certain members abstained or were absent from time to time. Fifty-three votes were needed for an absolute majority. The voting went as follows:

January 9, 1899 (First Ballot): J. K. Toole, 30; Conrad, 29; Clark, 3
January 11, 1899: Conrad, 38; J. K. Toole, 20; Clark, 10
January 12, 1899: Conrad, 35; J. K. Toole, 11; Clark, 11
January 14, 1899: Conrad, 37; Clark, 23; T. C. Power, 15; J. K. Toole, 8

January 16, 1899: Conrad 36; Clark, 25; J. K. Toole, 7; O. F. Goddard

January 17, 1899: Conrad, 34; Clark, 25; J. K. Toole, 8; O. F. Goddard

January 18, 1899: Conrad, 32; Clark, 26; T. C. Power, 15; J. K. Toole, 8

January 19, 1899: Conrad, 33; Others, 28; Malone, 15; Clark, 12

January 20, 1899: Conrad, 37; Clark, 29; Malone, 15; Others, 14

January 21, 1899: Conrad, 33; Clark, 33; Others, 17; Tom Marshall, 14

January 24, 1899: Clark, 38; Conrad, 30; Grubb, 14; Others, 10

January 25, 1899: Clark, 39; Conrad, 30; Grubb, 14; Others, 14

January 26, 1899: Clark, 40; Conrad, 29; Grubb, 15; Others, 10

January 27, 1899: Clark, 41; Conrad, 30; Others, 20; Leonard, 16

January 28, 1899 (First Ballot): Clark, 41; Conrad, 27; Others, 10; Maginnis, 7

January 28, 1899 (Second Ballot): Clark, 54, Conrad, 27; Maginnis, 7; Others, 10

"Mr. W. A. Clark having received an absolute majority, has been elected to the United States Senate from the state of Montana."

So intoned gruff old Speaker of the House H. C. Stiff, in a growling and abbreviated manner, whereupon he promptly left the podium in disgust.

And thus the cold-eyed little man, through mind-boggling corruption, threats of violence, and cruel economic pressure caused the Montana Legislature to send him to the U.S. Senate.

One of the legislators, Edward H. Cooney, was a Great Falls businessman who represented the *Anaconda Standard* in that city. He was a supporter of Conrad. On the morning of the last balloting, he rapped on the door of John R. Toole's room in the Helena Hotel. John R. was not dressed yet, but called Cooney to come in. Cooney was in a state of extreme tension.

"My God, this is terrible," he said, according to C. P. Connally. "What's the matter?" asked John R.

"They have been after me all night. They shoved $20,000 in bills under my nose. They told me that Conrad would not be my friend after this is all over because they were going to win and I might as well have a friend in Mr. Clark. They have approached my wife and my children. It bothers me terribly to have them bothering my wife and family. They say over and over again, 'Here's $20,000. Don't be a fool; take it.' I've got to talk to someone about this."

John R. replied, "You have come to the wrong man if you have come to me for advice. I don't want your wife to ever say that I stood between you and $20,000. If you take Clark's money and I were sitting on a jury to try you for a crime, I would not vote to convict you. There are many men here who are in bad shape. This is a rough country. Some of their children are going barefoot; they can't give them the necessities of life. Some have heavy mortgages on their ranches, and they can't make the payments. Some sawmill men are broke because the price of lumber is down. You can't blame men for accepting large sums under these conditions. You might as well arrest a hungry boy for stealing a ripe apple hanging over the fence.

"But suppose you take a bribe from Clark's men. You won't have better meals; you won't sleep in a better bed. Here is what I will tell you: If you take that money, in time to come it will be a canker at your heart. Twenty thousand seems like a lot of money, but it won't last long, not as long as the stain of the thing. All these men in this Legislature who are taking money to vote for Clark will pay a penalty for it. They may not go to jail, but they will serve their time in the guilt they will feel for the rest of their lives."

Cooney settled down. He said it was exactly what he wanted to hear. He had stayed with Conrad through sixteen ballots and would stay with him on the last two. Reconciled to his poverty, he watched the wild scenes in the House chamber that day, the sobbing, the threats, the shouting, and reported that he felt calm and detached.

On the opening day of the session, John R. Toole had moved to create a Select Committee to Investigate Bribery that had gone on before the session and that he expected to continue during the balloting, as it did. W. J. Stephens of Missoula County was chosen chairman of the House delegation, and Sen. James T. Anderson of Meagher was named chairman of the Senate delegation. The physical danger was palpable; one man had already been killed, another wounded. The committee held its meetings in the wee hours at a house in Helena's suburbs. None other than Fred Whiteside turned out to be its first witness.

Whiteside, determined to expose bribery from whatever source, was a man not to be taken lightly. He had been a buffalo hunter and Indian fighter on the plains of eastern Montana. He was absolutely incorruptible, personally brave, and had everything to lose and nothing to gain. He was one of those lonely men who sometimes appear on the American political scene whose actions, based on principle and principle only, dwarf the men around them.

At first, W. A. Clark fell for Whiteside's tricks. The buffalo hunter was respected. He had fought corruption in state government on previous occasions. Now he seemed completely devoted to Clark's cause. Charlie Clark entrusted him with cash and sent him scurrying around to bribe legislators. It was canny Walter Bickford who smelled the rat.

The night after the session opened, Whiteside was joshing with friends in the Helena Hotel. A grim-faced Charlie Clark walked up to him and said, "Come out. I want to talk with you." Charlie led the way down to the *Helena Independent* office. John B. Wellcome joined them, his demeanor cold and threatening. In a basement room, all took seats except a burly armed guard named Ben Hill. Wellcome fixed Whiteside with an accusatory stare and said, "Whiteside, we know you're going to betray us. You've got $30,000 of Mr. Clark's money and you're going to show it on the floor of the House tomorrow. Now talk fast and if we don't like your talk, you'll never leave this room alive."

Whiteside played for time. "Why, John, that's not true and you know it. Now, fellows, I've done a lot for you. I've given you a lot of information about members of the Senate. I've made deals for you and I've accounted for every cent of Mr. Clark's money. Anyway, so far as the $30,000 is concerned, every cent of it is in a safety box at the Union Bank. Here's the key, and go to the bank in the morning and see for yourself." He tossed the key to John Wellcome.

Then he got harsh: "But listen, fellows. The people of Montana know how tough I am, and if you think I'll give in to threats, you've got another think coming."

Now it was Wellcome's turn to change his tune. Wellcome was a prominent family man. Murder was not one of his options. "We're not threatening you, Whiteside," he said quietly. "But, by God, if you do any such thing as has been repeated [meaning spill the beans], if you want ten times the amount in the bank, we'll give it to you. W. A. Clark would withdraw his candidacy tonight, and it will be in the morning papers."

"Now, fellows, you've got me all wrong," said Whiteside pleasantly. "I'm the best friend W. A. Clark has in the Legislature."

Charlie Clark spoke up, "I believe Whiteside, gentlemen."

The tension was relieved, but Whiteside now played it to the hilt. "You know, boys, I'm really afraid of that Daly crowd. Do you suppose that one of you boys could loan me a gun for a few days?" The Clark men looked at each other askance. Could it be the mild, professorial, bespectacled John R. Toole who frightened this Indian fighter?

But Whiteside knew that he was now in real danger. The safety-deposit box contained no money; the $30,000 was tacked to the bottom of a bureau drawer in Whiteside's room in the Warren Hotel.

The doughty buffalo hunter raced through Helena's deserted streets to the house at the edge of town where John R. Toole's committee was meeting, and mounted the stairs. The entire committee, fully armed, was there. Whiteside persuaded them to come with him up to his room at the Warren Hotel, where he proceeded to untack the bundle of money from the drawer. He handed it to Senator Anderson. An honest man, Anderson had turned down a

$25,000 bribe from Clark's men only a few days before. Immediately, the committee rousted out the Senate Sergeant-at-Arms and instructed him to provide an armed guard for Anderson. Then they returned to the matter of grilling Fred Whiteside.

The senator from Flathead had maneuvered himself into a hell of a position. He had just turned out to be in possession of $30,000 of Clark's money and had admitted arranging bribes to be given men in exchange for a vote for Clark. He had contacted Daly's men and asked for money in exchange for a vote for Conrad. The committee was in a quandary. Whiteside was either the most demonic criminal in the West, extorting money from both sides, or he was one of the most amazing and patriotic citizens in the Republic.

"You know," said Senator Anderson after Whiteside had left, "I find Senator Whiteside a very strange man."

January 10, 1899, was the day set for the report of the Committee to Investigate Bribery and for reading the sworn testimony of Whiteside and others. The $30,000 that Whiteside had given the committee had been turned over to the Clerk of the House, to relieve Senator Anderson of the danger of carrying it.

Speaker Stiff grumped, "The Joint Session is now prepared to hear the Select Committee to Investigate Bribery in the matter of the election of a United States Senator."

John R. Toole rose and stated, "I move that the Clerk be instructed to open an envelope given him by Senator Anderson this morning and reveal the contents thereof."

"Well, it's so ordered. The Clerk will produce the contents."

The Clerk held up $30,000 in currency, and Fred Whiteside rose.

Speaker Stiff monotoned, "The Chair recognizes the Senator from Flathead." The lean, wiry buffalo hunter began to speak.

I know there is a sentiment in this community which favors the election of Mr. W. A. Clark to the United States Senate by fair means or foul. I know that the course I have pursued will not be popular, but so long as I live I propose to fight the men who have placed the withering curse of bribery upon this state. I had rather go back to the carpenter's bench where I learned my trade and spend the rest of my days in toil and obscurity, and be able to hold my head erect and look the world in the face, than to be a silent party to the knowledge of this crime. The man who is weak will come out of this contest infamous, while he who is strong will emerge from it sublime. What has happened to the men who were bribed in the Legislature of 1893: They are shunned by their fellow citizens and even spurned by the very scoundrels who caused their downfall. This contest between two men has already culminated in murder in Silver Bow County, and the life of the man who dares to oppose the element that committed that crime is not safe. My own life has been threatened, but I defy the men who have made the threat; for, when weighed against honesty and honor, life has no value; and if this be the last act of my life, it is worth its price to the people of this state.

The committee then recommended that a grand jury be empaneled to investigate and make a determination as to whether or not a crime or crimes had been committed.

One source says that the Joint Session was shocked into deathly silence by Whiteside's speech. Another says there was pandemonium.

The Select Committee was dismissed, and the Joint Session cast its first ballot for Senator. The effect of Whiteside's speech was devastating. Even the recipients of bribes could not bring themselves to vote for Clark on the first ballot, and the deadly little man received only three votes. But little did the members realize how powerful was Clark's juggernaut, or that it would take eighteen more days of pressure, soul-searching, and threats before the issue would be decided and Clark would emerge the winner.

Clark's men moved with swiftness to pierce Whiteside in the jugular. The November 1898 vote for state senator in Flathead County had been extremely close. Whiteside defeated a man named John Geiger by just a handful of votes. Geiger was seeking a recount. The Clark men, means unknown, took charge of the count and arranged to switch the winning plurality from Whiteside to Geiger, who arrived in Helena in time to vote for Clark three times.

During the balloting, strong speeches were made by men who refused to be bribed: Speaker Stiff, Sen. E. G. Matts of Deer Lodge County and Sen. W. A. Clark (no kin to the villain of this piece). Matts and John R. Toole were close friends. In Washington, at the subsequent Senate investigation of the election, Fred Whiteside was asked by U.S. Senator Faulkner, "Did you also approach Mr. John R. Toole, representing Senator Matts, and ask for a bribe?"

"Yes, I did and Mr. Toole said that he had no money that he would spend in that way."

Matts was not a candidate for the U.S. Senate in the 1899 legislative session. He never threw his hat in the ring. This is a mystery. Why did Senator Faulkner use the words "representing Senator Matts?" In any event, Matts was incorruptible. The evidence points to Conrad as the man John R. was representing.

Fred Whiteside delivered a withering blast at the Montana Legislature the day before he went home. But he was never again prominent in Montana politics.

On the day of the final ballot, when Clark went over the top, a huge crowd of Helena citizens gathered around the capital, their eyes riveted on the windows of the House chambers. When the word came out that Clark was now Montana's Senator, the crowd roared its approval and Helena had another Roman holiday. The celebration cost Clark $30,000 for champagne.

Two days before the final balloting, a grand jury, composed of eight Helena citizens, brought in its report: "We have carefully weighed all the evidence submitted to us and while there has been some evidence which tends to show that money has been used in connection with the election of a United States Senator, it has been contradicted and explained in such a way that all the evidence introduced before us, taken together, would not warrant a conviction by a trial jury."

Sighed an exhausted Charlie Clark, "That'll help."

The decision of the grand jury had the effect of exonerating everyone connected with the affair. The decision seems incredible, until you recall that the grand jury was composed entirely of Helena residents. These people owed a debt to W. A. Clark. He had presented them with the permanent state capital in 1894. It was claimed that Clark spent $150,000 to bribe the jury, and although this claim was never substantiated, it should not be dismissed lightly. The decision kept Clark out of jail. The jury was probably worth that amount to him. One wonders what was going on in John R. Toole's head when this decision came down. It was he who had moved the Joint Session to empanel the jury.

Montana was a little jaded after this monstrous affair, but the Montana Supreme Court decided at least to institute disbarment proceedings against John B. Wellcome, who though he was one of Clark's agents happened to be a fellow townsman of John R. Toole. A man named Martin, from Deer Lodge, was a good friend of Clark's. Clark was perturbed about the disbarment for fear it would hurt his chances before the U.S. Senate Committee. He wrote to Martin:

> Dear Mr. Martin:
>   If you could see our mutual friend, [Supreme Court Justice] Judge Brantly, and relate to him what J.R.T. told you, outlining the plan of their campaign, which manifestly showed that everything was pre-arranged, I am sure he would have a better understanding of the whole proceedings, and not allow that splendid man to be disbarred. He has a lovely wife and children and it would be a shame that they should suffer the disgrace on the evidence of two such disreputable men as Whiteside and my namesake from Madison County.
>   Yours sincerely,
>   W. A. Clark

"Everything was prearranged." A lot of unanswered questions ride with that statement. But Clark at least seems to be accusing John R. of some kind of hanky-panky on behalf of the effort to keep Clark from becoming Senator. Though that would be a hilarious case of the pot calling the kettle black, was there anything to

Clark's insinuation? Was there a sinister "Daly crowd"?

Only the flimsiest of evidence suggests that the charge is true. A number of anti-Clark legislators were openly Daly men, and some may have benefited from that fact. Con Kelley, who would become the brilliant, ruthless chairman of Anaconda fifteen years later, was one of them—a lawyer in his twenties, just out of Michigan Law School. Others, both in and out of the Legislature, were John R. Toole, Fred Whiteside, E. G. Matts, W. G. Conrad, H. C. Stiff, and Daly himself. It was said that Congressman A. J. Campbell of Helena owed his job to Daly, and Campbell took an interest in the 1898 legislature elections, but he is not recorded as attending any Daly crowd meetings or passing money secretly.

In fact, none of the subsequent investigations speak of clandestine meetings, plots, or throwing currency over the transom when reporting the activities of the Daly crowd.

Naturally John R. supported this interpretation. In testimony before the U.S. Senate Committee on Privileges and Elections after Clark's election, John R. said: "In terms of a campaign led by someone, an organized campaign, that is simply not so. Mr. Daly led no such campaign. He returned to New York, confident that Mr. Clark could not be elected by the 1898 legislature. Any statement that there was an organized campaign is a pipedream."

My brother, the historian K. Ross Toole, once wrote that John R. must have had his tongue in his cheek when he said that, and added that John R. "turned and twisted" when he was talking about the organization of the Daly crowd. Perhaps so. But the strange lack of disclosed action on the part of the Daly crowd indicates that John R. was trying to hide nothing before the U.S. Senate.

The fact is that the Daly crowd was completely bowled over by Clark's swift and massive lunge. The 1899 Legislature was strongly anti-Clark. The Daly crowd settled back to watch the downfall of W. A. Clark, confidently expecting each ballot to be the end of his ambitions. They got promises from members to vote against Clark on the following day, only to have the Clark forces push the currency in the middle of the night and steal another vote. Never have so many been so venal in so short a time.

Toward the end of the 1899 session and after Clark had been elected, Daly returned to Anaconda. He was angry. His followers had let him down and permitted Clark to be elected. He gathered them together to let them know he had not yet given up the fight, and would keep Clark out of the Senate "by fair means or foul." His helpers felt ashamed.

In the waning days of the session, one James Rhoades from Custer County came to Helena and sought out John R. Toole. He said that Custer County was about to be split and a new county named Rosebud was to be created out of the western part of Custer. Rhoades and his neighbors didn't like the idea because their homes would be in the new county. They lived near Miles City and residence in Rosebud would mean a trip to Forsyth whenever they visited the county seat. Rhoades asked John R. to deliver the Daly vote in a motion to forestall the creation of Rosebud County.

The next evening John R. met Rhoades and made a quid pro quo deal with him. He would deliver the Daly vote if Rhoades would find half a dozen Republicans in eastern Montana who would go to Washington and testify to Clark's chicanery at a U.S. Senate hearing. John R. told Rhoades that the Republicans would be reimbursed for their trips.

Rhoades declined, saying that the Clark-Daly feud was the Democratic party's problem and he would not mix his Republican friends in it. End of story? No.

Clark's forces somehow got hold of Rhoades and paid his expenses for a trip to Washington so that he could relate to the U.S. Senate the chicanery of John R. Toole. Testifying before the Senate Committee, John R. denied everything.

Under oath before the Senate Committee in Washington, Marcus Daly testified that he had spent $40,000 to defeat Clark. He offered to open his books of account so that the committee members might see for themselves. It was not necessary. The evidence against Clark was so overwhelming that, after three months of hearings and 1,500,000 words of testimony, the committee threw Clark out of the Senate. He rose before that body and said:

Conscious of the rectitude of my own conduct, after a critical examination of all the evidence taken by the Committee, convinced that my friends . . . did not resort to dishonorable or corrupt means to influence the action of the Legislature in their choice of a Senator, I am yet unwilling to occupy a seat in the Senate of the United States under credentials which its Committee has declared rest for their authority upon the action of a Legislature which was not free and voluntary in its choice of a Senator. I propose to leave to my children a legacy worth more than gold, that of an unblemished name.

Whereupon William Andrews Clark resigned from the United States Senate. "Jeezes!" one senator exclaimed out loud.

But the little man was by no means finished. His machinery in Montana cranked up to attack the enemy's flank. Gov. Robert Burns Smith received a telegram from a prestigious law firm in San Francisco stating that the firm had a large title problem in Montana and needed an expert title attorney to examine an abstract for them immediately. Smith was a title attorney; the fee offered was substantial, and he was a man of modest means. He took the next train for San Francisco. Lieutenant Governor

Spriggs, a Clark lackey, was at a Populist Convention in Omaha. A signal from Charlie Clark put him on the next train for Helena. Charlie handed Spriggs a copy of Clark's letter of resignation, and Spriggs immediately appointed Clark to fill his own vacancy!

Clark hung around Washington for the fun. Shortly after his appointment, he was walking through the Senate foyer. A senator noticed him and paused. "My word, Mr. Clark," he said, "I see you are back again and this time with an appointment which, as I perceive it, is perfectly legal."

Clark replied with a reptilian smile, "Yes, Senator, isn't that nice? A complete vindication, I would say."

The senator hurried off, shaking his head.

But Clark chose not to accept the appointment. He simply wanted to show everybody how powerful he could be. Governor Smith was frantic with rage. There was no title fee waiting for him in San Francisco. He had been tricked. He fired off a telegram rescinding Clark's appointment and appointed Martin Maginnis. The U.S. Senate refused the Maginnis appointment and Montana was once more without a senator.

And here's a footnote to the whole affair. A recently discovered receipt in John R. Toole's files reads as follows: "Received of John R. Toole Five Thousand Dollars—a/c/ Kalispell Bee. November 10, 1903." The receipt was signed by Fred Whiteside. After the trauma of the 1899 session, Whiteside's fortunes fell. W. A. Clark's revenge was harsh. Whiteside tried to start a newspaper in Kalispell, but the attempt failed in spite of the financial help from John R. By the time this money was advanced, Marcus Daly had been dead for three years, W. A. Clark had finally battered his way into the United States Senate, and John R. Toole had moved to Missoula. This money therefore came from his personal funds. The plight of the courageous Whiteside moved him.

At the turn of the century, two important changes overtook Anaconda Copper. First, Marcus Daly sold it to the Standard Oil Company of New Jersey, and Anaconda became part of Standard's Amalgamated Copper Company. Second, Daly himself died, on November 12, 1900.

After that, Clark had nothing to fear from Daly and his popularity with the Butte miners. Instead a remarkable new face appeared on center stage in Butte. F. Augustus ("Fritz") Heinze was a trained geologist, a crooked buccaneer, and a politician par excellence. He was popular in Butte. Young and dynamic, he had bought all the politicians in Silver Bow County, including the two district judges, and was giving Anaconda—now Amalgamated Copper—fits. He had several mines on Butte Hill and was stealing Anaconda ore underground.

233

Clark watched Heinze and concluded that the young miner would be a useful ally. They got together. Heinze scented an opportunity to get his hands on a little Clark money. He would help Clark have another try at the U.S. Senate, and this time Clark would walk down the Senate aisle with honor, having been legally elected in such a way that no stain could show. Heinze would handle the politics; Clark would provide the money.

The first order of business was to get control of the labor vote in Montana. Marcus Daly had always had a lock on it, but his successor, Standard Oil, was viewed with suspicion. Amalgamated had almost twenty thousand workers directly and indirectly employed in the state. Both Heinze and Clark had substantial mines on the Butte Hill, but they employed only five thousand miners. Their opening blow was to reduce the hours in the working day from ten to eight and increase wages in their own mines. Heinze made the announcement with a bombastic speech in which he dared Amalgamated to do the same. The cost to Amalgamated would be huge and the Company temporized, but after a time it had to make the same move to keep its good crews. The money Clark spent for the wage increase and the reduced hours was more effective for him than dozens of the crude bribes he had arranged in the 1899 session of the Legislature. In speeches, Heinze praised Clark to the skies. On Miner's Union Day, Clark and Heinze rode in the same carriage to the tumultuous applause of the miners.

The next move was to get control of the Democratic party in Montana. Clark's money was used to send large sums to local Central Committees. Heinze and Clark sent bands all over the state, hired musical comedy performers, and sent out brochures, hats, pens, pencils, badges, banners, and on and on—all free. They infiltrated local Central Committees, dumping incumbent precinct committee members and installing their own. Everyone who didn't join their wing of the party was called a stooge of Amalgamated. Both men marched in torchlight parades. The Clark money poured out, and Clark found himself enjoying it. And it was all legal, at least on the surface.

Special attention was paid to the Republican country in eastern Montana, and when the election time came, the Republicans were simply overwhelmed. During the first month of the twentieth century, the Legislature sent William Andrews Clark to the United States Senate, and turned absolute political power in Montana over to F. Augustus Heinze.

As Clark headed for the Capitol, it appeared that he now had clear sailing; but though he didn't know it, a potentially lethal obstacle still lay ahead. When he got to Washington, he received a call from H. H. Rogers in New York. He was asked to come to New York for a meeting with Rogers, who named the date, the place,

Henry H. Rogers

and the time. Clark was totally unused to being summoned peremptorily, and felt outraged. Then he considered the facts. He decided to comply with the request.

H. H. Rogers was the Chief Executive Officer of the entire Rockefeller empire, including Standard Oil. It was the largest industrial combine in America, and it had added the Anaconda Company to its crown jewels. Rogers was bold, brilliant, ruthless, and next to John D. Rockefeller the most powerful man in the United States. After 1900, W. A. Clark became immoral and lascivious—not H. H. Rogers. For forty years, he occupied the front pew at his church, not missing a Sunday. He was a handsome man with bold features, iron gray hair, and a bushy mustache. He was feared and hated, but respected. When W. A. Clark arrived in his office at the appointed hour, Rogers got right down to business.

"Good day, Mr. Clark. Please sit down." He paused, looked directly at Clark through green eyes and went on:

> Mr. Clark, I have no objection to your taking your seat in the United States Senate. But, Mr. Clark, you have formed an alliance with Fritz Heinze in Montana which is absolutely unacceptable to me. Heinze is causing us great difficulties in Montana. I intend to destroy Heinze, Mr. Clark. However, I have no particular desire to destroy you if you demonstrate a willingness to cooperate with me. I will, however, use my influence to prevent your being seated as the next Senator from Montana unless you terminate your arrangement with Fritz Heinze immediately. I have ample power in the United States Senate to accomplish this and I have enough confidential information about you, the disclosure of which would render the task quite simple. I request that you communicate with Fritz forthwith and sever all relations with him and provide me with evidence that you have done so. And, I might add, any attempt by you to resume a relationship with Heinze in the future will be disclosed to me through my own apparatus, and I am prepared to move against you in the future so as to interrupt your term in the Senate at any time during the next six years. Do I make myself clear?

Clark was absolutely seething. He hadn't been talked to like this since he was a schoolboy. All of a sudden, he came to realize that the man sitting across from him exercised a degree of power that no U.S. senator could ever exercise. Clark was a small man; now he felt even smaller.

Within twenty-four hours, Fritz Heinze received a telegram from Clark that produced a complete rupture between them. Heinze was mystified and angry and turned viciously against Amalgamated. There were epochal battles, but, within six years, Rogers would have the pleasure of nailing Fritz Heinze's hide to the wall by buying him out.

Clark's service in the Senate was unspectacular. He managed to wangle a seat on the Senate Foreign Relations Committee, but he was often absent. When an issue came before the Senate that affected one of his own businesses, his arguments for or against were based on what was best for himself. A statement he made about one of Theodore Roosevelt's measures on conservation may interest the environmentalists of today: "Those who succeed us," he said, "can well take care of themselves."

Cataclysmic events came upon Montana as the twentieth century opened. The day of the cowboy was over, and barbed wire started spinning across the plains. Loggers could no longer find vast stands of timber so close to the rivers that they could skid it to the water and watch it float down to the mill. Railroads had reached almost every lonesome village. Butte Hill, under the spur of great infusions of capital investment, produced more fabulously than ever.

The government had declared the frontier closed in 1890, and the Indians, after one last dying effort at Wounded Knee, South Dakota, stayed cowed on their reservations. People were experimenting with horseless carriages; the telephone was in common use; electric lights adorned every city; and typewriters wrote every business letter.

Theodore Roosevelt was President. Sen. Mark Hanna said disgustedly: "I tried to keep that damn cowboy out of the way by shunting him into the Vice Presidency and now, for God's sake, he's in the White House!"

Many Montanans looked out upon the world with optimism and saw a brilliant future of growth, prosperity, and ease. John R. Toole was tired, but once again he filed for the Legislature. As of filing date, Marcus Daly was alive, but he died four days after the election. It is doubtful that John R. would have filed had he suspected that Daly would be dead before the session opened. He and Daly had been through many wars together and the genial Irishman was responsible for whatever fortune John R. had been able to accumulate.

Upon Daly's death, John R. came into ownership of the majority of the stock in Marcus Daly's bank, the Daly Bank & Trust Company of Anaconda, and he became its president. It is not known whether the transfer took place before Daly died or whether it was done by will. The bank paid substantial dividends until the debacle of 1929.

Then something happened to John R. that he found most displeasing. He came into the limelight. None of Marcus Daly's enemies, even W. A. Clark, dared attack Marcus Daly personally, but John R. Toole was fair game. He now worked for Standard Oil! Heinze wasted no time and in a speech called him "oily and slimy." Cartoons poured out from Heinze's newspaper, the *Reveille*. Gov. J. K. Toole, a namesake with whom John R. had worked closely in struggle after struggle, turned on him. Not only John R. suffered. His children were attacked at school. My father told me that after Clark and Heinze took over political dominance, life was difficult for the Toole children in Anaconda. The pretty daughters were spat upon. The Toole boys and the sons of the smeltermen threw rocks at each other. The boys savagely defended their sisters when they were harassed, and one night when John R. was patching a wound in the head of his eldest son Allan, my father heard him say: "I'm afraid we're going to have to leave Anaconda."

In one Heinze cartoon, John R. is shown hefting large packages of construction plans. The cartoonist implies that John R. was about to embark on a series of construction projects for Amalgamated that would profit him greatly. A picture of a prospector's mule carrying gold bricks made the accusation that John R. would receive large payments for doing nothing. Perhaps the cartoonist was simply reminding people about the construction jobs handed to John R. six years back when he built the B.A.&P. for Marcus Daly. If he accomplished any construction jobs for Amalgamated, nothing is known about them. Another of Heinze's cartoons shows him playing the organ of the press for Sen. Thomas Carter. Carter was defeated for the U.S. Senate by W. A. Clark in 1900.

After Clark and Heinze seized control of the Democratic party in Montana, John R. and a few others filed on the Independent Democratic ticket. He obviously would not receive any support from Clark and Heinze in the regular Democratic party. Heinze orated in Butte: "Every candidate on the Independent Democratic ticket has been put there by John R. Toole." Could be. There's no law against that. The Independent Democrats, perhaps, didn't care much whether they were put there by the ruthless millions of H. H. Rogers or by the scheming, bribing, murdering Fritz Heinze and W. A. Clark.

Joseph K. Toole was an ambitious politician, but when he ran for

MEPHISTOPHOLIC JOHN FOOLS THE NURSE WHILE FAUST DEBAUCHES THE MAIDEN

238

governor in 1900, he was boxed in. If he ran on the regular Democratic ticket, he was a prisoner of Clark and Heinze. If he ran on the Independent Democratic ticket, he would be called a stooge of Amalgamated. So Joe Toole settled down into the comfortable embrace of W. A. Clark and Fritz Heinze. The pages of Clark's *Butte Miner* afforded him the opportunity to advance his political fortunes. Clark was only too happy to welcome Joe Toole aboard. Both the Tooles had maintained a sort of respectability in a decade when practically everyone else was tainted by bribery, murder, or chicanery of one kind or another.

In his new role of carrying water for Clark and Heinze, J. K. Toole spotted an opportunity to advance his cause by wrenching himself from his friend and namesake, John R. Toole, whose reputation, J. K. thought, was being tarnished by his new association with Amalgamated Copper. J. K. Toole made the break in a marvelously florid and learned-sounding speech in Billings:

On several occasions of late I have been mistaken for John R. Toole. To those who have known John R. in the past, it will be quite unnecessary to say that he is a gentleman of thin skin and fine feelings, who has seen better days—politically, of course.

Together we have hunted the gentle Republican and like holy men have shown him the error of his way. Together we have figured up the narrow margin between victory and defeat and with wine and song have celebrated the general result.

We have often climbed the genealogical tree and surveyed its every branch to strike the trail of lineal or collateral descent, but never found a limb on which to hang a hope. True, there was said to be slight personal resemblance, that was all, nothing more. In those days John R. was a veritable Jupiter Tonans in the democratic fold. In sentiment and spirit we were always one. What Damon was to Pythias, John was to me, what Castor was to Pollox, I was to John, but John has changed. Time, great vandal as it is, is not so destructive as man, for while time destroys the works of man, man sometimes destroys himself. In the transformation he has traded off old friends for new; the enviable place I once occupied in John R.'s esteem is now held ostensibly by Mr. Hogan, but in reality by Mr. Folsom, as subsequent events will show.

It is a great responsibility to father two such lusty sons of different political pedigrees, and it is only fair to say that the weight of this new paternity is telling on John R., to say nothing of its disastrous effects on "The Heavenly Twins," one of which I am told is already sick at the stomach. John R., once fair of feature, with a smile that lighted up his face like an oasis in the desert of life, is now sicklied o'er with the pale cast of thought and today is older, "older by a score than many gone, gone, gone long before, if sorrow be the sum of life."

But I started out to say that we have often been mistaken for each other, a fact that came near breaking up my meeting recently at Ubet, in Fergus county, where the report was current that John R.

John R. Toole Makes the Tunes the Amalgamated Copper Standard Oil Press of the State Plays
and Tommy Carter Furnishes the Wind With Standard Oil Money.

would advocate the free and unlimited coinage of copper. In fact, our identity was so pronounced that once upon a time it actually deceived John R. himself into being interviewed by several press reporters as the governor and ex-governor of Montana, all the way from San Francisco to the City of Mexico, and he did not discover the mistake until his return to Montana and his attention was called to it.

I do not mention this incident in any spirit of complaint (for John R. can give me cards and spades in an interview) but simply to illustrate how a man, big with great responsibilities, might do a thing without being conscious of it, and so I am trying, against the weight of evidence, to persuade myself that when John R. fell from the sublime heights of democracy into the tank of the Standard Oil company, he knew not what he did, but I am afraid he is lost.

He might cry, "Help, help, Cornelius," or "I sink" but it is too late. "Amalgamated copper" will not save him and "Standard Oil" will not preserve him.

Be it far from me to say that John R. is better or worse than the average man. I have no right to take such liberty. Nor is it for me to moralize or with prophetic vision penetrate the future. When the dark shades of political despondency and political death shall over-

240

take him as it has overtaken others it will be interesting to learn whether his spirit has taken up its abode with the other seven or eight wreckers of the year of our Lord 1900, or whether it has winged its way to that realm of joy and peace where Jefferson democracy rollicks with the redeemed.

Nor is it material whether the pathway to his political tomb is lighted by Standard Oil or kerosene. It is enough to know, in this house of party disloyalty and the state's betrayal, that John R. is dead, dead, politically dead. Requiescat in pace.

In order that the present and generations yet unborn may take note of the waywardness of man and that, by accident or mistake, I may never be accused of laying claim to that which belongs exclusively to John, is my excuse for dropping like Silas Wegg into poetry.

> My head and John's are just alike,
> I can prove it in one minute.
> My head has nothing on the top,
> While John's has nothing in it.
>
> Kind nature made us all alike,
> As far as can be seen,
> In some folks' head she put true brains,
> In others Kerosene.
>
> All men can see what I lack here,
> Be I standing still or walking,
> But strangers never see John's need
> Until he goes to talking.
>
> By more than one way may we know,
> The Toole we call John R.
> For when he comes you'll smell the oil
> Though washed in soap of tar.

John R. characteristically made no response; he let his constituents respond for him. A month after Joe Toole's snide attempt to discredit him, the smeltermen of Anaconda sent him to Helena as a member of the Legislature for the sixth time, notwithstanding the albatross of H. H. Rogers around his neck, and notwithstanding the assaults of Clark, Heinze, and J. K. Toole. If he resented the tactics used against him, it is not apparent. J. K. Toole was elected governor, and John R. cooperated with him in the legislative session on measures with which he could agree. John R. was a strange man. He shunned publicity; he seemed incapable of holding resentments; and personalities did not interest him except insofar as they provided an opportunity for some sort of case study.

Just before the election of 1900, the *Northwest Tribune*, Clark's paper in Helena, defended its owner by detailing the Marcus Daly-Anaconda assets that had been inherited by Amalgamated

Copper Company and noting that "in addition, these corporations have acquired as political assets John R. Toole, former chief engineer of the Anaconda Copper Mining Company's slush fund." All of Clark's and Heinze's newspapers assailed Thomas Hogan, who was J. K. Toole's opponent for governor in the 1900 election.

Political events in Montana had reached such a crescendo that in 1900 the eyes of the nation were on the state. The *St. Paul Tribune* showed a cartoon which portrayed William Jennings Bryan in a state of collapse on his desk as he read of the prostitution of the democratic process in Montana, all brought about by his own party.

Shortly after the adjournment of the Legislature in 1901, H. H. Rogers came to Butte. He had a meeting with John R. Toole. He asked, "What do you intend to do now, John?"

"Well, I am tired of the monkeyshines in Butte and Anaconda and I'm thinking of moving. I think I'll move to Missoula and establish my home there where my children can attend the University."

"Well, John," Rogers said, "if you'll come back to New York, I can give you any job in the Rockefeller organization that you wish."

"I don't want to do that, although I appreciate the offer. If the Company has anything for me to do in Montana, I'd be glad to undertake it."

"Well," said Rogers, "we have large interests in western Montana, as you know. If you wish to go to Bonner and look out for our interests over there, we can give you a fine position." John R. accepted.

Margaret Hotel in Bonner, built in 1892 and razed in 1957. J. R. Toole and Kenneth Ross lived here.

Bonner School collection, original owned by Toivo Hamma

The friendship of John R. Toole and this mightiest of nineteenth-century robber barons is curious. John R. frequently went to New York, and when he did he always stayed in Rogers' house. Rogers did not extend this courtesy to Con Kelley or William Scallon or John D. Ryan—all Amalgamated Copper presidents during this period. Instead, he chose as his personal companion a business subordinate who had voluntarily left the centers of power to live in Montana lumber country. When Rogers was asked why he had John R. Toole around so much, he replied, "He's the only man who never asks me for anything."

And so it came about that John R. left Anaconda after almost twenty years of danger and strife. He retained his presidency in the Daly Bank & Trust Company, and by now was on his own financially. Thus he could spurn Rogers' offer to go to New York, an offer that would have been snapped up by most men. It wasn't without some emotion that he departed the little smelter town whose residents had supported him so assiduously and where he was so constantly in the eye of the hurricane. Nevertheless, he was glad to move to Missoula.

He built the gracious big house that still stands at 1005 Gerald Avenue. The house was a complete departure from Missoula's customary great Victorian piles, some of which still adorn that street. An inspection of his library indicates that he had an interest in the history of the Confederacy. Perhaps that interest stimulated his desire to build a southern colonial mansion.

As we have seen in Chapter 4, this is the point in the life of my grandfather John R. Toole when he became the close associate, both as friend and boss, of my other grandfather, Kenneth Ross—the period when each in succession undertook to build a stretch of the Milwaukee railroad, and then found that he would not be permitted to do so.

John R.'s life became placid for the first time in twenty years. During his early years in Missoula, he lived in the Margaret Hotel at Bonner and went home on weekends. The distance between Bonner and Missoula at that time was seven miles, too far to commute daily by horse and buggy.

Then W. A. Clark came to his aid, though only accidentally. Clark's business empire was burgeoning all over the West, and one of his minor enterprises was the construction of a street railway in Missoula and environs. The line extended to Bonner, and one could now make the trip in twenty minutes. John R. and Kenneth Ross were delighted, and enriched the Senator with fares of 40 cents per day.

W. A. Clark had a private railroad car in France, but in the United States, he had a private train. When his train passed through Missoula, he always stopped and invited John R. Toole to dinner with him. Apparently John R. was incapable of hatred. In 1910 Sen. Joseph M. Dixon, the implacable foe of Amalgamated, the man who would, in 1924, beat Amalgamated into the ground and fasten on it a severance tax on metal mines, wrote in a letter to his wife: "I had dinner with John R. Toole last night. Very fine man."

The new position that H. H. Rogers assigned to John R. was the presidency of the Big Blackfoot Milling Company. This company was a wholly-owned subsidiary of Amalgamated Copper. At the time of John R.'s arrival, Big Blackfoot owned 375,000 acres of land upon which grew three billion board feet of timber. About 50 percent of this went to the mines in Butte; the rest was sold on the open market. One of the great problems that had been encountered by the Anaconda Company was keeping a continuous flow of timbers into the Butte mines. Without the timbers to prop up the miles of tunnels, not a pound of copper could be mined, and the Company had resolved to maintain a major lumber operation so that the mines would never be caught short.

One of the principle tasks of John R. Toole was the acquisition of more timberland. An important source was the Northern Pacific Railway. The N.P. had been granted a veritable empire of timber under the land-grant program, to induce the railroad to extend its line from St. Paul to the Pacific Coast. The railroad had more timber than it thought it could ever conceivably use, so it entered into negotiations with Big Blackfoot Milling. John R. Toole thus acquired another 250,000 acres of land upon which grew two billion feet of timber.

Another method of acquisition used by Big Blackfoot took advantage of the Timber and Stone Act of 1872.

Congress, in its wisdom, decided to pass a law allowing citizens to acquire timberland in the public domain, using the formula of the Homestead Act of 1862. A citizen could go out and file on 160 acres of federal timberland, occupy it, do what he could to harvest the timber, and within five years he would own it. The acreage was the same as that of the Homestead Act, by which citizens acquired dry Montana wheat land. These acts were abominable from the economic standpoint, from the environmental standpoint, and from the social standpoint. The acreage was too small to make a living on. Everyone knows what happened to the "honyockers" (homesteaders) in eastern Montana. What about the homesteaders in western Montana?

They moved onto their 160 acres and were surrounded by a huge cathedral-like forest. First they cut enough trees to build a house; then they cut all the firewood they needed; then they went hunting or fishing. At length they started giving attention to harvesting their timber and getting it to a mill. But they usually found that it was so remote that no logger wanted to mobilize the teams, the sawyers, the camps, and the men to log it. Some of the homesteaders stuck it out by raising chickens, a cow, and a few hogs; but many simply let their land and buildings revert to the government or the banks.

Judge George B. Winston had been a district judge in Anaconda and a good friend of John R. Toole's. He came to see John R. one day in Bonner and said that he had been defeated for reelection and was broke. He wondered whether John R. could help.

John R. walked over to a big map hanging on the wall and said, "Judge, I think there's a way we might help you. Do you see this quarter section marked in red down near Thompson Falls? That piece of land has a good stand of timber on it. My company would like to own it. But the government can't sell it to us, and they won't let us acquire it under the Timber and Stone Act.

"Now, if you go down there and live on that piece of land, build yourself a house and stick it out for three years, the company will buy that quarter section from you at a reasonable figure. In the meantime, I will advance you enough money so you can get by. How does that strike you?"

Things like that happened often on the Montana frontier. There were no social programs of any kind to help Judge Winston out of the morass into which he had fallen. If events followed their logical progression, he and his family would go hungry. He accepted John R.'s offer with a delighted shake of the hand.

During the term of Sen. W. A. Clark, Congress was sent a bill to repeal the Timber and Stone Act. Clark fought it vigorously. He also was acquiring timber in that way. But Clark used different tactics. He squeezed homesteaders out, and picked up the timber for a song.

By the time of John R. Toole's death, Big Blackfoot had acquired over one million acres and five billion feet of timber. Any way you look at it, the acquisition of this large block of timber was constructive. It put Anaconda (the Company reverted to this name in 1915) on a sustained yield. The mill at Bonner could not cut the timber as fast as it grew, therefore Anaconda was in no particular hurry to "rape the land" for quick profits or because of strident demands from Butte for more mine timbers. Anaconda was accused of many things, but it was never criticized for rapacious use of its timber assets. When the Company's lumber interests were sold to Champion Industries in 1969, there were four billion feet of timber standing on Anaconda's lands. Champion cut it out almost completely in ten years.

John R. seemingly foresaw this exploitation. A few months before his death, in a remarkable speech before the Federal Trade

Kenneth Ross and Guss Gorier (sitting) enjoy the afternoon sun in this 1911 scene at McNamara's Landing. John R. Toole stands at left, smoking a cigar.

UM Mansfield Library, Dengler collection

Commission in Spokane, he castigated his own industry. Here are his words:

> The manufacturing of lumber is wasteful, shamefully wasteful, and there is no other resource of the country that needs more to be protected. The government must some day be cognizant of it. It should be cared for. Our trouble, our sickness, is over-production and unlimited competition.
>
> In my state, the beautiful lakes surpass anything except the Great Lakes; as beautiful as anything in Europe, as told to me by people who have traveled there for recreation and health. European lakes are providing good living for the people there in the years to come. People are already making their summer homes on our Montana lakes.
>
> Why shouldn't the government retain a mile around these lakes for the future welfare and happiness of the people, and say: "You cannot cut trees here except as marked by the government as fit and right to cut."
>
> It is a shame now to see how these bodies of water look after the lumbermen get through with them. It looks like a volcano after they have passed . . . these beautiful lakes that should be preserved.
>
> My company owns the Northern Pacific land-grant timber. I estimate that 20 percent of it is fit for agriculture, 20 percent

perhaps for pasture, 60 percent is fit for nothing but the growing of timber.

Why should they not conserve the timber on these high mountains? Why should not the government say: "We will take them? . . ."

Now perhaps you may ask me the question, "What would I say that would be the remedy for this state of affairs?"

I think we should admit, without going into detail, that the lumber business is sick.

I have been trying to get some of my friends in Congress to make some arrangements whereby the government could acquire some of this land for growing timber and nothing else, 60 percent of it. Why not say, "All right, we will condemn it for 50 or 60 cents an acre and grow timber for the next one hundred years, guard it, and protect it from fire."

Now I tell you, there is no remedy in any other way. You have the machinery here already at hand for government supervision. The Forest Service knows the business of my company as well as I know it myself. They are in a position at any time to tell us what to do.

Why should not the government take charge of this great interest? Why should they not conserve it until the time that we have two or three hundred million people in this country? If they don't do it, and it goes on as it is, falls into the hands of two or three bondholders and a trust is formed, then the government will have to take charge of it as they did when the railroads combined. Why should not the government take charge of these resources?

These are my notions, and it may be that I am a visionary, but I want to impress on you gentlemen that all of the side issues here do not get to the root of the matter. It is overproduction, unlimited competition, and shameful waste of one of the greatest natural resources of this country.

Like Kenneth Ross, John R. Toole had a brush with the Industrial Workers of the World — the Wobblies. Here is the story as told me by Hjalmar Karkanen, Anaconda security guard at Bonner. He witnessed the incident.

I think it was in 1914 or 1915. It was about 4:30 in the afternoon. The Wobblies had one of their gangs and on this night they made a march on the Bonner office. A bunch of them started for the office, yelling dirty names and so on. They all had clubs or axes and I was told some of them had guns, but I never saw any. They edged up to the little picket fence in front of the office. It was just about time for the streetcar to come in and your Grandpa Toole came out on the porch to go home. He just leaned up against one of the posts and put his hands in his pockets. I thought the Wobblies would jump him, but they didn't. They made an aisle for him and he went on up to the roundhouse and got on the streetcar. He either was the luckiest or the craziest man I ever knew.

In a recently published pictorial history book, called *The Big Blackfoot Railway*, one photo (reproduced on page 246) is captioned, "Kenneth Ross at McNamara's Landing, 1914." The photo shows Ross in a chair on top of a flat car, his legs crossed, his cigar held imperiously. He is monarch of all he surveys. Over at one side of the picture is a nondescript-looking man dressed in a rumpled black suit. He is standing beside the track, a feather in the brim of his hat. He is leaning over, intently studying a flower. He is not identified. This man is John R. Toole.

When John R. came to Bonner, he walked into a difficult situation. Kenneth Ross had always been the undisputed boss. He had demonstrated that he would quit if he didn't get his way. He was a hard driver, a good manager, and a good producer. The two men had different and somewhat conflicting titles. John R. was president of Big Blackfoot Milling; Ross was the general manager of Anaconda Lumber Department, charged with supplying timbers for the mines. Still, there wasn't much question as to who would be the boss in case of a showdown, for John R. was at Bonner by reason of the wishes of the all-powerful H. H. Rogers. But he didn't do much bossing. He let Kenneth Ross run his show and the result was a friendship and a working relationship of a rare quality.

John R. spent more time with Kenneth Ross than with any other man during those long evenings in the Margaret Hotel at Bonner.

Home of John R. Toole, 1005 Gerald Avenue, Missoula
Sketch by Allan Toole

Kenneth Ross handed out few bouquets, but these words in his journal tell us a great deal: "I never knew there was such a broad-minded, honest, Christian man as Mr. John R. Toole."

E. C. Mulroney was an attorney who lived just two blocks up Connell Avenue from the Toole mansion. On warm summer nights in 1915, he and his wife frequently took evening strolls, and often they walked by the home of the Toole family. Mrs. Mulroney noted the scene: the Toole yard was merry with the laughter of scampering, white-suited grandchildren. And from the summer house south of the main building came the high-pitched piping of John R. Toole practicing on his flute.

Mrs. Mulroney never forgot the sensation. It was, she said, a picture of serenity, of happiness and security. It had the sounds and sights of permanence, rather as though it would go on like that forever.

But only a few months later, John R. began to decline. That fall he went to Madison, Wisconsin, to visit a sister whom he had not seen for many years. Howard Toole's letters to my mother express concern about John R. traveling alone, because of his poor health. In January 1916, another letter from my father says, "I'm terribly worried about Father. I walked to church with him today and he could scarcely make it home."

John R. and Anna journeyed to California in February in hopes that he could regain his health in a balmy climate, but he died in Riverside on March 6, 1916.

The *Anaconda Standard* headlined: JOHN R. TOOLE IS NO MORE ON EARTH. For his children he left some final words:

> Missoula, Montana
> Sept. 5th 1914
>
> My Beloved Children:
>   I have, this day, made my will leaving all my property to your dear Mother.
>   I have also left her a letter which you can read, giving my wishes as to what share she shall divide with you.
>   The Blessed Lord has been good to me all my life and his chiefest blessing has been a dear wife and you, my children. All that I have experienced in pleasure and pain, joy and sorrow, hope and disappointment, has been for the best.
>   It is my wish that you do not grieve for me for my work in this life is done and I have not left you forever.
>   Rather have I laid aside the body that has served its purpose, to enter into a larger and more beautiful life where I shall meet those who have gone before and where I shall welcome you all in God's good time.
>   Praying His gracious blessing to be with you always, I am,
>   Your Father

In 1931, Anna Toole who for fifteen years had been a rich widow, took granddaughter Virginia Weisel on a tour around the world aboard the American luxury liner *President Pierce*. Their voyage began in San Francisco, touched all the famous Oriental ports of call, and at length arrived in Egypt, where the ship docked at Alexandria.

As the *President Pierce* got under way again, and the ancient city slipped astern, Anna settled into a deck chair. It was a blazing-hot morning, but the sea breeze kept her cool, and she watched the rocky coast of North Africa slide by on the port side. She was content. As a baby she crossed the immense American Plains to Virginia City in a covered wagon. Her girlhood years had been spent in rough mining camps and tough little smelter towns, but her parents had been determined to bestow on her all the love and good things that were in their power to give. Then she had married a man of rare kindness and sagacity who had made a great deal of money. She had much to be thankful for and was aware of it every day of her life.

A purser came by and delivered her a newspaper. On the front page a banner headline screamed: CREDIT-ANSTALT COLLAPSES. Anna had never heard of the Credit-Anstalt Bank, and she certainly was not aware that it was one of the largest commercial banks in the world. She noted that the bank was located in Vienna, and therefore could not possibly be very important.

Nevertheless, she was vaguely troubled. Things had not been going well in the United States when she left. The stock market had declined precipitously and millions of men were thrown out of work. For the first time in many months, Anna gave some thought to her own finances.

Above all, there was the Daly Bank & Trust Co. of Anaconda. Her husband, John R. Toole, had been president and principal stockholder. It was an excellent little bank. Substantial dividends had come to her every quarter, and in 1928, the Northwest Bank Corporation of St. Paul had made her an attractive offer for her shares. She thereupon turned them over for shares in Northwest, which yielded much higher dividends. Her sons and E. J. Bowman, the manager of the Daly Bank, recommended that she sell. Also, it was pointed out, W. L. Murphy and Fred Sterling had sold their bank, the Western Montana National of Missoula, to First Bank Stock Corporation. Several other banks in Montana had exchanged shares. It was just a good business proposition. Northwest was huge and solid. No, Anna told herself, there was nothing to worry about in the bank stock.

Anna Toole with children: (upper left, moving clockwise): Nora, Thula Howard, Allan

Then there were the Chilean government bonds. Certainly nothing to worry about here. The bonds had been recommended to her by Con Kelley and John D. Ryan, and Mr. Ryan was the president of Anaconda. Mr. Ryan had said the bonds were a good buy because Anaconda was making huge investments in Chile and that nation would prosper as a result. Furthermore, Anaconda needed a stable government in Chile. No. With men like Mr. Kelley and Mr. Ryan recommending the bonds, there was nothing to worry about there. And the interest checks on the bonds had been coming in regularly.

Then there were her holdings in Anaconda stock. Before she left, the price of the stock had declined sharply, but the dividends had held firm, and her brokers with connections in Wall Street recommended that she retain her shares, citing an anticipated resurgence in the world demand for copper and the fundamental financial soundness of Anaconda's position. No. Nothing serious could ever happen to Anaconda. Wasn't it the largest mining company in the world?

Anna's review of her finances pleased and comforted her. Why were the newspapers making such a fuss over a little bank in Austria?

Virginia came up and sat down in a nearby deck chair. The course of the *President Pierce* paralleled the North African coast. They were now opposite Libya, and they gazed at the white-walled cities of Tobruk and Benghazi. Anna reflected with pleasure on her ordered and prosperous life, oblivious that, hour by hour, day by day, it was all slipping away.

And it was the collapse of the Credit-Anstalt that was the begin-

251

ning of the end for her. In ten years the white-walled cities across the bay would disappear, blasted to rubble by the raging battles of the British armies and the Afrika Corps of the German Field Marshall Erwin Rommel. The Credit-Anstalt bankruptcy triggered the bankruptcies of all the huge banking houses in western Europe, bringing inflation and poverty, and the rise of Adolf Hitler with his horrors.

Now the ship turned north and sailed for Naples. On the dock of this teeming city, Anna and Virginia were greeted by their uniformed chauffeur and a limousine. They traveled northward through France and Germany to Holland, where they met Virginia's younger sister, the delicate and fairy-like Anna Afton, who was visiting at the home of Jan Boissevain in Amsterdam.

Jan Boissevain was the scion of a rich and famous Dutch family. His father was the burgermeister of Amsterdam, and the name Boissevain was known throughout Holland. Jan was a tall, elegantly handsome young man with a clipped mustache. His dress was impeccable; highly polished knee-length boots, expensive riding trousers, and English tweed jackets. He had attended school in England, and his use of the English language was so cultivated and so perfect that it was a pleasure just to hear him speak. He was courtly and gentlemanly, and epitomized the European upper class of that day.

Jan Boissevain

Jan was desperately in love with lissome, eighteen-year-old Anna Afton. He also loved Montana and its Blackfoot Valley, and would make of it a dude ranch. He was perhaps the most impractical man who ever lived, but Anna highly approved this union of her granddaughter and the wealthy, dashing Dutchman.

After a stay in Amsterdam, Anna and her two granddaughters booked passage for New York on the Holland-America Line, a steamship company in which the Boissevain family had a financial interest.

As the days of the summer of 1931 came to a close, Howard Toole became terribly concerned about his mother's finances. Badly wounded by the failure of the money systems in Europe, the United States plunged even deeper into the Depression. President Hoover labored mightily, but he had lost control of Congress in 1930.

Howard felt frustrated by his inability to get any information. At length he called his brother in Spokane. "Allan, can you come over here? We need to talk about Mother's finances."

Allan took the next train for Missoula, and the two were closeted in Howard's office. Howard opened the conversation:

"Allan, Mother's situation looks extremely dangerous. Northwest Bank passed its last dividend, and no interest checks have been received on the Chilean bonds for four months. Anaconda's last dividend came in but the stock is down to twenty-seven and she has a huge paper loss."

Allan asked, "What is the price of Northwest stock shares?"

Howard replied, "It's not quoted."

Allan was startled. "Not quoted?"

"No, it's not quoted, Allan," Howard replied, "but I have a good friend, Shirley Ford, who is Vice President of Northwest, and he tells me over the phone that he thinks the holding company is sound. You realize, don't you, that Mother does not have possession of her shares in Northwest? The certificates are held by the bank." Shirley Ford was the son of Robert Ford who, with Mathew Dunn, drove four hundred head of cattle through the Sun River Valley in 1875.

Allan rubbed his chin, "Mother will be shocked at what has happened to her."

Howard said, "Allan, I'm going back to the Twin Cities, get those certificates, and see Shirley Ford. Will you come with me?"

Allan nodded and the next day, both men climbed onto the luxurious Olympian of the Milwaukee Road, bound for St. Paul.

Shirley Ford met them at the offices of Northwest. He was distraught and apologetic, but he displayed his customary friendliness and hospitality. Howard asked about the custodianship of Anna Toole's shares and he promptly produced them. Howard asked him what they were worth and Ford replied, "I guess they're worth whatever you can get for them."

They took the train back to Missoula and when they had settled down in the observation car, Howard said gloomily, "Well, that finishes the story of the Daly Bank & Trust Co. as far as the Toole family is concerned." Allan looked sadly out the window and murmured, "I'm glad Father wasn't here to witness this."

Then Allan looked straight at Howard and said, "Mother has to sell the house." The house he referred to is the great colonial structure at 1005 Gerald Avenue. It is now occupied by the Kappa Kappa Gamma sorority.

Howard replied, "She'll get virtually nothing for that house in Missoula now."

"Nevertheless, I think it must be sold," Allan said, "She can keep the barn and move in there." Howard nodded. The "barn" was the house at 105 Connell Avenue, once the horse barn for 1005 Gerald. It had been remodeled into a spacious home after the demise of the horse and buggy.

And that was what Anna did. But both of these normally ebullient men were saddened and bewildered by what was happening. Besides, both had financial emergencies in their own lives.

When Anna, Virginia and Anna Afton had piled off the train that fall, they were greeted by their noisy, happy, kissing family

253

amid an exciting clutter of steamer trunks, expensive luggage, and many flowers. It was only a few days until Howard walked up to 1005 Gerald and broke the news to Anna that virtually her entire fortune had been wiped away.

What manner of man was John R. Toole?

One cannot come to grips with him. He was a man whose political activities could be called questionable, and yet a man whose transparent honesty reveals itself time and again. A man who walked always in the shadows, yet a man whose influence was immense. A man who was the subject of pernicious political cartoons, yet a man with whom cartoonists and reporters longed to sit down and visit. A man forsaken by his best friend and namesake, and yet a man upon whom this namesake could count when the welfare of the state was at stake. He was a man who enjoyed working and associating with the great movers and doers of his time, but who never seemed to have a craving to be a mover and doer himself. The answers to the riddles behind the turbulent events of his times seem to be just inside his door, yet historians have never succeeded in opening that door. They approach him obliquely or just in passing.

In the history of Montana, John R. Toole remains an enigma. And he would want it that way. He never craved recognition or publicity, and in fact he shunned it.

His politics and his business were inextricably linked in a way that would today be frowned on, but his was a different time with different values.

Schoolteacher, miner, harness maker—metallurgist, mathematician, lumberman—religious scholar, environmentalist, and historian—he moved through life with a seemingly serene and calm demeanor. He was respected and liked by all, yet he confessed to his wife that he was "smooth."

There were terrible conflicts within him about the political morals of the day and the part he was playing in them. Why then, did he not simply pick up and leave and go to a place where his morals would not be so tortured? The answer is simple. He had a wife, six children and an aging father-in-law. He would give his children monetary assistance that had been denied him

He emerged from the time of troubles respected and wealthy. But one suspects that he paid a high price. By 1902 his health had been badly damaged.

He had an intense intellectual curiosity, and he was a man of the physical sciences, yet he embraced the concept of an eternal life. Religion was part and parcel of his being.

One bright light emanated from John R. Toole. That was love: love for his in-laws, love for his brothers and sisters and above all, love for his wife and children. In 1978, I called on Dr. Norman Maclean, Professor of English at the University of Chicago and author of *A River Runs Through It*, also a story of the Blackfoot Valley. Dr. Maclean is one of the few who remember John R. Toole. I asked him his impression of John R. He looked out the window and replied, "I would say that he was a man of infinite grace."

9   *1937: Fire and Temptation*

9   1937: Fire and Temptation

In the summer of 1937 fighting fire sounded to me like a much more exciting and challenging enterprise than drudging away in a logging camp.

The timberlands in the Blackfoot Valley were not owned by the U.S. Forest Service, and fire protection was afforded by a cooperative known as the Blackfoot Forest Protective Association or, as everyone called it, the B.F.P.A. Its operations were financed by a small tax levy on all the property in the valley, and since Anaconda owned most of the valley, Anaconda paid about 80 percent of the cost and pretty well ramrodded the organization. It had "ranger stations" in Bonner, Greenough, Ovando, Lincoln, and Drummond. It had been founded by Kenneth Ross in 1920 and he was its first president.

The buildings and equipment of the B.F.P.A. were scarcely like the lavish, olive-drab facilities of the Forest Service. Its ranger stations were, in some instances, located in deserted farm buildings or in abandoned commercial buildings. Its equipment seemed old and nondescript. But the B.F.P.A. had much esprit de corps and the men were proud of their fire-fighting successes. And the B.F.P.A. had one major advantage over the Forest Service. The B.F.P.A. could call on the Anaconda lumberjacks for a fire-fighting

259

crew at a minute's notice. The lumberjacks, with their disciplined work habits and their skill with tools, were like an elite military corps compared with the dregs of the Missoula bars dredged up by the Forest Service. The B.F.P.A. could mobilize 300 of these excellent men in minutes.

The boss of the B.F.P.A. was Les Tarbet. Les was a Marine in World War I, and held the Marine light-heavyweight boxing championship. He was off again in World War II to fight the Japanese in the Pacific. He was a pugnacious, ferocious worker and a hard driver. In fact, Les flung himself with such abandon into his work that he always worked himself into some sort of illness.

My first assignment was at Bonner, where there was a headquarters, a bunkhouse, and a telephone dispatcher who sent the crews out on the fires. It was in the old Odd Fellows Hall, and we had to do our own cooking.

The first job was marvelous. The B.F.P.A. gave me a red shirt and a huge silver badge inscribed with the words FIRE WARDEN. In a Studebaker pickup I drove up and down the Blackfoot River visiting campgrounds. I had a little carbon-paper pad and wherever I found someone camping, I would approach ostentatiously and fill out a camping permit. I would hand the original to a camper and give him a canned speech about putting out his campfire and being careful. I felt authoritative and important. And, after I learned not to be so stuck-up, I made many friends and they are friends to this day.

But this pleasant pastime didn't last long. One day, Les Tarbet came roaring up in a big truck with four horses in the back. I thought he would drive the truck right through our headquarters, but he slammed on the brakes and stopped in a flurry of gravel. He hopped out and said: "Come on, John, we've got to go up and clear the trail from the Circle W Ranch to the Chamberlain Meadows. Get your gear." I thought: This is great.

The Chamberlain Meadows were a series of little openings in the forest, remote, mysterious, and unknown. Chamberlain Creek had its source there, and Douglas Creek was only five miles south. An endless forest spread around them for miles, the home of elk, deer, coyotes, and wolverines.

Les drove the big truck over the gravel road at high speed. When we reached the ranch, Aunt Thula came out to greet us cordially, but Les was in a rush, so we saddled pack horses and saddle horses and headed up the trail, with Les mercilessly switching his horse's rump. I wondered what the hell the hurry was.

We made camp that night on a crystal clear branch of Chamberlain Creek.

Les said, "I'll fix up some grub. You go get some wood."

After dinner, Les flopped down on his sleeping bag.

Les Tarbet

"I don't feel so hot," he said.

"It's no wonder, Les," I said. "You work too hard."

"Naw," he said. "It's heat exhaustion. I'll be O.K. in the morning."

Morning came and he seemed all right, so we headed up the trail. Then we hit the windfalls. Every time we'd encounter a log across the trail, Les would be off his horse in a flash and start chopping the log in two. This went on until about two in the afternoon. Finally he sat down and looked at me with a kind of desperate expression.

"Goddamn, I don't know what the hell's wrong with me."

I said, "Les, let's camp here tonight. This is a good spot, water and everything."

He nodded.

I was getting worried about him. I didn't know whether I could get him out of this wilderness or not if he passed out.

That night he didn't move from his sleeping bag, and I had to get dinner.

In the morning he said, "I gotta go back to town. Damn! I don't know what we'll do if we have to bring a fire crew in here!"

He mounted his horse, put both hands on the saddlehorn and hung his head down. We stumbled 15 miles back to the Circle W. Aunt Thula met us with a worried look on her face. She wanted us to stay, but Les staggered into the big truck. I somehow got the horses loaded up and climbed in behind the wheel. I'd never driven the truck before, but Les was in such a bad way that I managed. He just sat in the seat with his head down.

When we pulled up in front of his house in Missoula, Mrs. Tarbet came out shaking her head. Then I drove the horses and equipment back to Bonner.

One day in June, Les came charging up in a pickup and said: "Come on, Johnny. We're going to string a telephone wire into old lady Potter's ranch. The old gal doesn't deserve it but she's goin' to pay us through the nose for the service and make our bank account a little fatter! Ha!"

I climbed into the back of the pickup, which was filled with spools of wire and rope. As usual, Les charged up the road at full speed. Mrs. Potter's ranch was the E Bar L, a beautiful, well-managed dude ranch overlooking the Blackfoot Valley near Clearwater. A magnificent place.

We headed down for the river below the ranch, toiling under the spools of wire and rope. Tom Harper was with us. The Blackfoot was at full flood. The muddy water boiled and roiled with a tremendous roar, pouring its cascades over huge rocks. Les reached down and picked up three twigs.

"Now, boys," he said with an evil leer, "one of us is going to swim

*Frank
("Rattlesnake")
Inman*

that river with a rope tied to him. Then we'll hook the wire to the rope and pull it across. Frank Inman has brought up wire on the other side of the river in a speeder on the Milwaukee tracks." I looked across and there was Frank standing on the opposite bank. Les went on and grasped three twigs in his fist.

"Now the guy that draws the short twig of these three is gonna swim the river with the rope tied to him. Here, Johnny, you draw first." I drew a twig and Les threw the other two twigs away. He laughed and leered at me again: "You got the short one, Johnny! Peel off your clothes." What a lousy deal, I thought. Les and Tom never intended to swim that river! I stripped to my trunks.

The river looked formidable. I stood uncertainly on the bank. Les wasted no time. He tied the rope around my waist and commanded: "O.K., boy. Dive in!"

I have never been a particularly strong swimmer, but I dove. The river was ice cold, freshly melted snow. The plunge was a shock.

I closed my eyes and flailed madly. The big rope was a burdensome drag that got worse as water soaked it. The current hurtled me downstream, and I banged my arms and legs on rocks. Already, I was 75 yards down from my starting point, but I was making it across. The rope pulled me under, but I gave a mighty heave and felt sand in my hands. I opened my eyes. Les and Tom were way back up the river paying out the rope. Frank Inman came running down to give me a hand, and I crawled out on the bank like a gasping porpoise.

Big joke! They were all laughing to beat hell. Frank gave me some dry clothes, and I lay down gasping for breath. Frank busied himself tying the wire to the rope and Les and Tom pulled it across. I thought: "I hope Mrs. Potter appreciates her telephone."

Frank and I were to return to Bonner on the railroad speeder, but first we ate our lunch. We watched the roaring torrent of the Blackfoot River, the blue skies, the huge pines, and the tiny figures of Les and Tom as they toiled up the slope to the E Bar L ranch. It was pure adventure, adventure tinged with danger, accomplishment, and all in the midst of magnificent beauty.

"Well, come on, Johnny," Frank said. "Let's get that speeder loaded."

We climbed up to the tracks and put our gear on the speeder. Frank cranked it up, the little gas engine coughed, and we were soon clicking down the tracks of the Blackfoot branch of the Chicago, Milwaukee, St. Paul & Pacific Railway Company, headed for Bonner, Montana.

Frank drove the speeder at a leisurely pace, and all I had to do was watch the great wild beautiful country go by as we went around and around the curves in the tracks. Then I thought of something.

262

It was Friday afternoon. The Milwaukee logging train would be heading up the valley late this afternoon and we were heading down. I hollered at Frank:

"Frank, that train is coming up the canyon today."

"Yeah, I know. But we'll be in Bonner before she even starts.

He took a drag on his cigarette, giving me a snag-toothed smile.

I was uneasy now. All these curves, that huge locomotive. I peered ahead but all I could see was miles of track, twisting and turning as it paralleled the river. Frank didn't seem to have a care in the world. He sang lustily and kept the speeder put-putting along at medium speed.

We met the train below McNamara's Landing. First I saw the white plume of steam, then I heard the roar of the great steam whistle. The train was thrusting along at top speed. I hollered at Frank:

"There's that goddamn train, Frank! Let's get the hell off this vehicle!"

He shook his head and advanced speed to high, heading straight for the oncoming train.

I shouted: "What the hell are you doing?"

But he just held the throttle open, and the gap between the train and the speeder narrowed rapidly. The engineer spotted us and laid on the whistle, and the colossal noise filled the canyon from rim to rim. Then he dynamited his brakes, and the big drive wheels on the engine locked, spraying sparks from the track. I was getting ready to jump. Frank was obviously insane, racing into the path of the locomotive. But no. He stopped the speeder with a jerk and piled off, yelling at me: "Get off quick, Johnny, grab the handles and wrestle this thing off the track!" Now the locomotive was bearing down on us, wheels locked, brakes screaming. And I saw what Frank had in his head.

Next to the track was a mound of earth, and on top of it were two parallel railroad ties placed at right angles to the rails. It was the only place where you could pivot a speeder off the track. I swear that engine would have busted us into little pieces in another five seconds if we hadn't reached that haven. I looked up just in time to see the locomotive engineer shouting at us and shaking his fist. I'll bet *he* had a good scare too.

Frank sat down on the speeder and lit a cigarette, saying, "You see what I was aimin' at, Johnny: I knew what I was doin.' We saved a B.F.P.A. speeder!" I was irked and replied: "That's bunk, Frank! If you'd stepped on it a little, we'd have made Bonner before the train left!"

Now he was really angry.

"Listen, pretty boy! We damn near had to buy a new speeder for the B.F.P.A. and who would of paid for it? Not me. You woulda paid for it 'cause your old man's got a lot of money and I ain't got a Christly cent!"

July brought hot weather and sultry nights, and the skies lit up in brilliant, eerie flashes, with thunder rolling off in the distance like the boom of huge guns.

Tom Harper, our boss at Bonner said, "All hell's gonna break loose any time. Nobody leave the building."

In the middle of one night, Frank Inman awakened me by shaking my shoulder.

"Get up, Johnny. There's a fire at Potomac!"

I staggered out and jumped into a pickup. Frank drove east up the river over the gravel road to Potomac. When we broke into the Potomac Valley, the fire was in full view. It was nothing but a brightly burning blaze in the top of a big ponderosa pine that had been struck by lightning.

"This'll be easy," Frank said.

The pine was not far off the road. As we gathered up a saw and two axes, Frank said:

"Now, kid, we've got to cut that pine, and the top might come down any minute. While you're workin' keep your eye cocked over your head so you won't get conked."

As we eased the saw into the wood, flaming branches kept coming down, and we hopped here and there to avoid them. No hard hats in those days. We made our undercut, then moved back of the tree. Our saw was sharp, and pretty soon Frank hollered, "Timber!" The pine came crashing down, and the top scattered burning wood all over the forest.

"Get on them little blazes quick, kid!" Frank shouted, and we attacked the small fires with shovel and pulaskis (a fire fighting tool with an axe for one blade and a hoe for the other, developed for the Forest Service by a man named Pulaski). We had everything smothered in short order, then we went down to the creek, got 80 gallons of water and put it out but good.

I said, expansively and authoritatively, "Well! That wasn't much!"

Frank said, "Kid, you talk like you knew all about fightin' fire. Fact is, you don't know nothin'!"

A few nights later our dispatcher, old Frank Shaeffer, answered the phone. He turned to us and said, "A lady in Missoula says there's a fire burning on the top of University Mountain."

This mountain is the next big hump behind Mount Sentinel, just back of the University of Montana. It is brutally steep, rising over 2,000 feet from the valley floor. Tom Harper said he was too old and tired to make that climb and told me to take a couple of men up and put out the fire. It was long before the days of smokejumpers, but we were young and we raced down the streets of Bonner, crossed the Milwaukee Railroad Bridge and went up on a bee line to the top. We pawed the trees aside, slipped on the big clumps of grass, and after two hours clawed our way into the clearing on the mountain's top. We couldn't believe what we saw. There was a huge steel tower on top of the mountain and on top of it was a brilliant white and red light slowly revolving.

One boy said, "I'll be goddamned, what the hell is that?"

I watched the tower for a while, then it suddenly came to me, "Hell, I know what it is. It's a beacon to guide airplanes."

But it didn't look anything like a forest fire, and there was no forest fire anyplace.

We picked our way down the mountain and got to headquarters at daylight. I told Frank Shaeffer, "Hell, Frank, there's no fire up there. It's a light to guide airplanes!"

He replied, "What the hell are you talking about?"

I said, "Call up the airport and ask 'em."

Frank made the call, then turned to me: "By God you're right. They just installed it yesterday. What's the world coming to? Think of the cost of that light, and all at the taxpayer's expense!"

The rest of us were all mad about our wild goose chase, and plumb worn out. We slept the rest of the day.

Then, about the first of August, we had some real action. One day, Les Tarbet roared up to headquarters in a pickup, scattering dust and gravel from hell to breakfast. He jammed on the brakes, jumped out, and rushed into the office yelling commands:

"Frank, call Don MacKenzie at Woodworth and tell him to send three hundred men down to Greenough and have them unload two miles downstream from the Sunset bridge. There's a big fire burning on the mountain south of the river. Tom, go to the store and call the Milwaukee and tell them that the railroad will be plugged up tonight and not to send the logging train up. MacKenzie will have to send his men down by train. Frank, put all the pumps in a pickup and get goin' for Greenough. Set your pumps up by the riverbank and see if you got enough hose to reach that fire. Johnny, get the big truck and head for Missoula and load it up with men. First, head for Johnson's office [Hjalmar Johnson was the Missoula representative of the B.F.P.A.] on North Higgins and get all the men he's got. Then make the bars, hotels, and whorehouses. Try the Atlantic, the Western, the joints on Woody Street, and the whorehouses on West Front. Jam in as many as you can! Here's a pad of employment agreements."

The phone rang. Les answered and said, "Yeah, yeah, yeah. I know. The hell you say!" Then he turned and said, "That's Union Peak Lookout. The fire's runnin' uphill fast and beginning to crown."

265

Les ran out and jumped in his pickup. Nobody knew where he was headed. "Jeezes," I thought, "Will he ever be sick after this is over."

The big truck wasn't big by today's standards, but you could probably crowd in 30 men if you made them all stand.

Just before I left Bonner, a stroke of genius hit me. I got my big, tin FIRE WARDEN badge and pinned it prominently on my shirt. Johns had only a few men, so I hit the bars and whorehouses. The bartenders blanched when I entered with the huge badge. Everyone apparently thought it was some kind of a raid. No one thought about looking at the wording on the badge. The bartenders cooperated obsequiously. I raced upstairs. The whores squealed and retreated to the "ladies' rooms." The patrons stared at me vacantly, nodded, got their clothes together, and obediently signed the employment agreements. I herded them out to the truck. I covered the town and was gripped by the power of command. Every establishment was the same. I found myself giving harsh orders, all of which were promptly obeyed. Within fifteen minutes I had thirty specimens of the dregs of humanity pressed into the truck, all standing. Some were wearing slippers, some had no shirts, and many were suffering from monumental hangovers.

As I started the truck up the Blackfoot, I felt myself to be the most powerful man in the world.

When I topped the Potomac hill, I could see the fire. Great balls of gray smoke enveloped the mountains and the evil, yellow tongues of flame whipped venomously at the tops of the trees.

As I approached the fire, the county road paralleled the railroad for a few yards. I could hear a familiar sound. Sure enough, it was the puffing little Shay locomotive from Woodworth. Behind it were several flat cars upon which rode the lumberjacks of Don MacKenzie. We approached the fire, and I had to stop; burning trees blocked the road. The train also stopped, and MacKenzie's men piled off. I was appalled when I compared my miserable load of humanity from the fleshpots with MacKenzie's lumberjacks. Joe Grace was their foreman, and they took off for the fire at double time. Every man was equipped. They stayed closed up. Joe seemed to know exactly where to lead them, and they disappeared rapidly into the smoke. They looked almost like a company of Marines. When my men dismounted from the truck, I felt my importance disappearing. They sort of flowed out over the tailgate. Many simply sat down and held their heads in their hands. Others staggered about aimlessly. "Good God," I said to myself. "What good are these men to anybody?"

The B.F.P.A. had a supply dump from which the ill-prepared might obtain such apparel as they needed to fight fire.

At length, Herbert Jones, the foreman at Greenough, showed up

266

and whipped them into shape. He gave them all a big mug of coffee, and some of Joe Kingham's famous cookies. They straggled off in the direction of the fire and disappeared into the smoke.

Frank Inman showed up and told me to head back for Bonner for a load of grub and tools. I thought: The B.F.P.A.'s got too many bosses.

It was dark now, and as I wheeled the truck back to Bonner, I thought: This is great! This is more fun than anything I've done in the Blackfoot Valley.

When I returned, Tom Harper grabbed me and said: "Get up on that fire line, Johnny!" I got a pulaski and an axe and headed into the smoke. Almost at once I was in a fit of coughing and wheezing; then I noticed that many men had bandanna handkerchiefs, soaked with water, tied around their mouths and noses. This made breathing bearable. I found what I thought was an appropriate place and started in scraping the earth with the pulaski.

In fighting a fire, you had to "get a line" around the blaze. This was done by cutting a wide swath through the trees ahead of the fire; then you scarified the earth so that the fire could not cross the line. If the fire broke across, you tried to surround the point where it had crossed and contain it by making another line. This fire broke across the line repeatedly, and groups of men were continually running up to the breached areas and attempting to contain it. Les Tarbet was dashing about and giving commands. I heard him and Joe Grace arguing over starting a "backfire." A backfire is a series of fires a long distance ahead of the main fire, deliberately set in the hope that the two fires will meet and extinguish each other. Les said:

"No way are we gonna backfire! Can't you tell which way the wind's blowin', you dumb ox!" Obviously, if the wind blows the backfire away from the main fire, you will have two fires on your hands.

"Quittin' time" never came. We worked on into the night, but eventually the crew cooks showed up with army marmite cans loaded with stew and hot coffee. Finally I got so tired that I just lay down on the ground and went to sleep.

The next night was cool, and the flames started to die down. We had gotten a line all the way around the fire. Les started to pull the men off, and the little Shay tooted down from the camp to pick up Don MacKenzie's lumberjacks. Les was always cost-conscious. The B.F.P.A. funds were limited, and he couldn't pour the money out like the Forest Service did. It seemed to me that Les spent half his time cussing about the cost of everything. I was told to crank up the truck and start hauling my degenerates back to Missoula. But they weren't degenerates any more. They looked better and talked animatedly. Forty-eight hours in the smoke and flames had im-

267

proved their health, and each had a wad of currency. About one hundred men stayed on to mop up the fire.

Les had a relapse, and I found him, head in hands, sitting on the running board of a pickup. He looked pale and raised his head when I came by. "Goddamn it, Johnny. We lost a thousand acres of good timber."

In a few days all of the fire crew was relieved, but I had to stay at Greenough and patrol the line in case a spark flew up and caused the fire to flare up. They gave me a saddle horse, and all I did was ride round and round the fireline. It was a long, monotonous ride, and I went about it sleepily.

One hot windy day, I was startled out of my wits. A little Douglas fir tree outside the line suddenly flared up like a torch, then another went off, then another. I galloped my horse down, grabbed a shovel and started to work like mad. I had been taught to fling dirt off my shovel in a horizontal manner, and I used this technique in a frenzy. Then I grabbed my axe and began to cut the young trees.

It was obvious that if I did not control this outbreak, the entire country would be ablaze. Gradually, I got a line around the fire. With evening came coolness and the wind died down. Now all I had to do was keep an eagle eye out for a spark. It was midnight before Herbert Jones came up looking for me. When we left, the little fire was out for good.

I went back to Bonner for a few days. Les had recovered, and one day he came to the office with news.

"Johnny," he said, "there's a fire up on Henderson Creek. It's on Forest Service ground, but its headed for company timber. They'll fight it but they haven't got a truck handy to get their crew up there. Take the truck down to the Palace Hotel and pick up their crew and head for Henderson Creek. As of now you're workin' for the United States Forest Service! We got to cooperate with those guys and I always like to get my hands on a little of the Forest Service money. Ha!"

I picked up the crew in Missoula, and a Forest Service ranger got in the front seat with me. I was always worried about wrecking that old truck, and I drove extra carefully because of the ranger. We reached the end of the road and could spot the fire. It was a tiny, smoldering blaze and we had a line around it in a few hours. The ranger gave me a voucher that I could turn in for cash at Regional Headquarters in Missoula.

Frank ("Rattlesnake") Inman was a gaunt, lanky guy, another of those wanderers whose origins were obscure. Like all the others, he was a man of the outdoors. Frank had come down on the log drive from Seeley Lake in 1911. This adventure always interested

268

me, and he regaled me with hundreds of stories while I worked with him:

"Well, Johnny, one day in June of 1911, we had made it almost to Bonner and the logs started to pile up. Fella named Jack climbed out on the jam and went to work with his peavey. The water was backin' up and more logs come downstream, rode up over the top of the jam, and rolled down on the downstream side. Jack was workin' like hell, see, to find the key log [the log in a jam that when extricated causes the whole jam to break], and he never noticed when a big log come tumblin' over the jam. This log hit him, see? It pinned his foot to another log and he hollered for help; meantime, more logs are pilin' over him, and the water's comin' up.

"Well, Johnny, I took one look at him and I grabbed me a good axe. I clumb out on that jam with the water and the logs fallin' all around. I got to Jack and I could see there was no way to get his foot out from between them two logs and things was gettin' worse every minute, so I took careful aim with that axe and cut his foot off just above the ankle with one blow. Jack hollered bloody murder and the blood was shootin' every place, but I dragged him ashore and put a turnikee on his leg. Jack's alive to this day. Sends me a Christmas card now and then."

I said: "I don't believe you, Frank."

"Ya don't, huh. Well, let me ast ya this; what would you have done?"

That was a good response. What would I have done?

My last job that summer was a jim dandy. Every day I drove a pickup to the top of Sunset Hill, climbed a watch tower, and surveyed hundreds of square miles of the Blackfoot Valley through binoculars for the telltale smoke of a budding forest fire. I didn't spot a fire. All I did was read magazines.

While on this job, I stayed with Herbert Smith, his wife, and his daughter in a log cabin at Greenough. I slept in a lean-to at the rear of the cabin. Herbert's daughter, Sally, slept in the same lean-to, and our beds were separated only by a canvas tarpaulin. I was a puritanical character, and this situation seemed fraught with peril.

Sally was a kind of dumpy, sexy little beast who was always flouncing around the cabin, striking poses, and running her fingers through my hair. My parents had indoctrinated me thoroughly in the evils that accompanied illicit sexual adventures and lectured me sternly about the dangers of unwanted pregnancies, venereal disease, and blackmail. And here I was, sleeping in the same room with a highly provocative little babe, our beds separated by only a little canvas. I didn't like Sally very well and she wasn't much to look at, but she had a kind of animal-like attraction.

One night Herbert and I were listening on the radio to the World Heavyweight Championship bout between Billy Conn, the English champion, and Joe Louis, the Brown Bomber. Sally kept hanging around, caressing me. At length Herbert said to her irritably: "Quit bothering Johnny, Sally. He wants to hear the fight."

But a few days later he said: "Johnny, nights are gettin' kinda' cool. If you get cold, crawl into bed with Sally. She'll warm you up! Ha! Ha!"

"Jeezes," I thought, "What's Herbert up to anyway?"

Well, things went on. I could hear Sally's gentle breathing behind the tarp. I thought of Father Juvenal, a Catholic priest in Alaska. He was up against the same kind of problem. He gave in and had to go out in the street and commit suicide! Then I told myself, "Hell, you're not a Catholic priest!"

The credit or blame, whichever you choose, for this situation can be laid at the door of Father Juvenal and my parents. She and I slept apart until I finally went home to school.

Epilogue

After World War II, the state built a highway from Helmville to Great Falls through Rogers Pass, and I drove over. I broke out of the mountains onto the plains with a startling suddenness, and there before me swept the immensity of Charlie Russell's country: the magnificent rolling land, the ocean of waving green grass, and the cottonwood-lined Sun River shimmering in the sun. And nowhere to be seen was the hand of man.

As you drive down this great, broad valley, you come to a little town called Sun River. Up on a hill to the south, where you can get a view of the verdant prairies reaching for mile after mile in all directions, is the Sun River Cemetery, and in that cemetery under a modest stone, lies the body of Kate Furnell, the sister of Mathew Dunn. Kate Furnell died at the age of thirty. You stand there, your body leaning into the wind, and you wish you knew more about her. There are so many such stones in the cemeteries of the small towns in Montana. Young people cut down—young people full of enthusiasm and joy in their determination to better themselves in this beautiful but strange and savage land. Cut down far too young, and now the memory of them is lost forever. There is only the stone, only the stone in a little cemetery on a little hill, enveloped in the vastness of the Montana plains.

Kate Furnell's husband, shown on a nearby stone only as Matthew Furnell, came to the Sun River in 1864, at a time when

271

The First Three Generations

I	Alan Hardenbrook m Thula Walker	C. C. ("Baron") O'Keefe m Anna Lester	William Dunn m Bridget Fogarty
II	Anna Hardenbrook m John R. Toole	Mary ("Mollie") O'Keefe m Kenneth Ross	Barbara E. Brown m Mathew Dunn
III	Nora Clifton Howard Toole Thula Weisel Brice Toole Allan Toole Johnny Toole	Marjorie Ross Toole Kenneth Ross II Bruce W. Ross	Edith Dunn Keith Josephine Dye Harry Dunn

(As a member of the fourth generation, I am the son of Howard and Marjorie Ross Toole. My wife Barbara is the granddaughter of Barbara and Matthew Dunn.)

The Arrivals

Ancestor	Date	Route	Settled
C. C. ("Baron") O'Keefe	1859	Sailing vessel around Cape Horn	Missoula
Dave O'Keefe	1862	Across the Isthmus of Panama	Missoula
Alan Hardenbrook	1864	Across the Plains by wagon	Anaconda-Deer Lodge
Anna Lester	1864	Across the Plains by wagon	Missoula
Thula Walker	1865	Across the Plains by wagon	Anaconda-Deer Lodge
Anna Hardenbrook	1865	Across the Plains by wagon	Anaconda-Deer Lodge
Mary ("Mollie") O'Keefe	1865	Born in Missoula	Missoula
Margaret ("Maggie") O'Keefe	1866	Born in Missoula	Missoula
Thomas Dunn	1870	Stagecoach from Promontory Point	Sun River
Mathew Dunn	1874	Stagecoach from Promontory Point	Sun River
John R. Toole	1882	Montana Central	Anaconda-Deer Lodge
Kenneth Ross	1883	Northern Pacific	Missoula
Barbara Brown Dunn	1888	Great Northern	Great Falls

the Sun River Valley was indisputedly owned by the tall, fierce horsemen of the Blackfeet tribe.

Montana is a place for golden moments, moments when you find yourself suddenly overwhelmed by the beauty and mystery around you.

You can go back to the places where you experienced the golden moments, but you cannot recreate them. Trees grow, roads are built, streams dry up. Golden moments visit only once. Yet you realize that the moments have created something in your consciousness, something that stays with you for a lifetime, a vision of something, a wonderful, pleasant, adventuresome vision. When you probe hard enough and force yourself back to those days, you know that the golden moments were few—a sunset, the sighing of the wind in the trees, a mountain peak, a gold nugget. Mostly you were working, enduring hard, boring, unremitting toil. But God has arranged it so that the memories of the toil fade, leaving only the golden moments.

In 1918 blind old Uncle Dave O'Keefe often went tapping, tapping up Gerald Avenue to visit his friend, Alan Hardenbrook. They talked of Blackfeet, Arapahoes, and Nez Perce. And freighting, blizzards, Vigilantes, covered wagons, brave women. Their thoughts went back to 1864, and they agreed that it was miserable and dangerous. But the misery and the danger had been dulled, and existed only in their words. It was the sharing of the golden moments that brought Uncle Dave tapping, tapping up Gerald Avenue. And this he did every day until Alan Hardenbrook died.

Granville Stuart, Dave O'Keefe, and Alan Hardenbrook

Acknowledgments

Many people had a hand in this book.

It was my brother, K. Ross Toole, who provided the inspiration. He shared with me a sense of wonder and curiosity about our pioneer forebears, and talked always of writing about them, but died before he could. My daughter Edith Toole Oberley provided the backbone of Chapter 2 on Baron O'Keefe. My cousin Mollie Fitzell Matteson, in a series of telephone calls from her home in Tampa, Florida, told me more about the Baron, her grandfather.

Marian Herzer Wolfe talked to me at length about her father Dick Herzer, and provided photographs. Pat McDonald, nephew of Marvin McDonald, also gave me photos and told me that Marvin is living in Arizona. John M. Clifton Jr. and my son, Howard Toole III, obtained the long-lost letters of John R. Toole and had them photographed.

My father Howard had a lively historical bent and probed the lives of everyone in this book. His tales led me into ranches, mines and logging camps when I was young. It was my mother, Marjorie, who told me of the women on the frontier, their bravery and their steadfastness. I had the good fortune to live for several months in 1941 with William Scallon at the Montana Club in Helena. Judge Scallon opened my mind to the incredible days of the Copper Kings and John R. Toole's participation in their wars. Norman Maclean painted me a word picture of John R. My grandfather Kenneth Ross's written recollections were priceless in the chapter about him. Don MacKenzie, who is still going strong at ninety-seven, helped me to piece together my summer in Blackfoot Valley lumber camps. Don is the best man alive who worked at Seeley Lake in 1911. His contribution was invaluable.

George Weisel II and Virginia Weisel Johnson supplied me with the numerous photos of the Circle W Ranch and provided me with much information about those years. Alice Finnegan of the Tri-County Historical Society in Anaconda was indefatiguable in running down for me the sparse information about John R. Toole and Alan Hardenbrook.

My wife Barbara not only endured the endless mess in our basement and the clicking of an ancient typewriter far into the night, but also made her grandparents, Mathew and Barbara Dunn, spring alive. I must thank Denny Louquet of the Copy Center and fully a dozen good stenographers. My editor, Bill Forbis, helped organize the book and make it readable, understandable, and accurate.

Index

Page references in italics indicate illustrations.

Finnegan, Alice, 275
First Bank Stock Corporation, 250
First Chance Gulch, 52, 55–56
Fisher, Ed, 60–61, 80
Fitzell, Margaret ("Maggie") O'Keefe, v, 35–37, 39–41
Flathead Indian Agency, 41–42
Flathead Reservation, 38–39
Flathead Tribe, 24
Ford, Robert, 165
Ford, Shirley, 253
Forest Service, United States, 119, 121, 124, 129, 147, 159, 264, 268
Fort Benton, 21, 40, 43, 166
Furnell, Kate Dunn, vi, 271

Gambler Gulch, 78
Garnet, 51, *64* (in 1897), 61, *65* (in 1959), 66, 71, *86*, 159, 188–91
Gibson, Paris, 167
Girard, Jim, 121, 123, 181
Grace, Joe, *86*, 183, 186, 188, 266
Grant, Ulysses, 166
Great Depression, 3, 6, 32, 57, 59, 69, 84, 170
Great Falls Tribune, 28, 31
Great Northern Railroad, 111, 117, 167
Greene Cananea Mine, 211–13
Greene, William C., 211–12
Gros Ventre Tribe, 111
gyppos, 122, 184, 192

Haggin, James Ben Ali, 209, 217, 219
Hammond, A.B., 90, 101, 113–14
Hanna, Mark, 236
Hanson, Pearl, 61, 78–79, 81
Hardenbrook, Alan, v, 35, 71–78, *77*, 81, 85, 199–200, 203, 208–09, *210*, 213, 272–73
Hardenbrook, Thula Walker, 72–77, 200, 273
Harriman, E.H., 116–17
Harrison, Benjamin, 211
Harper, Tom, 261, 264
Hauser, S.T., 201
Hearst, George, 219
Heinze, F. Augustus, 203, 206, 233, 235–36, 239, 241, 267
Helena Daily Herald, 29
Helena Hotel, 198, 223, 225–26
Helena Independent, 227
Helmville rodeo, 11
Henderson, Al, 183–84, 186–88, *187*
Herndon, Sarah Raymond, 72–78, 81–82, 213
Herzer, Dick, *51*, 52–60, *59*, 82, 155, 159, 274
Higgins-Worden store, 30
Hill, Jim, 117
Hogan, Thomas, 239, 242
Hoover, Jake, vi, 169
horses, *120*, 179, 191

house at 105 Connell Avenue, 253
house at 905 Gerald Avenue, 44, *143*
house at 1005 Gerald Avenue, 6, 7, 84, 210, 243, *248*, 253–54
House, Montana, 210, 226, 229
Houtsdale, Pennsylvania, 91–92, 95
Hudson's Bay Company, 22
Huntington, C.P., 115

Independent Democratic Party, 237, 239
Industrial Workers of the World, 90, 93, 130–33, 136–37, 187, 247
Inman, Frank, 262–69, *262*

Jocko River, 40, 42, 110
Jones, Herbert, 268
Johns, Hjalmar, 265
Johnson, Virginia Weisel, 5, 7, 250–53, 275
Joseph, Chief, v, *34*, 36, 47, 220
Judith River, vi, 168

Kappa Kappa Gamma sorority, 253
Karkanen, Hjalmar, 131, 247
Keith, Barbara. *See* Toole, Barbara Keith
Keith, Edith Dunn, 167, 170, *171*, *174*, 273
Kelley, Con, 231, 243, 251
Kerfoot, Ezra, 74
Kerfoot, Frank, 77
Kerfoot, Neelie, 72, 74–75, 77
Kingham, Joe, 180, 267
Koessler, Horace, 11
Kohrs, Conrad, 165

Larson, Fred, 181–82
Legislature, Montana, 204, 210–11, 220–21, 224–25, 227–29, 231–32, 234, 241–42
Legislature, Territorial, 28, 47, 202–03, 211
Lennon, Chris, 53, 57
Levine, Louis, 206
Liberty, Billy, 66, 191
log drives, 125, *126*, 127, *128*
loggers, 179, 184
logging camp at Seeley Lake, *119*
logging headquarters at Seeley Lake, *118*
logging with sleighs, 119–20, 122
log rollways, *127*
logs at Bonner, *129*, *132*
long-butting logs, 120
London Sapphire Syndicate, 169, 174
Lubrecht, W.C., 192–93
lumberjacks at lunch, *132*, *134*

MacKenzie, Don, *178*, 178–92 *passim*, 265–66, 275
Maclean, Norman, 255, 275
Madden, Slim, 56, 60–61, 63, 67–69, 136
Madsen, Dave, 137–39, 145–46
Maginnis, Martin, 28, 211, 233
Malone, Jim, 61–62
Mansfield, Mike, 197